175 HOT & SPICY
CHILLI RECIPES

175 HOT & SPICY CHILLI RECIPES

A fiery and delicious collection of chilli-inspired recipes
for all occasions, featuring more than 180 photographs

Editor: JENNI FLEETWOOD

southwater

This edition is published by Southwater, an imprint of
Anness Publishing Ltd,
Blaby Road, Wigston,
Leicestershire LE18 4SE

Web: www.southwaterbooks.com; www.annesspublishing.com

If you like the images in this book and would like to investigate using them
for publishing, promotions or advertising, please visit our website
www.practicalpictures.com for more information.

Publisher: Joanna Lorenz
Project Editor: Anne Hildyard
Designer: Sarah Rock
Production Controller: Christine Ni

ETHICAL TRADING POLICY

At Anness Publishing we believe that business should be conducted in an ethical and ecologically sustainable way, with respect for the environment and a proper regard to the replacement of the natural resources we employ. As a publisher, we use a lot of wood pulp to make high-quality paper for printing, and that wood commonly comes from spruce trees. We are therefore currently growing more than 750,000 trees in three Scottish forest plantations: Berrymoss (130 hectares/320 acres), West Touxhill (125 hectares/305 acres) and Deveron Forest (75 hectares/185 acres). The forests we manage contain more than 3.5 times the number of trees employed each year in making paper for the books we manufacture. Because of this ongoing ecological investment programme, you, as our customer, can have the pleasure and reassurance of knowing that a tree is being cultivated on your behalf to naturally replace the materials used to make the book you are holding. Our forestry programme is run in accordance with the UK Woodland Assurance Scheme (UKWAS) and will be certified by the internationally recognized Forest Stewardship Council (FSC). The FSC is a non-government organization dedicated to promoting responsible management of the world's forests. Certification ensures forests are managed in an environmentally sustainable and socially responsible way. For further information about this scheme, go to www.annesspublishing.com/trees

© Anness Publishing Ltd 2011

All rights reserved. No part of this publication may be reproduced, stored in a retrieval system, or transmitted in any way or by any means, electronic, mechanical, photocopying, recording or otherwise, without the prior written permission of the copyright holder.

PUBLISHER'S NOTE

Although the advice and information in this book are believed to be accurate and true at the time of going to press, neither the authors nor the publisher can accept any legal responsibility or liability for any errors or omissions that may have been made nor for any inaccuracies nor for any loss, harm or injury that comes about from following instructions or advice in this book.

NOTES

Bracketed terms are intended for American readers.
For all recipes, quantities are given in both metric and imperial measures and, where appropriate, in standard cups and spoons. Follow one set of measures, but not a mixture, because they are not interchangeable. Standard spoon and cup measures are level. 1 tsp = 5ml, 1 tbsp = 15ml, 1 cup = 250ml/8fl oz. Australian standard tablespoons are 20ml. Australian readers should use 3 tsp in place of 1 tbsp for measuring small quantities.
American pints are 16fl oz/2 cups. American readers should use 20fl oz/2.5 cups in place of 1 pint when measuring liquids.
Electric oven temperatures in this book are for conventional ovens. When using a fan oven, the temperature will probably need to be reduced by about 10–20°C/20–40°F. Since ovens vary, you should check with your manufacturer's instruction book for guidance. The nutritional analysis given for each recipe is calculated per portion (i.e. serving or item), unless otherwise stated. If the recipe gives a range, such as Serves 4–6, then the nutritional analysis will be for the smaller portion size, i.e. 6 servings. The analysis does not include optional ingredients, such as salt added to taste. Medium (US large) eggs are used unless otherwise stated.

Main front cover image shows Spiced Guinea Fowl Curry - for recipe, see page 45

Previously published as part of a larger volume, *500 Chilli Recipes*

Contents

Introduction

Chillies come in all shapes and sizes, and range in colour from yellow, orange and green to red and black. There are hundreds of types of chilli, grown in the Far East, Mexico and India, and each has their own flavour and heat level. As a general guide, small chillies tend to be hotter, but it

is not always the case, since even chillies from the same plant can vary in degrees of hotness. Also with the advent of hybrids and new varieties, size is not such a good indicator of whether a chilli is fiery or not. Chillies have been rated on the Scoville scale, which measures the heat of each type of chilli. Results can vary from mild to intense: 0 for a sweet pepper to 300,000 for an extremely hot variety. The heat is caused by a volatile oil called capsaicin, which as well as causing a burning sensation when eaten, also leads to the secretion of endorphins, and hence a sense

of well-being. This has been confirmed by results from brain scans of people who have eaten chillies, and there appears to be an application for capsaicin in the treatment of disorders such as arthritis and psoriasis. In these conditions, topical capsaicin was found to alleviate pain. Other advantages

include reducing blood cholesterol, clearing congestion and helping to prevent stomach ulcers.

Because they contain large amounts of vitamin A and are a potent antioxidant, chillies can boost the immune system. Another benefit is that they are believed to increase the metabolic rate and burn off calories at a faster rate than normal. An extra flow of saliva occurs when eating food with chillies, which can get the gastric juices flowing and aid digestion. However, chillies should be handled with care because capsaicin remains on the hands for several hours and can

cause a painful sensation on the skin, eyes or nose. The seeds and membranes of chillies are the hottest parts and are usually removed before cooking, unless a very hot result is required. If the cooked chilli is too hot, it can be tempered by drinking a glass of milk rather than water, which reacts with the capsaicin and actually increases the heat. Some cultures serve sour cream or yogurt to counteract the heat of chillies in food.

Although chillies are prized for the heat they impart to dishes, they also have a distinctive flavour; some taste smokey, others are fruity, while earthy, sweet or lemony scents are not uncommon. Chillies are hugely popular and are cultivated in many countries of the world, from South and Central America to India, the Caribbean and the Far East, including China, Thailand and Indonesia, and many vibrant cuisines worldwide are based on the stimulating flavours and palate-pleasing effects of these plants.

In this book you will find more than 175 recipes that include chillies in various guises, added to recipes from every continent. There are dishes using fresh chillies, chilli powder, chilli oil, dried chillies, chilli paste, cayenne pepper, and harissa, a fiery North African sauce that is served with tagines. Countries in the Far East use chillies widely and there are superbly fiery dishes from Thailand, Vietnam, Indonesia, Burma, China, Malaysia, the Philippines, Korea and Japan. Rice Seaweed Roll with Spicy Squid is typical of Korea, while Chicken with Basil and Chilli is a popular repast in Thailand. From India, the spice basket of the world, comes Lamb Dhansak with Green Chillies, a popular curry, and favourites from Mexico are Tortillas with Salsa and Guacamole and Chipotle Chilli Sauce, with smoked and dried chillies, perfect served with barbecued food. The Mediterranean regions provide Spicy Spanish Chicken, Italian Lamb Meatballs with Chilli Tomato Sauce and Spiced Walnut and Red Chilli from Turkey. Dip into this inspirational volume to help you fire up your cooking – and discover a whole new world of flavour and warmth.

Fiery Tomato Soup with Red Pepper Cream

This dazzling soup can be as fiery or as mild as you like. Simply increase or reduce the amount of chilli.

Serves 4

1.5kg/3¼lb plum tomatoes, halved
5 red chillies, seeded
1 red (bell) pepper, halved
   and seeded
2 red onions, roughly chopped
6 garlic cloves, crushed
30ml/2 tbsp sun-dried
   tomato paste
45ml/3 tbsp olive oil
400ml/14fl oz/1⅔ cups
   vegetable stock
salt and ground black pepper
wild rocket (arugula) leaves,
   to garnish

For the pepper cream

1 red (bell) pepper, halved
   and seeded
10ml/2 tsp olive oil
120ml/4fl oz/½ cup crème frâiche
few drops of Tabasco sauce

1 Preheat the oven to 200°C/400°F/Gas 6. Place the tomatoes, chillies, pepper, onions, garlic and tomato paste in a roasting pan. Toss the vegetables, drizzle with the oil and toss again. Roast for 40 minutes, until tender and the pepper skin is slightly charred.

2 Meanwhile, make the pepper cream. Lay the pepper halves skin-side up on a baking tray and brush with the oil. Roast with the mixed vegetables for about 30–40 minutes, until blistered.

3 Transfer the pepper for the pepper cream to a bowl when cooked. Cover with clear film (plastic wrap) and leave to cool. Peel the skin and purée the flesh in a food processor or blender with half the crème frâiche. Pour into a bowl and stir in the remaining crème frâiche. Season and add a dash of Tabasco.

4 Process the roasted vegetables in batches, adding enough stock to each batch to make a thick purée. Press the purée through a sieve (strainer) into a pan and add more stock if you want a thinner soup. Heat the soup gently and season well.

5 Ladle the soup into bowls and spoon red pepper cream into the centre. Pile wild rocket leaves on top to garnish.

Corn and Red Chilli Chowder

Corn and chillies make good bedfellows, and here the cool combination of creamed corn and milk is the perfect foil for the raging heat of the chillies.

Serves 6

2 tomatoes, skinned
1 onion, roughly chopped
375g/13oz can creamed corn
2 red (bell) peppers, halved
   and seeded
15ml/1 tbsp olive oil, plus extra
   for brushing
3 red chillies, seeded
   and chopped
2 garlic cloves, chopped
5ml/1 tsp ground cumin
5ml/1 tsp ground coriander
600ml/1 pint/2½ cups milk
350ml/12fl oz/1½ cups
   chicken stock
3 corn on the cob, kernels
   removed
450g/1lb potatoes, finely diced
60ml/4 tbsp double
   (heavy) cream
60ml/4 tbsp chopped fresh parsley
salt and ground black pepper

1 Process the tomatoes and onion in a food processor or blender to a smooth purée. Add the corn and process again, then set aside. Preheat the grill to high.

2 Put the peppers, skin sides up, on a grill (broiler) rack and brush with oil. Grill (broil) for 8–10 minutes, until the skins blacken and blister. Transfer to a bowl and cover with clear film (plastic wrap), then leave to cool. Peel and dice the peppers, then set them aside.

3 Heat the oil in a large pan and add the chopped chillies and garlic. Cook, stirring, for 2–3 minutes, until softened.

4 Add the ground cumin and coriander, and cook for another minute. Stir in the corn purée and cook for about 8 minutes, stirring occasionally.

5 Pour in the milk and stock, then stir in the corn kernels, potatoes, red pepper and seasoning to taste. Cook for 15–20 minutes, until the corn and potatoes are tender.

6 Pour into deep bowls and add the cream, then sprinkle over the chopped parsley. Serve immediately.

Fiery Tomato Soup Energy 319kcal/1330kj; Protein 5.3g; Carbohydrate 23.5g; of which sugars 22g; Fat 23.4g; of which saturates 10g; Cholesterol 34mg; Calcium 67mg; Fibre 6.2g; Sodium 72mg.
Corn and Chilli Chowder Energy 294kcal/1347kj; Protein 9.4g; Carbohydrate 43.2g; of which sugars 15.7g; Fat 13.5g; of which saturates 5g; Cholesterol 18mg; Calcium 119mg; Fibre 5g; Sodium 500mg.

Chilli and Yogurt Soup

With the addition of bhajias, this soup can be served as a substantial main dish.

Serves 4 to 6

450ml/³⁄₄ pint/1¹⁄₂ cups natural (plain) yogurt, beaten
60ml/4 tbsp gram flour
2.5ml/¹⁄₂ tsp chilli powder
2.5ml/¹⁄₂ tsp ground turmeric
2–3 green chillies, finely chopped
60ml/4 tbsp vegetable oil
4 whole dried red chillies
5ml/1 tsp cumin seeds
3 garlic cloves, crushed
5cm/2in piece fresh root ginger, crushed
3–4 curry leaves
salt
fresh coriander (cilantro) leaves, chopped, to garnish

1 Mix together the yogurt, gram flour, chilli powder, and turmeric. Add salt to taste. Pass the mixture through a sieve (strainer) into a pan.

2 Add the green chillies and cook gently over a low heat for about 10 minutes, stirring occasionally. Be careful not to let the soup boil over.

3 Heat the oil in a frying pan and add the dried chillies, cumin, garlic, ginger and curry leaves. Fry until the chillies turn black.

4 Pour the contents of the frying pan over the yogurt soup. Cover the pan, then remove it from the heat and leave to rest for about 5 minutes.

5 Mix the soup well and gently reheat for a further 5 minutes. Serve hot, ladled into bowls and garnished with the chopped coriander leaves.

Cook's Tip
Gram flour, also known as besan, is a pale-yellow flour made from ground chickpeas. More aromatic and with less starch content and higher protein than wheat flour, it is used widely in Indian cookery for doughs, batters and for thickening sauces. Look for it in large supermarkets or Asian food stores.

Tomato, Chilli and Egg Drop Soup

Popular in southern Vietnam and Cambodia, this spicy soup with eggs is probably adapted from the traditional Chinese egg drop soup. Served on its own with chunks of crusty bread, or accompanied by jasmine or ginger rice, this is a tasty dish for a light supper.

Serves 4
30ml/2 tbsp groundnut (peanut) or vegetable oil
3 shallots, finely sliced
2 garlic cloves, finely chopped
2 Thai chillies, seeded and finely sliced
25g/1oz galangal, shredded
8 large, ripe tomatoes, skinned, seeded and finely chopped
15ml/1 tbsp sugar
30ml/2 tbsp Thai fish sauce
4 lime leaves
900ml/1¹⁄₂ pints/3³⁄₄ cups chicken stock
15ml/1 tbsp wine vinegar
4 eggs
sea salt and ground black pepper

For the garnish
chilli oil, for drizzling
1 small bunch fresh coriander (cilantro), finely chopped
1 small bunch fresh mint leaves, finely chopped

1 Heat the oil in a wok or heavy pan. Stir in the shallots, garlic, chillies and galangal and cook until golden and fragrant. Add the tomatoes with the sugar, Thai fish sauce and lime leaves. Stir until it resembles a sauce. Pour in the stock and bring to the boil. Reduce the heat and simmer for 30 minutes. Season.

2 Just before serving, bring a wide pan of water to the boil. Add the vinegar and half a teaspoon of salt. Break the eggs into individual cups or small bowls.

3 Stir the water rapidly to create a swirl and drop an egg into the centre of the swirl. Follow immediately with the others, or poach two at a time, and keep the water boiling to throw the whites up over the yolks. Turn off the heat, cover the pan and leave to poach until firm enough to lift. Poached eggs are traditional, but you could use lightly fried eggs instead.

4 Using a slotted spoon, lift the eggs out of the water and slip them into the hot soup. Drizzle a little chilli oil over the eggs, sprinkle with the coriander and mint, and serve.

Chilli and Yogurt Soup Energy 226kcal/924kJ; Protein 18.8g; Carbohydrate 9.1g, of which sugars 5.9g; Fat 14.4g, of which saturates 2.3g; Cholesterol 29mg; Calcium 177mg; Fibre 0.5g; Sodium 90mg.
Tomato and Egg Soup Energy 181kcal/756kJ; Protein 8g; Carbohydrate 12.3g, of which sugars 11.5g; Fat 11.7g, of which saturates 2.4g; Cholesterol 190mg; Calcium 52mg; Fibre 2.3g; Sodium 280mg.

Spiced Mango Soup with Yogurt

This delicious, light soup comes from Chutney Mary's, the Anglo-Indian restaurant in London. It is best when served lightly chilled.

Serves 4
2 ripe mangoes
15ml/1 tbsp gram flour
120ml/4fl oz/½ cup natural (plain) yogurt
900ml/1½ pints/3¾ cups water
2.5ml/½ tsp grated fresh root ginger
2 red chillies, seeded and finely chopped
30ml/2 tbsp olive oil
2.5ml/½ tsp mustard seeds
2.5ml/½ tsp cumin seeds
8 curry leaves
salt and ground black pepper
fresh mint leaves, shredded, to garnish
natural (plain) yogurt, to serve

1 Peel the mangoes, remove the stones (pits) and cut the flesh into even chunks. Purée the flesh in a food processor or blender until smooth.

2 Pour the puréed mango into a pan and stir in the gram flour, yogurt, water, ginger and chillies. Bring the mixture slowly to the boil, stirring occasionally. Simmer for about 4–5 minutes until the mixture has thickened slightly. Remove the pan from the heat and set aside.

3 Heat the olive oil in a frying pan. Add the mustard seeds and cook for a few seconds until they begin to pop, then add the cumin seeds.

4 Add the curry leaves to the frying pan and then cook for 5 minutes. Stir the spice mixture into the soup, return it to the heat and cook for 10 minutes.

5 Press the soup through a sieve (strainer), if you like, then season to taste.

6 Leave the soup to cool completely, then chill in the refrigerator for at least 1 hour.

7 Ladle the soup into bowls, and top each with a dollop of yogurt. Garnish with shredded mint leaves and serve.

Chilli Coconut Soup with Pumpkin and Bamboo

This tasty soup is from Java, where it is served on its own with rice or as an accompaniment to a poached or grilled fish dish. In some parts of Java, the dish includes small prawns but, if it is packed with vegetables alone, it makes a satisfying vegetarian meal. Generally, such dishes are accompanied by a chilli sambal, which can be made by pounding chillies with shrimp paste and lime juice.

Serves 4
30ml/2 tbsp palm, groundnut (peanut) or corn oil
150g/5oz pumpkin flesh
115g/4oz yard-long beans
220g/7½oz can bamboo shoots, drained and rinsed
900ml/1½ pints coconut milk
10–15ml/2–3 tsp palm sugar (jaggery)
130g/4½oz fresh coconut, shredded
salt

For the spice paste
4 shallots, chopped
25g/1oz fresh root ginger, chopped
4 red chillies, seeded and chopped
2 garlic cloves, chopped
5ml/1 tsp coriander seeds
4 candlenuts, toasted and chopped

1 Make the spice paste. Using a mortar and pestle, grind all the ingredients together to form a smooth paste, or whizz them together in an electric blender or food processor.

2 Heat the oil in a wok or large, heavy pan, stir in the spice paste and fry until it smells fragrant. Toss the pumpkin, yard-long beans and bamboo shoots in the paste and pour in the coconut milk.

3 Add the sugar and bring to the boil. Reduce the heat and cook gently for 5–10 minutes, until the vegetables are tender. Season the soup and stir in half the fresh coconut.

4 Ladle the soup into individual warmed bowls, sprinkle with the remaining coconut and serve with bowls of cooked rice to spoon the soup over, and chilli sauce.

Spiced Mango Soup Energy 121kcal/508kJ; Protein 2.8g; Carbohydrate 14.7g, of which sugars 12.7g; Fat 6.2g, of which saturates 1g; Cholesterol 0mg; Calcium 73mg; Fibre 2.4g; Sodium 28mg.
Chilli Coconut Soup Energy 333kcal/388kJ; Protein 6g; Carbohydrate 26g, of which sugars 23.8g; Fat 23.6g, of which saturates 11.7g; Cholesterol 0mg; Calcium 115mg; Fibre 4.9g; Sodium 258mg.

Hot and Sour Prawn Soup

This is a classic Thai seafood soup called *tom yam kung*, and it is one of the most popular and best-known Thai soups.

Serves 4 to 6

450g/1lb raw king prawns (jumbo shrimp), thawed if frozen
1 litre/1¾ pints/4 cups chicken stock or water
3 lemon grass stalks, roots trimmed
10 kaffir lime leaves, torn in half
225g/8oz can straw mushrooms, drained
45ml/3 tbsp Thai fish sauce
60ml/4 tbsp fresh lime juice
30ml/2 tbsp chopped spring onion (scallion)
15ml/1 tbsp fresh coriander (cilantro) leaves
4 fresh red chillies, seeded and thinly sliced
salt and ground black pepper

1 Peel the prawns, reserving the shells. Devein the prawns and set aside until needed.

2 Rinse the prawn shells under cold water, then put them into a large pan along with the chicken stock or water. Bring the pan gently to the boil.

3 Bruise the lemon grass stalks and add them to the stock with half the lime leaves. Simmer gently for 5–6 minutes, until the stock is fragrant.

4 Strain the stock through a sieve (strainer), return it to the clean pan and gently reheat.

5 Add the drained mushrooms and the prawns, then cook until the prawns turn pink.

6 Stir the Thai fish sauce, lime juice, spring onion, coriander, chillies and the remaining lime leaves into the soup.

7 Taste and adjust the seasoning if necessary. The soup should be sour, salty, spicy and hot.

8 Simmer the soup for a further 5 minutes. Divide among soup bowls and serve immediately.

Hot and Sour Pineapple Prawn Broth

This simple dish is served as an appetite enhancer because of its hot and sour flavour. It is also popular as an accompaniment to plain rice or noodles. In some restaurants, the broth is presented in a hollowed-out pineapple, halved lengthways.

Serves 4

30ml/2 tbsp vegetable oil
15–30ml/1–2 tbsp tamarind paste
15ml/1 tbsp sugar
450g/1lb fresh prawns (shrimp), peeled and deveined
4 thick fresh pineapple slices, cored and cut into bitesize chunks
salt and ground black pepper
fresh coriander (cilantro) and mint leaves, to garnish
steamed rice or plain noodles, to serve

For the spice paste
4 shallots, chopped
4 red chillies, chopped
25g/1oz fresh root ginger, peeled and chopped
1 lemon grass stalk, trimmed and chopped
5ml/1 tsp shrimp paste

1 Using a mortar and pestle or a food processor, grind the shallots, chillies, ginger and lemon grass to a paste. Add the shrimp paste and mix well.

2 Heat the oil in a wok or heavy pan. Stir in the spice paste and fry until fragrant. Stir in the tamarind paste and the sugar, then pour in 1.2 litres/2 pints/5 cups water. Mix well and bring to the boil. Reduce the heat and simmer for 10 minutes. Season the broth with salt and pepper.

3 Add the prawns and pineapple to the broth and simmer for 4–5 minutes, or until the prawns are cooked. Using a slotted spoon, lift the prawns and pineapple out of the broth and divide them among four warmed bowls. Ladle over some of the broth and garnish with coriander and mint leaves.

4 The remaining broth can be served separately as a drink, or spooned over steamed rice or plain noodles, if they are accompanying this dish.

Hot and sour **Prawn Soup** Energy 103kcal/434kj; Protein 21.5g; Carbohydrate 1.1g; of which sugars 0.7g; Fat 1.4g, of which saturates 0.2g; Cholesterol 219mg; Calcium 100mg; Fibre 0.8g; Sodium 892mg.
Pineapple Prawn Broth Energy 192kcal/808kJ; Protein 20.4g; Carbohydrate 14.2g, of which sugars 13.9g; Fat 6.4g, of which saturates 0.8g; Cholesterol 219mg; Calcium 111mg; Fibre 1.3g; Sodium 216mg.

Tomato Soup with Chilli Squid and Tarragon

Oriental-style seared squid mingles with the pungent tomato and garlic flavours of the Mediterranean.

Serves 4
4 small squid (or 1–2 large squid)
60ml/4 tbsp olive oil
2 shallots, chopped
1 garlic clove, crushed
1.2kg/2½ lb ripe tomatoes,
  roughly chopped
15ml/1 tbsp sun-dried
  tomato paste
450ml/¾ pint/2 scant cups
  vegetable stock
about 2.5ml/½ tsp sugar
2 red chillies, seeded
  and chopped
30ml/2 tbsp chopped
  fresh tarragon
salt and ground black pepper
crusty bread, to serve

1 Wash the squid under cold water. Grasp the head and tentacles and pull the body away with the other hand. Discard the intestines that come away. Cut the tentacles away from the head in one piece and reserve; discard the head. Pull the quills out of the main body and remove any roe. Pull off the fins from the body pouch and rub off the semi-transparent, mottled skin. Wash the squid under cold water. Cut into rings and set these aside with the tentacles.

2 Heat 30ml/2 tbsp of the oil in a heavy pan. Add the shallots and garlic, and cook for 4–5 minutes, until softened. Add the tomatoes and tomato paste. Season, cover and cook for 3 minutes. Add half the stock and simmer for 5 minutes, until the tomatoes are soft. Cool the soup, then rub it through a sieve (strainer) and return it to the rinsed-out pan. Stir in the remaining stock and sugar, and reheat gently.

3 Meanwhile, heat the remaining oil in a frying pan. Add the squid rings and tentacles, and the chillies. Cook for 4–5 minutes, stirring, then remove from the heat and stir in the tarragon.

4 Adjust the seasoning if necessary. If the soup tastes slightly sharp, add a little extra sugar. Ladle the soup into bowls and spoon the chilli squid in the centre. Serve with crusty bread.

Crab and Chilli Soup

Prepared fresh crab is readily available and perfect for creating an exotic soup in minutes.

Serves 4
45ml/3 tbsp olive oil
1 red onion, finely chopped
2 red chillies, seeded and
  finely chopped
1 garlic clove, finely chopped
450g/1lb fresh white crab meat
30ml/2 tbsp chopped
  fresh parsley
30ml/2 tbsp chopped fresh
  coriander (cilantro)
juice of 2 lemons
1 lemon grass stalk
1 litre/1¾ pints/4 cups good fish
  or chicken stock
15ml/1 tbsp Thai fish sauce
150g/5oz vermicelli or angel hair
  pasta, broken into 5–7.5cm/
  2–3in lengths
salt and ground black pepper

For the coriander relish
50g/2oz/1 cup fresh coriander
  (cilantro) leaves
1 green chilli, seeded and chopped
15ml/1 tbsp sunflower oil
25ml/1½ tbsp lemon juice
2.5ml/½ tsp ground roasted
  cumin seeds

1 Heat the oil in a pan and add the onion, chillies and garlic. Cook for 10 minutes until the onion is soft. Transfer to a bowl with the crab meat, parsley, coriander and lemon juice. Set aside.

2 Bruise the lemon grass and add to a pan with the stock and fish sauce. Add the lemon grass and bring to the boil, then stir in the pasta. Simmer, uncovered, for 3–4 minutes or cook for the time suggested on the packet, until the pasta is tender but al dente.

3 Meanwhile, make the coriander relish. Place the coriander, chilli, oil, lemon juice and cumin in a food processor or blender and process to form a coarse paste. Add seasoning to taste.

4 Remove and discard the lemon grass from the soup. Stir the chilli and crab mixture into the soup and season it well. Bring to the boil, then reduce the heat and simmer for 2 minutes.

5 Ladle the soup into four deep, warmed bowls and put a spoonful of the relish in the centre of each. Serve the soup immediately.

Tomato Soup Energy 186kcal/777kj; Protein 8.1g; Carbohydrate 10.9g; of which sugars 10.2g; Fat 12.6g; of which saturates 2g; Cholesterol 48mg; Calcium 30mg; Fibre 1.7g; Sodium 386mg.
Crab and Chilli Soup Energy 228kcal/951kj; Protein 23.6g; Carbohydrate 5.4g; of which sugars 5g; Fat 12.6g; of which saturates 6g; Cholesterol 90mg; Calcium 199mg; Fibre 1.1g; Sodium 767mg.

Hot and Sour Filipino Fish Soup

Chunky, filling and spicy, the Filipino fish soups are meals in themselves. There are many variations on the theme, depending on the region and the local fish, but most contain a lot of shellfish, and are flavoured with tamarind mixed with hot chilli, and served with coconut vinegar that is flavoured by garlic. Served on its own or with rice, this soup awakens the senses.

Serves 4 to 6
2 litres/3½ pints/8 cups fish stock
250ml/8fl oz/1 cup white wine
15–30ml/1–2 tbsp
  tamarind paste
30–45ml/2–3 tbsp patis
  (fish sauce)
30ml/2 tbsp palm sugar (jaggery)

50g/2oz fresh root ginger, grated
2–3 red or green chillies, seeded
  and finely sliced
2 tomatoes, skinned, seeded and
  cut into wedges
350g/12oz fresh fish, such as
  trout, sea bass, swordfish or
  cod, cut into bitesize chunks
12–16 fresh prawns (shrimp),
  in their shells
1 bunch fresh basil leaves,
  roughly chopped
1 bunch flat leaf parsley,
  roughly chopped
salt and ground black pepper

To serve
60–90ml/4–6 tbsp
  coconut vinegar
1–2 garlic cloves, finely chopped
1–2 limes, cut into wedges
2 red or green chillies, seeded
  and quartered lengthways

1 In a wok or large pan, bring the stock and wine to the boil. Stir in the tamarind paste, patis, sugar, ginger and chillies. Reduce the heat and simmer for 15–20 minutes.

2 Add the tomatoes to the broth and season with salt and pepper. Add the fish and prawns and simmer for a further 5 minutes, until the fish is cooked.

3 In a bowl, mix the coconut vinegar and garlic for serving and set aside. Stir half the basil and half the parsley into the broth.

4 Ladle into bowls. Garnish with the remaining basil and parsley and serve with the spiked coconut vinegar to splash on top, the lime wedges to squeeze into the soup, and the chillies to chew on for extra heat.

Spicy Indonesian Chicken Broth

Colourful and crunchy, this South-east Asian soup can be served as an appetizer or as a dish on its own.

Serves 4 to 6
30ml/2 tbsp palm, groundnut
  (peanut) or corn oil
25g/1oz fresh root ginger,
  finely chopped
25g/1oz fresh turmeric, finely
  chopped, or 5ml/1 tsp
  ground turmeric
1 lemon grass stalk, finely chopped
4–5 kaffir lime leaves, crushed
4 candlenuts, coarsely ground
2 garlic cloves, crushed
5ml/1 tsp coriander seeds
5ml/1 tsp shrimp paste
2 litres/3½ pints chicken stock

corn or vegetable oil, for deep-frying
2 waxy potatoes, finely sliced
350g/12oz skinless chicken
  breast fillets, thinly sliced
  widthways
150g/5oz leafy green cabbage,
  finely sliced
150g/5oz mung beansprouts
3 hard-boiled eggs, thinly sliced
salt and ground black pepper

To serve
1 bunch fresh coriander (cilantro)
  leaves, roughly chopped
2–3 spring onions (scallions),
  finely sliced
2–3 hot red or green chillies,
  seeded and finely sliced
2 limes, cut into wedges
kecap manis

1 Arrange the ingredients for serving attractively on a platter or in serving bowls.

2 Heat the oil in a pan, stir in the ginger, turmeric, lemon grass, kaffir lime leaves, candlenuts, garlic, coriander seeds and shrimp paste. Fry until the mixture darkens and becomes fragrant. Pour in the stock, bring to the boil, then simmer for about 20 minutes.

3 Meanwhile, heat the oil for deep-frying in a wok. Fry the potato slices until crisp. Remove with a slotted spoon, drain on kitchen paper and put aside. Strain the chicken stock and reserve. Pour back into the pan and season. Return to the boil, reduce the heat and add the chicken. Simmer for 2–3 minutes.

4 Sprinkle the cabbage and beansprouts into the base of the serving bowls. Ladle in the broth and top with the eggs and potatoes, and serve. Diners help themselves to the ingredients for serving, and the kecap manis to drizzle over the top.

Hot and Sour Filipino Fish Soup Energy 137kcal/576kJ; Protein 17.7g; Carbohydrate 8.1g, of which sugars 8g; Fat 1g, of which saturates 0.1g; Cholesterol 92mg; Calcium 76mg; Fibre 1.3g; Sodium 644mg.
Spicy Indonesian Broth Energy 296kcal/1238kJ; Protein 21.1g; Carbohydrate 14.8g, of which sugars 3g; Fat 17.5g, of which saturates 2.8g; Cholesterol 136mg; Calcium 63mg; Fibre 2.7g; Sodium 96mg.

Chilli Chicken Noodle Soup

Nowadays a signature dish of the city of Chiang Mai, this delicious noodle soup originated in Burma, now called Myanmar, which lies only a little to the north. It is also the Thai equivalent of the famous Malaysian laksa.

Serves 4 to 6
600ml/1 pint/2½ cups coconut milk
30ml/2 tbsp Thai red curry paste
5ml/1 tsp ground turmeric
450g/1lb chicken thighs, boned
 and cut into bitesize chunks
600ml/1 pint/2½ cups
 chicken stock

60ml/4 tbsp Thai fish sauce
15ml/1 tbsp dark soy sauce
juice of ½–1 lime
450g/1lb fresh egg noodles,
 blanched briefly in boiling water
salt and ground black pepper

To garnish
3 spring onions (scallions), chopped
4 fresh red chillies, chopped
4 shallots, chopped
60ml/4 tbsp sliced pickled
 mustard leaves, rinsed
30ml/2 tbsp fried sliced garlic
coriander (cilantro) leaves
4–6 fried noodle nests (optional)

1 Pour about one-third of the coconut milk into a large, heavy pan or wok. Bring to the boil over a medium heat, stirring frequently with a wooden spoon until the milk separates.

2 Add the curry paste and ground turmeric, stir to mix completely and cook until the mixture is fragrant. Add the chunks of chicken and toss over the heat for about 2 minutes, making sure that they are thoroughly coated with the paste.

3 Add the remaining coconut milk, the chicken stock, fish sauce and soy sauce. Season with salt and pepper to taste. Bring to simmering point, stirring frequently, then lower the heat and cook gently for 7–10 minutes. Remove from the heat and stir in lime juice to taste.

4 Reheat the fresh egg noodles in boiling water, drain and divide among four to six warmed bowls. Divide the chunks of chicken among the bowls and ladle in the hot soup. Top each serving with spring onions, chillies, shallots, pickled mustard leaves, fried garlic, coriander leaves and a fried noodle nest, if using. Serve immediately.

Roasted Garlic and Pork Soup with Chilli

Made with pork or chicken, this warming and sustaining rice soup combines ancient traditions of the Filipino rice culture with Spanish colonial techniques of browning and sautéeing.

Serves 4 to 6
15–30ml/1–2 tbsp palm or
 groundnut (peanut) oil
1 large onion, finely chopped.
2 garlic cloves, finely chopped
25g/1oz fresh root ginger,
 finely chopped
350g/12oz pork rump or
 tenderloin, cut widthways into
 bitesize slices

5–6 black peppercorns
115g/4oz/1 cup plus 15ml/1 tbsp
 short grain rice
2 litres/3½ pints/8 cups pork or
 chicken stock
30ml/2 tbsp patis (fish sauce)
salt

To serve
2 garlic cloves, finely chopped
2 spring onions (scallions), white
 parts only, finely sliced
2–3 green or red chillies, seeded
 and quartered lengthways

1 Heat the oil in a wok or deep, heavy pan that has a lid. Stir in the onion, garlic and ginger and fry until fragrant and beginning to colour. Add the pork and fry, stirring frequently, for 5–6 minutes, until lightly browned. Stir in the peppercorns.

2 Meanwhile, put the rice in a sieve (strainer), rinse under cold running water until the water runs clear, then drain. Toss the rice into the pan, making sure that it is coated in the mixture.

3 Pour in the stock, add the patis and bring to the boil. Reduce the heat and partially cover with a lid. Simmer for 40 minutes, stirring ocassionally to make sure that the rice doesn't stick to the bottom of the pan. Season with salt to taste.

4 Just before serving, dry-fry the garlic in a small, heavy pan until golden brown, then stir it into the soup. Ladle the soup into individual warmed bowls and sprinkle the spring onions over the top. Serve the chillies separately, to chew on.

Chilli Chicken Soup Energy 606kcal/2569kj; Protein 39.5g; Carbohydrate 88.7g; of which sugars 10.1g; Fat 12.9g; of which saturates 3.7g; Cholesterol 135mg; Calcium 84mg; Fibre 3.3g; Sodium 1111mg.
Garlic and Pork Soup Energy 195kcal/813kj; Protein 14.8g; Carbohydrate 19.9g, of which sugars 3.4g; Fat 6.2g, of which saturates 1.3g; Cholesterol 37mg; Calcium 24mg; Fibre 0.8g; Sodium 399mg.

Spicy Tripe Soup with Lemon Grass and Lime

This popular Indonesian soup is packed with spices and the refreshing flavours of lemon grass and lime.

Serves 4

250ml/8fl oz/1 cup rice
  wine vinegar
900g/2lb beef tripe, cleaned
2 litres/3½ pints/8 cups beef
  stock or water
2–3 garlic cloves, crushed whole
2 lemon grass stalks
25g/1oz fresh root ginger,
  finely grated
3–4 kaffir lime leaves

225g/8oz mooli (daikon) or
  turnip, finely sliced
15ml/1 tbsp palm, groundnut
  (peanut) or vegetable oil
4 shallots, finely sliced
salt and ground black pepper

For the sambal

15ml/1 tbsp palm, groundnut
  (peanut) or vegetable oil
2 garlic cloves, crushed
2–3 hot red chillies, seeded and
  finely chopped
15ml/1 tbsp chilli and shrimp paste
25ml/1½ tbsp tomato
  purée (paste)

1 Fill a large pan with about 2.5 litres/4½ pints/11¼ cups water and bring to the boil. Reduce the heat and add the vinegar and the tripe. Season and simmer gently for 1 hour.

2 Prepare the sambal. Heat the oil in a pan. Stir in the garlic and chillies and fry until fragrant. Stir in the chilli and shrimp paste, then add the tomato purée and mix. Set aside.

3 When the tripe is cooked, drain and cut into bitesize squares or strips. Pour the stock or water into a pan and bring to the boil. Reduce the heat and add the tripe, garlic, lemon grass, ginger, lime leaves and mooli or turnip. Cook gently for 15–20 minutes, until the mooli or turnip is tender.

4 Meanwhile, heat the oil in a frying pan. Add the shallots and fry for 5 minutes or until golden brown. Drain on kitchen paper.

5 Ladle the soup into individual warmed bowls and sprinkle the shallots over the top. Serve the soup with the spicy sambal, which can be added in a dollop and stirred in.

Hot and Spicy Beef and Fern Frond Soup

Known as *yukgejang*, this is one of the most traditional Korean soups. The smoky taste of fern fronds gives it its unique flavour, and red chilli powder provides a fierce kick and fiery colour to the combination of beef and leek. It makes a perfect lunch dish when served with a bowl of rice.

Serves 2 to 3

75g/3oz dried edible fern fronds

75g/3oz enoki
  mushrooms, trimmed
250g/9oz beef flank
10ml/2 tsp sesame oil
30ml/2 tbsp chilli powder
1 garlic clove, peeled and
  finely chopped
15ml/1 tbsp vegetable oil
75g/3oz/½ cup
  beansprouts, trimmed
1 leek, sliced
1 spring onion (scallion),
  finely sliced
salt

1 Boil the dried fern fronds for about 3 minutes. Drain and rinse with cold water. Cut the fronds into thirds and discard the tougher stem pieces, along with the enoki mushroom caps.

2 Place the beef in a medium pan and cover with water. Bring to the boil, cover and cook over high heat for 30 minutes. Then remove the beef and strain the stock into a jug (pitcher).

3 Cut the beef into thin strips and place in a bowl. Add the sesame oil, chilli powder and chopped garlic, and coat the meat.

4 Heat the vegetable oil in a pan and add the meat with the fern fronds, beansprouts, leek and spring onion. Stir-fry for 2 minutes, then reduce the heat and pour in the beef stock. Cover and cook gently for 30 minutes or so until tender. Add the mushrooms and salt and simmer for 2 minutes. Serve.

Cook's Tip
If edible fern shoots are not available, the best alternative is an equivalent amount of shiitake mushrooms.

Spicy Tripe Soup Energy 160kcal/668kJ; Protein 19.2g; Carbohydrate 5.5g, of which sugars 4.8g; Fat 7g, of which saturates 1.1g; Cholesterol 163mg; Calcium 198mg; Fibre 1.9g; Sodium 299mg.
Hot and Spicy Beef Soup Energy 225kcal/935kJ; Protein 21.5g; Carbohydrate 3g, of which sugars 2g; Fat 14.1g, of which saturates 4g; Cholesterol 48mg; Calcium 28mg; Fibre 2.3g; Sodium 59mg.

Roasted Coconut Cashew Nuts with Chilli

Serve these hot and sweet cashew nuts in paper or cellophane cones at parties. Not only do they look enticing and taste terrific, but the cones help to keep clothes and hands clean and can simply be thrown away afterwards.

Serves 6 to 8

15ml/1 tbsp groundnut (peanut) oil
30ml/2 tbsp clear honey
250g/8oz/2 cups cashew nuts
115g/4oz/1⅓ cups desiccated
  (dry unsweetened
  shredded) coconut
2 small fresh red chillies,
  seeded and finely chopped
salt and ground black pepper

1 Heat the oil in a wok or large frying pan.

2 Stir the honey into the pan and heat for a few seconds, stirring constantly.

3 Add the nuts and the desiccated coconut and stir-fry until both are golden brown. Stir the mixture constantly to ensure that it does not stick to the base of the pan.

4 Add the chillies to the pan and season with a little salt and ground black pepper to taste. Toss until all the ingredients are well mixed.

5 Serve the nuts warm or cooled in rolled-up paper cones or on saucers.

Variations
• Almonds would also work well in this recipe. Cashew nuts can be expensive so you could also choose peanuts for a more economical snack.
• Desiccated coconut is a handy ingredient to have in your pantry as it has many uses, but if you can get hold of a fresh coconut then you can also use that in this recipe. Simply grate the flesh and substitute for the desiccated version.

Rice Cakes with Spicy Dipping Sauce

Prepare these rice cakes at least a day before you plan to serve them, as the rice needs to dry out overnight.

Serves 4 to 6

175g/6oz/1 cup Thai jasmine rice
350ml/12fl oz/1½ cups water
oil, for deep-frying and greasing

For the spicy dipping sauce
6 dried chillies, halved and seeded
2.5ml/½ tsp salt
2 shallots, chopped
2 garlic cloves, chopped
4 coriander (cilantro) roots
10 white peppercorns
250ml/8fl oz/1 cup coconut milk
5ml/1 tsp shrimp paste
115g/4oz minced (ground) pork
115g/4oz cherry tomatoes, chopped
15ml/1 tbsp Thai fish sauce
15ml/1 tbsp palm sugar (jaggery)
  or light muscovado (brown) sugar
30ml/2 tbsp tamarind juice
  (tamarind paste mixed with
  warm water)
30ml/2 tbsp coarsely chopped
  roasted peanuts
2 spring onions (scallions), chopped

1 For the sauce, soak the chillies in warm water for 20 minutes. Drain and crush in a mortar with the salt. Add the shallots, garlic, coriander and peppercorns. Pound to a coarse paste.

2 Boil the coconut milk in a pan until it separates. Add the chilli paste and cook for 2–3 minutes. Stir in the shrimp paste.

3 Add the pork and cook for 5–10 minutes. Stir in the tomatoes, fish sauce, sugar and tamarind juice. Simmer, stirring until thickened, then stir in the peanuts and spring onions. Leave to cool.

4 Preheat the oven to the lowest setting. Wash the rice in several changes of water. Put it in a pan, add the water, cover and bring to the boil. Reduce the heat and simmer for 15 minutes.

5 Fluff up the rice. Spoon on to a greased baking sheet and press down. Leave in the oven to dry out overnight.

6 Break the rice into cake-size pieces. Heat the oil in a wok or deep-fryer. Deep-fry the cakes, in batches, for about 1 minute, until they puff up. Remove and drain well. Serve with the sauce.

Roasted Nuts Energy 436kcal/1810kJ; Protein 9.7g; Carbohydrate 22.1g, of which sugars 16.6g; Fat 34.9g, of which saturates 14.8g; Cholesterol 0mg; Calcium 20mg; Fibre 4g; Sodium 128mg.
Rice Cakes Energy 316kcal/1508kJ; Protein 11.7g; Carbohydrate 42g, of which sugars 8.8g; Fat 16g, of which saturates 2.9g; Cholesterol 19mg; Calcium 38mg; Fibre 0.8g; Sodium 359mg.

Spiced Walnut and Red Chilli

Made primarily of walnuts, this spicy Turkish dip is usually served with toasted flatbread or chunks of crusty bread. It can also be served as an accompaniment to grilled, broiled or barbecued meats. Arabic in origin, this dish is traditionally made with pomegranate juice, but modern recipes often use lemon juice instead.

Serves 4 to 6
175g/6oz/1 cup broken
    shelled walnuts
5ml/1 tsp cumin seeds, dry-
    roasted and ground
5–10ml/1–2 tsp Turkish red
    pepper, or 1–2 fresh red

chillies, seeded and finely
    chopped, or 5ml/1 tsp
    chilli powder
1–2 garlic cloves (optional)
1 slice of day-old bread, sprinkled
    with water and left for a few
    minutes, then squeezed dry
15–30ml/1–2 tbsp tomato
    purée (paste)
5–10ml/1–2 tsp sugar
30ml/2 tbsp pomegranate syrup
    or juice of 1 lemon
120ml/4fl oz/½ cup olive or
    sunflower oil, plus extra
    for serving
salt and ground black pepper
a few sprigs of fresh flat leaf
    parsley, to garnish
strips of pitta bread, to serve

1 Using a large mortar and pestle, pound the walnuts with the cumin seeds, red pepper or the fresh red chillies and garlic.

2 Add the soaked bread and pound to a paste, then beat in the tomato purée, sugar and pomegranate syrup or the juice of a lemon, if using.

3 Now slowly drizzle in 120ml/4fl oz/½ cup oil, beating all the time until the paste is thick and light. Season with salt and ground black pepper, and spoon into a bowl.

4 Splash a little olive oil over the top to keep it moist, and garnish with parsley leaves. Serve at room temperature.

Cook's Tip
If you have an electric blender, whizz the ingredients together.

Roast Vegetables with Fresh Herbs and Chilli Sauce

Oven roasting brings out all the flavours of these classic Mediterranean vegetables. Serve them hot with grilled or roast meat or fish.

Serves 4
2–3 courgettes (zucchini)
1 large onion

1 red (bell) pepper
16 cherry tomatoes
2 garlic cloves, chopped
pinch of cumin seeds
5ml/1 tsp fresh thyme or
    4–5 torn basil leaves
60ml/4 tbsp olive oil
juice of ½ lemon
5–10ml/1–2 tsp harissa
fresh thyme sprigs, to garnish

1 Preheat the oven to 220°C/425°F/Gas 7. Cut the courgettes into long thin strips. Cut the onion into thin wedges and cut the pepper into fairly large chunks, discarding the seeds and core.

2 Place the vegetables in a roasting pan, add the tomatoes, garlic, cumin seeds and thyme or basil. Sprinkle with oil and toss to coat. Cook in the oven for 25–30 minutes until the vegetables are soft and slightly charred at the edges.

3 Blend the lemon juice and harissa and stir into the vegetables just before serving, garnished with the fresh thyme sprigs.

Variation
Try wedges of red and yellow (bell) peppers in place of one of the courgettes, or add chunks of aubergine (eggplant).

Cook's Tip
Harissa is a spicy paste made from a base of beetroot (beets) and carrots and flavoured with chillies, coriander seeds, caraway, garlic, salt and olive oil. It is a popular ingredient in northern African cooking and is sold in small pots – look out for its distinctive orangey red colour.

Spiced Walnut Energy 339kcal/1399kJ; Protein 4.8g; Carbohydrate 5.1g, of which sugars 2.8g; Fat 33.4g, of which saturates 3.5g; Cholesterol 0mg; Calcium 34mg; Fibre 1.2g; Sodium 32mg.
Roast Vegetables Energy 154kcal/635kJ; Protein 3.7g; Carbohydrate 8.2g, of which sugars 7.6g; Fat 12g, of which saturates 1.8g; Cholesterol 0mg; Calcium 48mg; Fibre 2.8g; Sodium 8mg.

Deep-fried Eggs with Red Chilli

Another name for this Chinese dish is mother-in-law eggs, which comes from a story about a prospective bridegroom who very much wanted to impress his future mother-in-law and devised a new recipe based on the only dish he knew how to make – boiled eggs.

Serves 4 to 6
30ml/2 tbsp vegetable oil
6 shallots, thinly sliced

6 garlic cloves, thinly sliced
6 fresh red chillies, sliced
oil, for deep-frying
6 hard-boiled eggs, shelled
salad leaves, to serve
sprigs of fresh coriander (cilantro),
*   to garnish*

For the sauce
75g/3oz/6 tbsp palm sugar
*   (jaggery) or light muscovado*
*   (brown) sugar*
75ml/5 tbsp Thai fish sauce
90ml/6 tbsp tamarind juice

1 Make the sauce. Put the sugar, fish sauce and tamarind juice in a pan. Bring to the boil, stirring until the sugar dissolves, lower the heat and simmer for 5 minutes. Taste and add more sugar, fish sauce or tamarind juice, if needed. Transfer to a bowl.

2 Heat the vegetable oil in a frying pan and cook the shallots, garlic and chillies for 5 minutes. Transfer to a bowl and set aside.

3 Heat the oil in a deep-fryer or wok to 190°C/375°F or until a cube of bread, added to the oil, browns in about 45 seconds. Deep-fry the eggs in the hot oil for about 3–5 minutes, or until they turn a golden brown colour. Remove from the oil and drain well on kitchen paper.

4 Cut the eggs into quarters and arrange them on a bed of salad leaves. Drizzle with the prepared sauce and sprinkle over the shallot mixture. Garnish with the coriander sprigs and serve immediately.

Cook's Tip
The level of heat varies, depending on which type of chillies are used and whether or not you include the seeds.

Chilli Potatoes

There are several variations on this chilli and potato dish, but the most important thing is the spicing, which is made even more piquant by adding a little vinegar. This recipe uses dried chillies, but fresh ones can be substituted.

Serves 4
675g/1½lb small new potatoes
75ml/5 tbsp olive oil

2 garlic cloves, sliced
3 dried chillies, seeded
*   and chopped*
2.5ml/½ tsp ground cumin
10ml/2 tsp paprika
30ml/2 tbsp red or white
*   wine vinegar*
1 red or green (bell) pepper,
*   seeded and sliced*
coarse sea salt, for sprinkling
*   (optional)*

1 Scrub the potatoes and put them into a pan of salted water. Bring to the boil and cook for 10 minutes, or until almost tender. Drain and leave to cool slightly. Peel, if you like, then cut into chunks.

2 Heat the olive oil in a large frying pan and fry the potatoes over a medium-high heat, turning them frequently, until they have turned a golden brown colour.

3 Meanwhile, crush together the garlic, chillies and cumin to a paste using a mortar and pestle.

4 Mix the paste with the paprika and red or white wine vinegar, then add to the potatoes with the sliced pepper and cook, stirring, for about 2 minutes. Sprinkle with sea salt, if using, and serve the potatoes hot as a tapas dish or cold as a side dish with a main course.

Cook's Tip
This potato dish is an essential part of a tapas meal in Spain, where the dish is known as patatas bravas, *literally meaning 'fierce potatoes' owing to the heat. The classic version is made as above with a spicy tomato and chilli sauce poured over before serving.*

Hot Spring Rolls

These Thai spring rolls are filled with a tasty garlic, pork and noodle mixture.

Makes 24
24 X 15cm/6in square spring roll
   wrappers, thawed if frozen
30ml/2 tbsp plain
   (all-purpose) flour
vegetable oil, for deep-frying
sweet chilli dipping sauce, to serve

For the filling
6 Chinese dried mushrooms, soaked
   for 30 minutes in warm water
50g/2oz cellophane noodles
30ml/2 tbsp vegetable oil

2 garlic cloves, chopped
2 fresh red chillies, seeded
   and chopped
225g/8oz minced (ground) pork
50g/2oz peeled cooked prawns
   (shrimp), thawed if frozen
30ml/2 tbsp Thai fish sauce
5ml/1 tsp sugar
1 carrot, grated
50g/2oz piece of canned bamboo
   shoot, drained and chopped
50g/2oz/²⁄₃ cup beansprouts
2 spring onions (scallions),
   finely chopped
15ml/1 tbsp chopped fresh
   coriander (cilantro)
ground black pepper

1 Drain the mushrooms. Cut off and discard the stems. Chop the caps finely. Cover the noodles with boiling water and soak for 10 minutes. Drain and snip them into 5cm/2in lengths. Heat the oil in a wok, add the garlic and chillies and stir-fry for 30 seconds. Transfer to a plate.

2 Stir-fry the pork until browned. Add the mushrooms, noodles and prawns. Stir in the fish sauce and sugar. Season with pepper. Pour into a bowl. Stir in the carrot, bamboo, beansprouts, spring onions and coriander. Mix in the reserved chilli mixture.

3 Stir a little water into the flour in a small bowl to make a paste. Place a spoonful of the filling in the centre of a wrapper. Turn the bottom edge over to cover the filling, then fold in the sides. Roll up almost to the top, then brush the top edge with the flour paste and seal. Fill the remaining wrappers.

4 Heat the oil in a deep-fryer or wok to 190°C/375°F, or until a cube of bread browns in about 45 seconds. Fry the spring rolls, in batches, until crisp and golden. Drain on kitchen paper and serve hot with sweet chilli sauce.

Seafood Fritters with a Fiery Pear and Chilli Dip

Succulent seafood is battered and lightly fried to create these golden fritters.

Serves 4
2 eggs, beaten
45ml/3 tbsp vegetable oil, for frying
75g/3oz/²⁄₃ cup plain (all-purpose)
   flour for dusting
salt and ground black pepper

For the dipping sauce
45ml/3 tbsp light soy sauce
45ml/3 tbsp sugar
1 garlic clove, crushed
10ml/2 tsp pear juice
2.5ml/½ tsp lemon juice
1.5ml/½ tsp Korean chilli powder

For the prawn fritters
5 medium-size prawns
   (shrimp), peeled

juice of ½ lemon
30ml/2 tbsp white wine
2.5ml/½ tsp sesame oil
1 dried shiitake mushroom,
   soaked in warm water for
   about 30 minutes until soft
1 green chilli, finely chopped

For the crab fritters
75g/3oz crab meat
3 oyster mushrooms, finely sliced
¼ green (bell) pepper, chopped
25g/1oz Korean chives, finely sliced
1 garlic clove, thinly sliced
2 eggs, beaten
45ml/3 tbsp plain (all-purpose) flour

For the cod fritters
300g/11oz cod fillet
7.5ml/1½ tsp dark soy sauce
5ml/1 tsp white wine
2.5ml/½ tsp sesame oil

1 Combine all the ingredients for the sauce in a small bowl. For the prawn fritters, season the prawns with salt, pepper, lemon juice, white wine and sesame oil. Chop the mushroom and mix with the chilli, season with sesame oil, and dust with flour. Set aside. Dust the prawns with flour. Coat with egg and set aside.

2 To make the crab fritters, season the crab meat and place in a bowl. Add the remaining ingredients, mix well and set aside. For the cod fritters, cut into bitesize pieces and mix with the other ingredients. Dust with flour, coat with egg and set aside.

3 Heat the oil in a frying pan. Fry the fritters until browned and then add mushroom mixture to the prawn fritters. Continue frying until all are golden brown. Serve with the dipping sauce.

Hot Spring Rolls Energy 135kcal/562kJ; Protein 3.1g; Carbohydrate 7.8g, of which sugars 0.5g; Fat 10.3g, of which saturates 1.4g; Cholesterol 10mg; Calcium 15mg; Fibre 0.4g; Sodium 41g.
Seafood Fritters Energy 294kcal/1227kJ; Protein 29.3g; Carbohydrate 9.1g, of which sugars 6.1g; Fat 15.3g, of which saturates 2.8g; Cholesterol 287mg; Calcium 103mg; Fibre 1.1g; Sodium 671mg.

Scallops in Hot Chilli Sauce

Shellfish are often cooked very simply in Mexico. Hot chilli sauce and lime are popular ingredients in many fish recipes.

Serves 4
20 scallops
2 courgettes (zucchini)
75g/3oz/6 tbsp butter
15ml/1 tbsp vegetable oil
4 garlic cloves, chopped
30ml/2 tbsp hot chilli sauce
juice of 1 lime
small bunch of fresh coriander
(cilantro), finely chopped

1 If you have bought scallops in their shells, open them. Hold a scallop shell in the palm of your hand, with the flat side uppermost. Insert the blade of a knife close to the hinge that joins the shells and prise them apart. Run the blade of the knife across the inside of the flat shell to cut away the scallop. Only the white adductor muscle and the orange coral are eaten, so pull away and discard all other parts. Rinse the scallops under cold running water.

2 Cut the courgettes in half, then into four pieces. Melt the butter in the vegetable oil in a large frying pan. Add the courgettes to the pand and fry for about 5 minutes, or until soft. Remove from the pan.

3 Add the garlic to the frying pan and fry until golden. Stir in the hot chilli sauce.

4 Add the scallops to the sauce. Cook, stirring constantly, for 1–2 minutes only.

5 Stir in the lime juice, chopped coriander and the courgette pieces. Serve immediately on heated plates.

Cook's Tip
Oil is capable of withstanding higher temperatures than butter, but butter gives fried food added flavour. Using a mixture of both ingredients, as here, provides the perfect compromise because the oil prevents the butter from burning.

Rice Seaweed Roll with Spicy Squid

This Korean favourite is cooked rice, wrapped in seaweed, and then served with spicy squid and mooli. This delicious snack is perfect when accompanied by a bowl of clear soup.

Serves 2
400g/14oz/4 cups cooked rice
rice vinegar, for drizzling
sesame oil, for drizzling
150g/5oz squid, trimmed,
    cleaned, and skinned
90g/3½oz mooli (daikon), peeled
    and diced
3 large sheets dried seaweed
    or nori

For the squid seasoning
22.5ml/4½ tsp Korean
    chilli powder
7.5ml/1½ tsp sugar
1 garlic clove, crushed
5ml/1 tsp sesame oil
2.5ml/½ tsp sesame seeds

For the mooli seasoning
15ml/1 tbsp sugar
30ml/2 tbsp rice vinegar
22.5ml/4½ tsp Korean
    chilli powder
15ml/1 tbsp Thai fish sauce
1 garlic clove, crushed
1 spring onion (scallion),
    finely chopped

1 Put the cooked rice in a bowl and drizzle over some rice vinegar and sesame oil. Mix well, then set aside. Use a sharp knife to score the squid with a criss-cross pattern, and slice into pieces about 5cm/2in long and 1cm/½in wide.

2 Bring a pan of water to the boil over high heat. Blanch the squid for 3 minutes, then drain under cold running water. Combine all the squid seasoning ingredients in a bowl, and then coat the squid. Set aside to absorb the flavours.

3 Put the mooli in a bowl, then drizzle over some rice vinegar. Leave for 15 minutes and then drain the mooli and transfer to a bowl. Add the mooli seasoning ingredients, mix well and chill in the refrigerator.

4 Place the rice evenly on each of the three seaweed sheets, roll each into a cylinder and slice into bitesize pieces.

5 Arrange the rolls on a serving plate and serve with the seasoned squid and mooli.

Spiced Whelks

This Korean salad is a popular appetizer, often eaten as a snack with drinks. The saltiness of the whelks mingles with the heat of the chilli and the refreshing coolness of the cucumber, creating a captivating combination of tastes and textures.

Serves 2

300g/11oz cooked
  whelks, drained
½ medium cucumber
1 carrot
2 spring onions (scallions)
1 red chilli, finely sliced
1 green chilli, finely sliced
½ onion, finely sliced

For the dressing

45ml/3 tbsp soy sauce
45ml/3 tbsp sugar
45ml/3 tbsp rice vinegar
30ml/2 tbsp Korean
  chilli powder
10ml/2 tsp garlic, crushed
5ml/1 tsp sesame seeds
2.5ml/½ tsp salt
2.5ml/½ tsp ground pepper
5ml/1 tsp sesame oil

1 Wash and drain the whelks and slice them into pieces roughly 1cm/½in long.

2 Seed the cucumber and then slice it into long, thin matchstick strips. Cut the carrot into thin julienne strips and slice the spring onions into thin strips.

3 Blend all the dressing ingredients in a bowl, mixing them together thoroughly.

4 Combine the whelks with the cucumber, carrot, spring onions, chillies and onion in a large salad bowl. Pour over the dressing and toss the salad before serving.

> **Cook's Tips**
> • Korean chilli powder, called gochugaru is one of the essential ingredients in Korean cooking. Almost all spicy dishes contain it. It is one of the main ingredients of kimchi. There are many varieties, some are very hot and some are mild. Look for it in Asian markets and food stores.

Fried Anchovies with Peanuts and Chilli Paste

The Malays love these fiery fried dried anchovies, known as *ikan bilis goreng*. They are often served as a snack with bread or with coconut rice. The Malays also enjoy them with rice porridge, for breakfast.

Serves 4

4 shallots, chopped
2 garlic cloves, chopped
4 dried red chillies, soaked in warm water until soft, seeded
  and chopped
30ml/2 tbsp tamarind pulp,
  soaked in 150ml/¼ pint/
  ⅔ cup water until soft
vegetable oil, for deep-frying
115g/4oz/1 cup peanuts
200g/7oz dried anchovies,
  heads removed, washed
  and drained
30ml/2 tbsp sugar
bread or rice, to serve

1 Using a mortar and pestle, food processor or blender, grind the shallots, garlic and chillies together until they form a coarse paste. Set the mixture aside.

2 Squeeze the tamarind pulp to help soften it in the water and press it through a sieve (strainer). Measure out 120ml/4fl oz/ ½ cup of the tamarind water.

3 Heat oil for deep-frying in a wok or large pan. Lower the heat and deep-fry the peanuts in a wire basket, until they colour. Drain them on kitchen paper and set aside.

4 Add the anchovies to the hot oil and deep-fry until they turn brown and become crisp. Drain the anchovies on kitchen paper and set aside.

5 Pour out most of the oil from the wok, reserving 30ml/2 tbsp. Stir in the spice paste and fry for about 1–2 minutes until the mixture releases its fragrant aroma.

6 Add the sugar, anchovies and peanuts. Gradually stir in the tamarind water, so the mixture remains dry. Serve hot or cold with bread or rice.

Spiced Whelks Energy 215kcal/907kJ; Protein 25g; Carbohydrate 17g, of which sugars 14.1g; Fat 5.7g, of which saturates 1.1g; Cholesterol 338mg; Calcium 69mg; Fibre 1.8g; Sodium 1737mg.
Fried Anchovies Energy 338kcal/1400kJ; Protein 17g; Carbohydrate 4.8g, of which sugars 2.6g; Fat 28g, of which saturates 4.4g; Cholesterol 24mg; Calcium 134mg; Fibre 2g; Sodium 1475mg.

Herring Cured with Chilli and Ginger

Generally served as an appetizer or snack in the Philippines, the herring is not cooked but cured and eaten raw. As with sushi or any other raw fish dish, the fish has to be absolutely fresh. Cured in coconut vinegar and lime juice, and flavoured with ginger and chillies, this is a delicious and refreshing snack.

Serves 4

150ml/¼ pint/⅔ cup
  coconut vinegar
juice of 2 limes
40g/1½oz fresh root ginger, grated
2 red chillies, seeded and
  finely sliced
8–10 herring fillets, cut into
  bitesize pieces
2 shallots, finely sliced
1 green mango, cut into
  julienne strips
salt and ground black pepper
fresh coriander (cilantro) sprigs,
  lime wedges, shredded red
  chillies and shredded fresh
  ginger, to garnish

1 Put the coconut vinegar, lime juice, ginger and chillies in a bowl and mix together. Season the mixture with salt and pepper, to taste.

2 Place the herring fillets in a shallow dish, sprinkle the shallots and green mango over, and pour in the vinegar mixture.

3 Cover with clear film (plastic wrap) and leave to marinate in the refrigerator for 1–2 hours or overnight, turning the fish several times.

4 Serve the fish garnished with coriander, lime wedges to squeeze over, shredded chillies and shredded ginger.

Variation
This dish can be made with many types of seafood, including octopus, halibut and salmon, although mackerel and herring are particularly suitable.

Fiery Chicken Wings with Blood Oranges

This is a great recipe for the barbecue – it is quick and easy, and best eaten with the fingers. The juicy oranges are there to suck after experiencing an explosion of fiery spices on the tongue. The oranges can be cooked separately or threaded alternately with the chicken wings on skewers.

Serves 4

60ml/4 tbsp fiery harissa
30ml/2 tbsp olive oil
16–20 chicken wings
4 blood oranges, quartered
icing (confectioners') sugar
small bunch of fresh coriander
  (cilantro), chopped
salt

1 Put the harissa in a small bowl with the olive oil and mix to form a loose paste. Add a little salt and stir to combine.

2 Brush the harissa mixture over the chicken wings so that they are well coated. Cook the wings on a hot barbecue once the coals are ready or under a hot grill (broiler) for 5 minutes on each side.

3 Once the wings begin to cook, dip the orange quarters lightly in icing sugar and grill them for a few minutes, until they are slightly burnt but not black and charred.

4 Serve the chicken wings immediately with the oranges, sprinkled with a little chopped fresh coriander.

Variations
• *Cherry tomatoes will also work well here in place of the oranges. It is the burst of juice that makes this dish so delicious.*
• *The fiery marinade on the chicken works well with the oranges, for less heat cut back on the harissa and use a little more oil – or try adding a splash of fresh orange juice to the paste before coating the chicken.*

Herring Energy 408kcal/1699kJ; Protein 36.4g; Carbohydrate 5.9g, of which sugars 5.7g; Fat 26.7g, of which saturates 6.6g; Cholesterol 100mg; Calcium 160mg; Fibre 1.9g; Sodium 260mg.
Fiery Chicken Wings Energy 500kcal/2077kJ; Protein 44.8g; Carbohydrate 0g, of which sugars 0g; Fat 35.6g, of which saturates 8.9g; Cholesterol 196mg; Calcium 74mg; Fibre 0g; Sodium 132mg.

Crisp Spring Rolls with Hot Chilli Sauce

These Indonesian spring rolls are packed with vegetables and strips of chicken.

Serves 3 to 4

15–30ml/1–2 tbsp palm or corn oil
2–3 garlic cloves, finely chopped
225g/8oz chicken breast fillets, cut into fine strips
225g/8oz fresh shrimp, shelled
2 leeks, cut into matchsticks
2 carrots, cut into matchsticks
½ green cabbage, finely shredded
175g/6oz fresh beansprouts
30ml/2 tbsp patis (fish sauce)
30ml/2 tbsp kecap manis (Indonesian sweet soy sauce)
1 egg, lightly beaten
corn or vegetable oil, for deep-frying
4 red or green Thai chillies, seeded and finely sliced, to serve

For the spring roll wrappers

115g/4oz/1 cup rice flour
30ml/2 tbsp cornflour (cornstarch)
2 eggs, beaten
15ml/1 tbsp palm or coconut oil
400ml/14fl oz/scant 2 cups water
corn or vegetable oil, for frying
salt

For the dipping sauce

200ml/7fl oz kecap manis
1 red chilli, seeded and chopped

1 Sift the flours for wrappers into a bowl. Add the eggs and oil, and beat in the water until a smooth batter forms. Set aside. Mix together the ingredients for the sauce into a serving bowl.

2 Heat a little oil in a frying pan. Ladle in a little batter and cook on one side until lightly browned. Lift the wrapper on to a plate. Repeat with the remaining batter.

3 Heat 15ml/1 tbsp oil in a wok. Fry the garlic, chicken and shrimp until cooked. Set aside. Heat the remaining oil and stir-fry the leeks, carrots and cabbage for 3 minutes. Stir-fry the beansprouts for 1–2 minutes. Add the chicken, shrimp, patis and kecap manis. Tip on to a plate and leave to cool.

4 Fill the wrappers by adding a spoonful of the filling on to one side. Spread to form a log, then roll the wrapper over, tuck in the sides and continue rolling. Seal the end with beaten egg.

5 Heat the oil in a wok. Fry two rolls at a time for 4 minutes, until golden. Remove, drain and serve with sauce and chillies.

Pork Satay with Pineapple Sauce

Satay is the Indonesian answer to kebabs. Marinated strips of meat are threaded on to skewers, grilled over charcoal and served with a piquant peanut sauce.

Serves 4

500g/1¼lb pork fillet, cut into bitesize strips, or cubes
salt and ground black pepper
bamboo or wooden skewers

For the marinade

4 shallots, chopped
4 garlic cloves, chopped
5ml/1 tsp ground coriander
5ml/1 tsp ground cumin
2.5ml/½ tsp ground turmeric
30ml/2 tbsp dark soy sauce
30ml/2 tbsp sesame oil

fresh coriander (cilantro) leaves, roughly chopped, to garnish

For the sauce

4 shallots, chopped
2 garlic cloves, chopped
4 dried red chillies, soaked in warm water until soft, seeded and chopped
1 lemon grass stalk, trimmed and chopped
25g/1oz fresh root ginger, chopped
30ml/2 tbsp sesame or groundnut (peanut) oil
200ml/7fl oz/scant 1 cup coconut milk
10ml/2 tsp tamarind paste
10ml/2 tsp palm sugar (jaggery)
1 fresh pineapple, peeled, cored and cut into slices

1 For the marinade, grind the shallots and garlic in a mortar and pestle to form a paste. Add the spices, soy sauce and oil. Rub the marinade into the meat. Cover and set aside for 2 hours.

2 Meanwhile, prepare the sauce. Using a mortar and pestle, grind the shallots, garlic, chillies, lemon grass and ginger to a paste. Heat the oil in a heavy pan and cook the paste for 2–3 minutes until fragrant, then stir in the coconut milk, tamarind paste and sugar. Bring to the boil, then simmer for 5 minutes. Season to taste and leave to cool. Using a mortar and pestle or a food processor, crush three pineapple slices and beat them into the sauce. Soak the skewers in cold water.

3 Prepare the charcoal grill. Thread the meat on to skewers and arrange over the coals. Place the remaining pineapple slices next to them until charred, then chop into chunks. Grill the meat for 3 minutes each side; serve with the pineapple and sauce.

Crisp Spring Rolls Energy 585kcal/2446kJ; Protein 35.4g; Carbohydrate 43.5g, of which sugars 7.2g; Fat 31.2g, of which saturates 4.5g; Cholesterol 292mg; Calcium 170mg; Fibre 5.1g; Sodium 744mg.
Pork Satay Energy 294kcal/1233kJ; Protein 27.5g; Carbohydrate 16.4g, of which sugars 16g; Fat 13.6g, of which saturates 3g; Cholesterol 79mg; Calcium 47mg; Fibre 1.4g; Sodium 145mg.

Spicy Shrimp and Scallop Satay

One of the tastiest satay dishes, this is succulent, spicy and extremely moreish. Serve with rice and a fruity salad or pickled vegetables and lime.

Serves 4
250g/9oz shelled shrimp or prawns, deveined and chopped
250g/9oz shelled scallops, chopped
30ml/2 tbsp potato, tapioca or rice flour
5ml/1 tsp baking powder
12–16 wooden, metal, lemon grass or sugar cane skewers
1 lime, quartered, to serve

For the spice paste
2 shallots, chopped
2 garlic cloves, chopped
2–3 red chillies, seeded and chopped
25g/1oz galangal or fresh root ginger, chopped
15g/½oz fresh turmeric, chopped or 2.5ml/½ tsp ground turmeric
2–3 lemon grass stalks, chopped
15–30ml/1–2 tbsp palm or groundnut (peanut) oil
5ml/1 tsp shrimp paste
15ml/1 tbsp tamarind paste
5ml/1 tsp palm sugar (jaggery)

1 Make the paste. In a mortar and pestle, pound the shallots, garlic, chillies, galangal, turmeric and lemon grass to form a paste.

2 Heat the oil in a wok or heavy frying pan, stir in the paste. Fry until fragrant. Add the shrimp paste, tamarind and sugar and cook, stirring, until the mixture darkens. Set aside to cool.

3 In a bowl, pound the shrimps and scallops together to form a paste, or whizz them in an electric blender or food processor. Beat in the spice paste, then the flour and baking powder, and beat until blended. Chill in the refrigerator for 1 hour. If using wooden skewers, soak them in water for about 30 minutes.

4 Meanwhile, prepare the barbecue, or, if you are using the grill (broiler), preheat 5 minutes before you start cooking. Using your fingers, scoop up lumps of the shellfish paste and wrap it around the skewers.

5 Place each skewer on the barbecue or under the grill and cook for 3 minutes on each side, until golden brown. Serve with the lime wedges to squeeze over them.

Chilli Satay Prawns

This delicious dish, inspired by Indonesian satay, combines mild peanuts, aromatic spices, fiery chilli, coconut milk and lemon juice in the spicy dip.

Serves 4 to 6
450g/1lb king prawns (jumbo shrimp), peeled and deveined
25ml/1½ tbsp vegetable oil

For the peanut sauce
25ml/1½ tbsp vegetable oil
15ml/1 tbsp chopped garlic
1 small onion, chopped
3–4 red chillies, seeded and chopped
3 kaffir lime leaves, torn
1 lemon grass stalk, bruised and chopped

5ml/1 tsp medium curry paste
250ml/8fl oz/1 cup coconut milk
1cm/½in piece cinnamon stick
75g/3oz/⅓ cup crunchy peanut butter
45ml/3 tbsp tamarind juice, made by mixing tamarind paste with warm water
30ml/2 tbsp Thai fish sauce
30ml/2 tbsp palm sugar (jaggery) or muscovado (brown) sugar
juice of ½ lemon

For the garnish
½ bunch fresh coriander (cilantro) leaves (optional)
4 fresh red chillies, finely sliced (optional)
spring onions (scallions), sliced

1 Make the peanut sauce. Heat half the oil in a wok or heavy frying pan. Add the garlic and onion and cook, stirring, for 3–4 minutes, until the mixture has softened but not browned.

2 Add the chillies, kaffir lime leaves, lemon grass and curry paste. Cook for 2–3 minutes, then stir in the coconut milk, cinnamon stick, peanut butter, tamarind juice, fish sauce, sugar and lemon juice. Bring to the boil, then reduce the heat to low and simmer gently for 15–20 minutes, until the sauce thickens.

3 Thread the prawns on to skewers and brush with a little oil. Cook under a preheated grill (broiler) for 2 minutes on each side until they turn pink and are firm to the touch. Alternatively, pan-fry the prawns, then thread on to skewers.

4 Remove the cinnamon from the sauce and discard. Arrange the prawns on a warmed platter, garnish with spring onions and coriander and red chillies, if liked, and serve with the sauce.

Spicy Shrimp Satay Energy 220kcal/922kJ; Protein 27.1g; Carbohydrate 11.5g, of which sugars 1g; Fat 7.3g, of which saturates 1g; Cholesterol 151mg; Calcium 99mg; Fibre 1.5g; Sodium 249mg.
Satay Prawns Energy 321kcal/1340kJ; Protein 24.6g; Carbohydrate 13.5g; of which sugars 8.2g; Fat 13.3g; of which saturates 3.6g; Cholesterol 219mg; Calcium 52mg; Fibre 1.2g; Sodium 794mg.

Red-hot Prawn and Fish Curry

Bengalis are famous for their spicy seafood dishes and always use mustard oil in recipes because it imparts a uniquely delicious taste, flavour and aroma. No feast in Bengal is complete without one of these celebrated fish dishes.

Serves 4 to 6
3 cloves garlic
5cm/2in piece fresh root ginger, peeled and roughly chopped
1 large leek, roughly chopped
4 green chillies, seeded and roughly chopped, plus two whole chillies, to garnish
60ml/4 tbsp mustard oil, or vegetable oil
15ml/1 tbsp ground coriander
2.5ml/½ tsp fennel seeds
15ml/1 tbsp crushed yellow mustard seeds, or 5ml/1 tsp mustard powder
175ml/6fl oz/¾ cup thick coconut milk
225g/8oz huss, skate blobs or monkfish, chopped into bitesize pieces
225g/8oz fresh king prawns (jumbo shrimp), peeled and deveined with tails intact
salt, to taste
115g/4oz fresh coriander (cilantro) leaves, chopped

1 In a food processor, grind the garlic, ginger, leek and chillies to a coarse paste.

2 In a frying pan, heat the mustard or vegetable oil with the paste until it is well blended. Keep the window open and take care not to overheat the mixture as any smoke from the mustard oil will sting the eyes.

3 Add the ground coriander, fennel seeds, mustard and coconut milk, stirring well until thoroughly combined. Gently bring the mixture to the boil and then simmer, uncovered, for about 5 minutes.

4 Add the fish pieces and simmer for 2–3 minutes, then fold in the prawns (shrimp). Cook over a medium heat until the prawns are cooked.

5 Season with salt to taste, fold in the chopped fresh coriander leaves and serve immediately, garnished with two whole green chillies.

Yellow Prawn Curry

Colour is an important part of Indonesian food and the word *udang*, meaning 'yellow', is used to describe this delicious and attractive prawn dish. Big, juicy prawns are particularly favoured in Bali and Java, but you can easily substitute them with scallops, squid or mussels, or a combination of all three, depending on what you have available.

Serves 4
30ml/2 tbsp coconut or palm oil
2 shallots, finely chopped
2 garlic cloves, finely chopped
2 red chillies, seeded and finely chopped
25g/1oz fresh turmeric, finely chopped, or 10ml/2 tsp ground turmeric
25g/1oz fresh root ginger, finely chopped
2 lemon grass stalks, finely sliced
10ml/2 tsp coriander seeds
10ml/2 tsp shrimp paste
1 red (bell) pepper, seeded and finely sliced
4 kaffir lime leaves
about 500g/1¼lb fresh prawns (shrimp), shelled and deveined
400g/14oz can coconut milk
salt and ground black pepper
1 green chilli, seeded and sliced, to garnish

To serve
cooked rice
4 fried shallots or fresh chillies, seeded and sliced lengthways

1 Heat the oil in a wok or heavy frying pan. Stir in the shallots, garlic, chillies, turmeric, ginger, lemon grass and coriander seeds and fry until fragrant.

2 Stir in the shrimp paste and cook the mixture for 2–3 minutes. Add the red pepper and lime leaves and stir-fry for a further 1 minute.

3 Add the prawns to the pan. Pour in the coconut milk, stirring to combine, and bring to the boil. Cook for 5–6 minutes until the prawns are cooked. Season with salt and pepper to taste.

4 Spoon the prawns on to a warmed serving dish and sprinkle with the sliced green chillies to garnish. Serve with rice and fried shallots or the fresh chillies on the side.

Red-hot Prawn Curry Energy 166kcal/695kJ; Protein 15.2g; Carbohydrate 6.2g, of which sugars 3.3g; Fat 9.2g, of which saturates 1.2g; Cholesterol 78mg; Calcium 108mg; Fibre 2.4g; Sodium 120mg.
Yellow Prawn Curry Energy 230kcal/965kJ; Protein 26.4g; Carbohydrate 16g, of which sugars 13.5g; Fat 7.2g, of which saturates 1g; Cholesterol 263mg; Calcium 226mg; Fibre 2.7g; Sodium 519mg.

Hot, Sweet and Sour Squid

The Indonesians and Malays love cooking prawns and squid in this way, expertly crunching shells and sucking tentacles to savour all the juicy chilli and tamarind flavouring. Sweetened with the ubiquitous kecap manis, the cooking aroma emanating from these scrumptious squid will make you drool.

Serves 2 to 4
500g/1¼lb fresh baby squid

30ml/2 tbsp tamarind paste
30ml/2 tbsp chilli sauce
45ml/3 tbsp kecap manis (Indonesian sweet soy sauce)
juice of 1 kalamansi or ordinary lime
25g/1oz fresh root ginger, grated
1 small bunch fresh coriander (cilantro) leaves
2–4 green chillies, seeded and quartered lengthways
ground black pepper

To serve
fresh coriander (cilantro) leaves

1 Clean the squid and remove the head and ink sac. Pull out the backbone and rinse the body sac inside and out. Trim the head above the eyes, keeping the tentacle intact. Dry the body sac and tentacles on kitchen paper and discard the rest.

2 In a bowl, mix together the tamarind paste, chilli sauce, kecap manis and lime juice. Add the ginger and a little black pepper.

3 Spoon the mixture over the squid and rub it all over the body sacs and tentacles. Cover and chill for 1 hour.

4 Meanwhile, prepare the barbecue or heat a ridged griddle. Place the squid on the rack or griddle and cook for 3 minutes on each side, brushing them with the marinade as they cook. Serve immediately, with fresh coriander leaves.

Variation
To make hot, sweet and sour prawns (shrimp), devein the prawns and remove the feelers and legs, then rinse, pat dry, and make an incision along the tail. Marinate and cook in the same way as the squid.

Squid in Hot Yellow Sauce

Simple fishermen's dishes such as this one are cooked the length and breadth of Malaysia's coastline. This recipe from Sabah, the northernmost state in Malaysian Borneo, includes enough chillies to set your tongue on fire. To temper the heat, the dish is often served with the local staple, sago porridge, and finely shredded green mango tossed in lime juice.

Serves 4
500g/1¼lb fresh squid
juice of 2 limes

5ml/1 tsp salt
4 shallots, chopped
4 garlic cloves, chopped
25g/1oz galangal, chopped
25g/1oz fresh turmeric, chopped
6–8 red chillies, seeded and chopped
30ml/2 tbsp vegetable or groundnut (peanut) oil
7.5ml/1½ tsp palm sugar (jaggery)
2 lemon grass stalks, crushed
4 lime leaves
400ml/14fl oz/1⅔ cups coconut milk
salt and ground black pepper
crusty bread or steamed rice, to serve

1 First prepare the squid. Hold the body sac in one hand and pull off the head with the other. Sever the tentacles just above the eyes, and discard the rest of the head and innards. Clean the body sac inside and out and remove the skin. Pat the squid dry, cut it into thick slices and put them in a bowl, along with the tentacles. Mix the lime juice with the salt and rub it into the squid. Set aside for 30 minutes.

2 Meanwhile, using a mortar and pestle or food processor, grind the shallots, garlic, galangal, turmeric and chillies to a coarse paste.

3 Heat the oil in a wok or heavy pan, and stir in the coarse paste. Cook the paste until fragrant, then add the palm sugar, lemon grass and lime leaves. Drain the squid of any juice and toss it around the wok, coating it in the flavourings. Pour in the coconut milk and bring it to the boil. Reduce the heat and simmer for 5–10 minutes, until the squid is tender. Season with salt and pepper and serve with chunks of fresh, crusty bread or steamed rice.

Sweet and Sour Squid Energy 110kcal/468kJ; Protein 20g; Carbohydrate 2.8g, of which sugars 1.1g; Fat 2.3g, of which saturates 0.5g; Cholesterol 281mg; Calcium 43mg; Fibre 0.6g; Sodium 943mg.
Squid in Yellow Sauce Energy 185kcal/780kJ; Protein 19.8g; Carbohydrate 9.4g, of which sugars 7.6g; Fat 8g, of which saturates 1.4g; Cholesterol 281mg; Calcium 50mg; Fibre 0.2g; Sodium 739mg.

Chargrilled Squid with Red Chilli and White Wine

The squid in this Spanish recipe, known as *calamares a la plancha* are traditionally cooked on the hot griddle that is an essential part of every Spanish kitchen. The method is fast and simple and really brings out the flavour of the squid. This dish is an ideal first course for four people, or can be served on a bed of rice as a main dish for two.

Serves 2 to 4

2 whole cleaned squid, with
    tentacles, about 275g/10oz each
75ml/5 tbsp olive oil
30ml/2 tbsp sherry vinegar
2 fresh red chillies, finely chopped
60ml/4 tbsp dry white wine
salt and ground black pepper
hot cooked rice, to serve
    (optional)
15–30ml/1–2 tbsp chopped
    parsley, to garnish

1 Make a lengthways cut down the side of the body of each squid, then open it out flat. Score the flesh on both sides of the bodies in a criss-cross pattern with the tip of a sharp knife. Chop the tentacles into short lengths. Place all the squid pieces in a non-metallic dish.

2 Whisk together the oil and vinegar in a small bowl until well combined. Season with salt and pepper to taste, pour over the squid and toss to mix. Cover the bowl and set aside to marinate for about 1 hour.

3 Heat a ridged griddle pan until hot. Add the body of one of the squid and cook over a medium heat for 2–3 minutes, pressing the squid down on to the ridges with a metal spatula to keep it flat. Repeat on the other side. Cook the other squid body in the same way.

4 Slice the bodies of the squid into diagonal strips. If serving with rice, arrange the strips over the rice and keep warm.

5 Add the chopped tentacles and chillies to the pan and toss over a medium heat for about 2–3 minutes. Stir in the white wine, then drizzle over the squid. Garnish with the parsley.

Saigon Shellfish Curry

There are many variations of this tasty curry all over the south of Vietnam. This recipe is made with prawns, squid and scallops but you could use any combination of shellfish, or even add chunks of filleted fish.

Serves 4

4cm/1½in fresh root ginger,
    peeled and roughly chopped
2–3 garlic cloves, roughly chopped
45ml/3 tbsp groundnut (peanut) oil
1 onion, finely sliced
2 lemon grass stalks, finely sliced
2 green or red Thai chillies,
    seeded and finely sliced
15ml/1 tbsp raw cane sugar
10ml/2 tsp shrimp paste
15ml/1 tbsp Thai fish sauce
30ml/2 tbsp curry powder or
    garam masala
550ml/18fl oz can coconut milk
juice and rind of 1 lime
4 medium squid, cleaned and cut
    diagonally into 3 or 4 pieces
12 king or queen scallops, shelled
20 raw prawns (shrimp), shelled
    and deveined
1 small bunch of fresh basil,
    stalks removed
1 small bunch of fresh coriander
    (cilantro), stalks removed, leaves
    finely chopped, to garnish
salt

1 Using a mortar and pestle, grind the ginger with the garlic until it almost resembles a paste. Heat the oil in a traditional clay pot, wok or heavy pan and stir in the onion. Cook until it begins to turn brown, then stir in the garlic and ginger paste.

2 Once the aromas begin to lift from the pot, add the lemon grass, chillies and sugar. Cook for 2 minutes before adding the shrimp paste, fish sauce and curry powder or garam masala. Stir the mixture well and allow the flavours to mingle and combine over the heat for 1–2 minutes.

3 Add the coconut milk, lime juice and rind. Mix well and bring the liquid to the boil. Simmer for 2–3 minutes. Season to taste with salt.

4 Gently stir in the squid, scallops and prawns. Bring the liquid to the boil once more. Reduce the heat and cook gently until the shellfish turns opaque. Add the basil leaves and sprinkle the coriander over the top. Serve immediately from the pot into individual bowls.

Squid with Chilli Energy 258kcal/1076kJ; Protein 23.5g; Carbohydrate 2g; of which sugars 0.2g; Fat 16.4g; of which saturates 2.6g; Cholesterol 338mg; Calcium 25mg; Fibre 0g; Sodium 167mg.
Saigon Shellfish Curry Energy 528kcal/2225kJ; Protein 68g; Carbohydrate 24g, of which sugars 14g; Fat 18g; of which saturates 4g; Cholesterol 699mg; Calcium 250mg; Fibre 2.5g; Sodium 1.3mg.

Lobster and Crab Steamed in Beer and Hot Spices

Depending on the size and availability of the lobsters and crabs, you can make this delicious spicy dish for as many people as you like, because the quantities are simple to adjust.

Serves 4

4 uncooked lobsters, about
    450g/1lb each
4–8 uncooked crabs, about
    225g/8oz each
about 600ml/1 pint/2½ cups beer
4 spring onions (scallions),
    trimmed and chopped into
    long pieces

4cm/1½in fresh root ginger,
    peeled and finely sliced
2 green or red Thai chillies,
    seeded and finely sliced
3 lemon grass stalks,
    finely sliced
1 bunch of fresh dill,
    fronds chopped
1 bunch each of fresh basil
    and coriander (cilantro),
    stalks removed, leaves
    chopped
about 30ml/2 tbsp Thai fish
    sauce, plus extra for serving
juice of 1 lemon
salt and ground black
    pepper

1 Clean the lobsters and crabs well and rub them with salt and pepper. Place half of them in a large steamer and pour the beer into the base. Sprinkle half the spring onions, ginger, chillies, lemon grass and herbs over the lobsters and crabs, and steam for 10 minutes, or until the lobsters turn red. Lift them on to a serving dish. Cook the remaining half in the same way.

2 Add the lemon grass, herbs and fish sauce to the simmering beer, stir in the lemon juice, then pour into a dipping bowl. Serve the shellfish hot, dipping the lobster and crab meat into the broth and adding extra splashes of fish sauce, if you like.

Cook's Tip
Whether you cook the lobsters and crabs at the same time depends on the number of people you are cooking for and the size of your steamer. However, they don't take long to cook so it is easy to steam them in batches.

Chargrilled Fish with a Fiery Sambal

A fiery sambal is the perfect complement to succulently grilled fish.

Serves 4

30ml/2 tbsp coconut oil
60ml/4 tbsp dark soy sauce
2 garlic cloves, crushed
juice of 1 lime
1 whole sea fish, such as grouper,
    red snapper, or sea bass, or
    4 whole smaller fish, such as
    sardines, gutted and cleaned
cooked rice, to serve

For the sambal
50g/2oz tamarind paste
150ml/¼ pint/⅔ cup boiling water
4 shallots, chopped
4 garlic cloves, chopped
5 red chillies, seeded and chopped
25g/1oz galangal, chopped
2 kaffir lime leaves, crumbled
10ml/2 tsp shrimp paste
10ml/2 tsp palm sugar (jaggery)
30ml/2 tbsp coconut or palm oil

1 In a small bowl, mix the coconut oil, soy sauce, garlic and lime juice together. Put the fish in a shallow dish and slash the flesh at intervals with a sharp knife. Spoon over the marinade and rub it into the skin and slashes. Leave for about 1 hour.

2 Meanwhile, make the sambal. Put the tamarind paste in a bowl, pour over the water and leave to soak for 30 minutes. Strain into a separate bowl, pressing the paste through a sieve (strainer). Discard the solids and put the tamarind juice aside.

3 Using a mortar and pestle, pound the shallots, garlic, chillies, galangal and lime leaves to a coarse paste. Add the shrimp paste and sugar and beat together until combined.

4 Heat the oil in a small wok, stir in the paste and fry for 2–3 minutes. Stir in the tamarind juice and boil until it reduces to a thick paste. Turn into a serving bowl.

5 Prepare the barbecue. Place the fish on the grill (broiler) and cook for 5 minutes each side, depending on the size of fish, basting it with any leftover marinade. Transfer the fish to a serving plate and serve with the sambal and boiled rice.

Lobster and Crab Energy 264kcal/1112kJ; Protein 48g; Carbohydrate 4g, of which sugars 1g; Fat 7g, of which saturates 1g; Cholesterol 210mg; Calcium 185mg; Fibre 0.5g; Sodium 1.3mg.
Chargrilled Fish Energy 359kcal/1507kJ; Protein 42.3g; Carbohydrate 11.8g, of which sugars 9.3g; Fat 16.4g, of which saturates 2.3g; Cholesterol 75mg; Calcium 117mg; Fibre 1.4g; Sodium 1263mg.

Spicy Swordfish and Green Chilli Tacos

It is important not to overcook swordfish, or it can be tough and dry. Cooked correctly, however, it is absolutely delicious and makes a great change from beef or chicken as a spicy filling for a taco.

Serves 6
3 swordfish steaks
30ml/2 tbsp vegetable oil
2 garlic cloves, crushed
1 small onion, chopped
3 fresh green chillies, seeded
    and chopped
3 tomatoes
small bunch of fresh coriander
    (cilantro), chopped
6 fresh corn tortillas
1/2 iceberg lettuce, shredded
salt and ground black pepper
lemon wedges, to serve
    (optional)

1 Preheat the grill (broiler). Put the swordfish on an oiled rack over a grill pan and grill (broil) for 2–3 minutes on each side. When cool enough to handle, remove the skin and flake the fish into a bowl.

2 Heat the vegetable oil in a pan. Add the garlic, onion and chillies and fry for 5 minutes, or until the onion has turned soft and translucent.

3 Cut a cross in the base of each tomato, place in a heatproof bowl and pour over boiling water. After 3 minutes plunge the tomatoes into another bowl of cold water. Drain the tomatoes. Their skins will have begun to peel back from the crosses. Remove the skins, halve the tomatoes and cut out the seeds. Chop the flesh into 1cm/1/2in dice.

4 Add the tomatoes and swordfish to the onion mixture. Cook for 5 minutes over a low heat. Add the coriander and cook for 1–2 minutes. Season to taste.

5 Wrap the tortillas in foil and steam on a plate over a pan of boiling water until they are heated through and pliable. Place some shredded lettuce and fish mixture on to each tortilla. Fold in half, covering the filling, and serve with lemon wedges, if liked.

Seared Tuna with Ginger, Chilli and Watercress Salad

Tuna steaks are wonderful seared and served slightly rare with a punchy spicy sauce or salad. In this recipe the salad is served just warm as a bed for the tender tuna. Add a dab of harissa as a condiment to create a dish that will transport you to the warmth of the North African coastline.

Serves 4
30ml/2 tbsp olive oil
5ml/1 tsp harissa
5ml/1 tsp clear honey
4 X 200g/7oz tuna steaks
salt and ground black pepper
lemon wedges, to serve

For the salad
30ml/2 tbsp olive oil
a little butter
25g/1oz fresh root ginger, peeled
    and finely sliced
2 garlic cloves, finely sliced
2 green chillies, seeded and sliced
6 spring onions (scallions), cut into
    bitesize pieces
2 large handfuls of watercress
juice of 1/2 lemon

1 Mix the olive oil, harissa, honey and salt, and rub it over the tuna. Heat a little oil in a frying pan and sear the tuna steaks for 2 minutes on each side. They should still be pink inside.

2 Keep the tuna warm while you prepare the salad: heat the olive oil and butter in a pan. Add the ginger, garlic, chillies and spring onions, cook for a few minutes, then add the watercress. When the watercress begins to wilt, toss in the lemon juice and season well with salt and black pepper.

3 Tip the warm salad on to a serving dish or individual plates. Slice the tuna steaks and arrange on top of the salad. Serve immediately with lemon wedges for squeezing over.

> **Variation**
> Prawns (shrimp) and scallops can be cooked in the same way. The shellfish will just need to be cooked through briefly – too long and they will become rubbery.

Seared Tuna Energy 383kcal/1604kJ; Protein 48.1g; Carbohydrate 2g, of which sugars 2g; Fat 20.4g, of which saturates 4g; Cholesterol 56mg; Calcium 59mg; Fibre 0.4g; Sodium 102mg.
Swordfish Tacos Energy 357kcal/1507kJ; Protein 32g; Carbohydrate 36g, of which sugars 3g; Fat 11g; of which saturates 2g; Cholesterol 105mg; Calcium 80mg; Fibre 2.1g; Sodium 400mg.

Catfish with a Chilli Coconut Sauce

In this popular Indonesian dish, fish is fried and served with a fragrant and spicy sauce. Serve with rice and pickled vegetables or a green mango or papaya salad.

Serves 4
200ml/7fl oz/scant 1 cup
   coconut milk
30–45ml/2–3 tbsp coconut cream
30–45ml/2–3 tbsp rice flour,
   tapioca flour or cornflour
   (cornstarch)
5–10ml/1–2 tsp ground coriander
8 fresh catfish fillets
30–45ml/2–3 tbsp coconut, palm
   groundnut (peanut) or corn oil

salt and ground black pepper
1 lime, quartered, to serve

For the spice paste
2 shallots, chopped
2 garlic cloves, chopped
2–3 red chillies, seeded
   and chopped
25g/1oz galangal, chopped
15g/½ oz fresh turmeric,
   chopped, or 2.5ml/½ tsp
   ground turmeric
2–3 lemon grass stalks, chopped
15–30ml/1–2 tbsp palm or
   groundnut (peanut) oil
5ml/1 tsp shrimp paste
15ml/1 tbsp tamarind paste
5ml/1 tsp palm sugar (jaggery)

1 Make the paste. Using a mortar and pestle, pound the shallots, garlic, chillies, galangal, turmeric and lemon grass to a paste.

2 Heat the oil in a wok or heavy pan, stir in the paste and fry until it is fragrant and begins to colour. Add the shrimp and tamarind pastes and sugar and stir until the mixture darkens.

3 Stir the coconut milk and cream into the paste and boil for 10 minutes, until the milk and cream separate, leaving behind an oily paste. Season the sauce with salt and pepper to taste.

4 Meanwhile, mix the flour with the coriander on a plate and season. Toss the catfish fillets in the flour until lightly coated.

5 Heat the oil in a heavy frying pan and quickly fry the fillets for about 2 minutes on each side, until golden brown.

6 Transfer the catfish fillets to a warmed serving dish and serve with the spicy coconut sauce and wedges of lime to squeeze over the fish.

Sardines in Spicy Coconut Milk

A deliciously spiced fish dish based on coconut milk. This dish is particularly fiery but its heat is tempered by the inclusion of herbs.

Serves 4
6–8 red chillies, according to
   taste, seeded and chopped
4 shallots, chopped
4 garlic cloves, chopped
1 lemon grass stalk, chopped
25g/1oz galangal, chopped
30ml/2 tbsp coconut or palm oil
10ml/2 tsp coriander seeds
5ml/1 tsp cumin seeds

5ml/1 tsp fennel seeds
1 small bunch fresh mint leaves,
   finely chopped
1 small bunch fresh flat leaf
   parsley, finely chopped
15ml/1 tbsp palm sugar (jaggery)
15ml/1 tbsp tamarind paste
4 sardines or small mackerel,
   gutted, but kept whole
300ml/½ pint/1¼ cups
   coconut milk
salt and ground black pepper
steamed rice, 1 large bunch fresh
   flat leaf parsley and fresh basil
   leaves, to serve

1 Using a mortar and pestle, pound the chillies, shallots, garlic, lemon grass and galangal to a paste.

2 Heat the oil in a wok or wide, heavy pan, stir in the coriander, cumin and fennel seeds and fry until they give off a fragrant aroma. Add the spicy paste and stir until it becomes golden in colour. Add the chopped mint and parsley and stir for about 1 minute, then add the sugar and tamarind paste.

3 Carefully place the fish in the pan and toss gently to coat it thoroughly in the paste. Pour in the coconut milk and stir gently. Bring to the boil, then reduce the heat and simmer the mixture for 10–15 minutes, until the fish is tender when flaked using a fork. Season the sauce with salt and ground black pepper to taste.

4 Cover the bottom of a warmed serving dish with sprigs of flat leaf parsley and place the fish on top, then spoon the sauce over the top. Serve with a bowl of steamed rice or sago and extra stalks of fresh parsley and basil leaves to cut the spice.

Catfish Energy 338kcal/1412kJ; Protein 38.1g; Carbohydrate 11.9g, of which sugars 4.9g; Fat 15.3g, of which saturates 5.7g; Cholesterol 92mg; Calcium 56mg; Fibre 0.9g; Sodium 190mg.
Sardines with Herbs Energy 287kcal/1199kJ; Protein 22.8g; Carbohydrate 11g, of which sugars 10.2g; Fat 17.2g, of which saturates 3.7g; Cholesterol 0mg; Calcium 167mg; Fibre 2.1g; Sodium 213mg.

Salmon in Coconut Chilli Sauce

This is an ideal dish to serve as an appetizer at dinner parties. The salmon is first marinated in a spicy coating before being cooked in a delicious coconut sauce.

Serves 4

10ml/2 tsp ground cumin
10ml/2 tsp chilli powder
2.5ml/½ tsp ground turmeric
30ml/2 tbsp white wine vinegar
1.5ml/¼ tsp salt
4 salmon steaks, about
   175g/6oz each

45 ml/3 tbsp oil
1 onion, chopped
2 green chillies, seeded
   and chopped
2 garlic cloves, crushed
2.5cm/1in piece fresh root
   ginger, grated
5 ml/1 tsp ground coriander
175 ml/6 fl oz/¾ cup
   coconut milk
spring onion rice, to serve
fresh coriander (cilantro) sprigs,
   to garnish

1 In a small bowl, mix 5ml/1 tsp of the ground cumin together with the chilli powder, turmeric, vinegar and salt.

2 Rub the paste over the salmon steaks and leave to marinate for about 15 minutes.

3 Heat the oil in a large frying pan and fry the onion, chillies, garlic and ginger for 5–6 minutes. Put into a food processor or blender and process to a paste.

4 Return the paste to the pan. Add the remaining cumin, coriander and coconut milk. Bring the mixture to the boil and simmer, stirring occasionally, for 5 minutes.

5 Add the salmon steaks to the sauce. Cover the pan and cook for 15 minutes until the fish is tender. Serve with spring onion rice and garnish with coriander sprigs.

> **Cook's Tip**
> *If coconut milk is unavailable, substitute coconut cream diluted with water to get the desired consistency.*

Steamed Fish with Spices and Chilli Sauce

Steaming is one of the best methods of cooking fish. By leaving the fish whole and on the bone, more flavour is retained and the flesh remains moist.

Serves 4

1 large or 2 medium firm fish
   such as sea bass or grouper,
   scaled and cleaned
30ml/2 tbsp rice wine
3 fresh red chillies, seeded and
   thinly sliced
2 garlic cloves, finely chopped

2cm/¾in piece fresh root ginger,
   peeled and finely shredded
2 lemon grass stalks, chopped
2 spring onions (scallions), chopped
30ml/2 tbsp Thai fish sauce
juice of 1 lime
1 fresh banana leaf

For the chilli sauce
10 fresh red chillies, seeded
   and chopped
4 garlic cloves, chopped
60ml/4 tbsp Thai fish sauce
15ml/1 tbsp sugar
75ml/5 tbsp fresh lime juice

1 Thoroughly rinse the fish under cold running water. Pat it dry with kitchen paper. With a sharp knife, slash the skin of the fish a few times on both sides.

2 Mix together the rice wine, chillies, garlic, shredded ginger, lemon grass and spring onions in a non-metallic bowl. Add the fish sauce and lime juice and mix to a paste. Place the fish on the banana leaf and spread the spice paste evenly over it, rubbing it in well where the skin has been slashed.

3 Put a rack or a small upturned plate in the base of a wok. Pour in boiling water to a depth of 5cm/2in. Lift the banana leaf, together with the fish, and place it on the rack or plate. Cover with a lid and steam for 10–15 minutes, or until the fish is cooked.

4 Meanwhile, make the sauce. Place all the ingredients in a food processor and blend until smooth. If the mixture seems to be too thick, add a little cold water. Scrape into a serving bowl.

5 Serve the fish hot, on the banana leaf if you like, with the sweet chilli sauce to spoon over the top.

Salmon in Coconut Sauce Energy 417kcal/1740kJ; Protein 37g; Carbohydrate 6g; of which sugars 4g; Fat 28g, of which saturates 4g; Cholesterol 88mg; Calcium 73mg; Fibre 0.6g; Sodium 200mg.
Fish with Spices Energy 123kcal/519kJ; Protein 23.3g; Carbohydrate 0.8g; of which sugars 0.7g; Fat 3g, of which saturates 0.5g; Cholesterol 95mg; Calcium 158mg; Fibre 0.1g; Sodium 616mg.

Fiery Fish in a Banana Leaf Parcel

This delicious Indian dish will make an excellent appetizer for a dinner party and your guests will enjoy opening up their own individual parcels and finding the spicy aromatic fish.

Serves 6

50g/2oz fresh coconut, skinned and grated, or 65g/2^1/$_2$oz/ scant 1 cup desiccated (dry unsweetened shredded) coconut, soaked in 30ml/2 tbsp water

1 large lemon, skin, pith and seeds removed, roughly chopped

4 large garlic cloves, crushed

3 large fresh mild green chillies, seeded and chopped

50g/2oz fresh coriander (cilantro), roughly chopped

25g/1oz fresh mint leaves, roughly chopped

5ml/1 tsp ground cumin

5ml/1 tsp sugar

2.5ml/^{1}/$_2$ tsp fenugreek seeds, finely ground

5ml/1 tsp salt

2 large, whole banana leaves

6 salmon fillets, total weight about 1.2kg/2^1/$_2$lb, skinned

1 Place all the ingredients except the banana leaves and salmon in a food processor. Pulse to a fine paste. Scrape the mixture into a bowl, cover and chill for 30 minutes.

2 Prepare the barbecue. While it is heating, make the parcels. Cut each banana leaf widthways into three and cut off the hard outside edge. Put the pieces of leaf and the edge strips in a bowl of hot water and soak for 10 minutes. Drain, wipe off any white residue, and rinse. Pour over boiling water to soften. Drain, then place the leaves, smooth side up, on a clean board.

3 Smear the top and bottom with coconut paste. Place a fillet on each leaf. Bring the trimmed edge over, then fold in the sides. Bring up the remaining edge to make a parcel. Tie with a leaf strip.

4 Lay each parcel on a sheet of foil, bring up the edges and scrunch the tops together to seal. When the coals are medium-hot, or with a moderate coating of ash, place the salmon parcels on the grill rack and cook for 10 minutes, turning once.

5 Place on individual plates and leave for 2–3 minutes. Remove the foil, then unwrap and eat the fish straight out of the parcel.

Mackerel with Red and Green Chilli

Oily fish such as mackerel is a perfect match for the clean, dry taste of sake. Garlic and chilli mute the strong flavour of the fish, while the diced mooli absorbs all the flavours of the cooking liquid for a unique and delicious taste.

Serves 2–3

1 large mackerel, filleted

300g/11oz mooli (daikon), peeled

120ml/4fl oz/^{1}/$_2$ cup light soy sauce

30ml/2 tbsp sake or rice wine

30ml/2 tbsp maple syrup

3 garlic cloves, crushed

10ml/2 tsp Korean chilli powder

^{1}/$_2$ onion, chopped

1 fresh red chilli, seeded and finely sliced

1 fresh green chilli, seeded and finely sliced

1 Slice the mackerel into medium pieces. Cut the mooli into 2.5cm/1in cubes, and then arrange evenly across the base of a large pan. Cover with a layer of mackerel.

2 Pour the soy sauce over the fish and add 200ml/7fl oz/ scant 1 cup water, the sake or rice wine, and the maple syrup. Sprinkle the crushed garlic and chilli powder into the pan, and gently stir the liquid, trying not to disturb the fish and mooli. Add the onion and sliced fresh red and green chillies, and cover the pan.

3 Place the pan over a high heat and bring the liquid to the boil. Reduce the heat and simmer for 8–10 minutes, or until the fish is tender, spooning the soy liquid over the fish as it cooks. Ladle the mixture into two or three warmed serving bowls and serve immediately.

Variation

If mooli is not available then potatoes make a good alternative. They will give a sweeter, more delicate flavour to the fish, while a handful of coriander (cilantro) leaves will add more of a Thai flavour to the recipe.

Fiery Fish in a Parcel Energy 225kcal/943kJ; Protein 27.6g; Carbohydrate 14.1g, of which sugars 10.4g; Fat 6.9g, of which saturates 1.2g; Cholesterol 58mg; Calcium 51mg; Fibre 2.5g; Sodium 79mg.
Mackerel Fillets Energy 207kcal/861kJ; Protein 13.4g; Carbohydrate 11.4g, of which sugars 10.9g; Fat 11g, of which saturates 2.3g; Cholesterol 36mg; Calcium 33mg; Fibre 1.2g; Sodium 81mg.

Sour Fish, Star Fruit and Chilli Stew

Somewhere between a stew and a soup, this refreshing dish is just one of many variations on the theme of sour fish stew found throughout South-east Asia. The star fruit are added towards the end of cooking so that they retain a bite.

Serves 4 to 6
30ml/2 tbsp coconut or palm oil
900ml/1½ pints/3¾ cups water
2 lemon grass stalks, bruised
25g/1oz fresh root ginger, finely sliced
about 675g/1½lb freshwater or saltwater fish, such as trout or sea bream, cut into thin steaks

2 firm star fruit (carambola), sliced
juice of 1–2 limes

For the spice paste
4 shallots, chopped
4 red chillies, seeded and chopped
2 garlic cloves, chopped
25g/1oz galangal, chopped
25g/1oz fresh turmeric, chopped
3–4 candlenuts, chopped

To serve
1 bunch fresh basil leaves
1 lime, cut into wedges
steamed rice

1 Using a mortar and pestle or food processor, grind all the spice paste ingredients together to form a coarse paste.

2 Heat the oil in a wok or wide, heavy pan, stir in the spice paste and fry until fragrant. Pour in the water and add the lemon grass and ginger. Bring to the boil, stirring all the time, then reduce the heat and simmer for 10 minutes.

3 Slip the fish steaks into the pan, making sure there is enough cooking liquid to cover the fish and adding more water if necessary. Simmer gently for 3–4 minutes, then add the star fruit and lime juice. Simmer for a further 2–3 minutes, until the fish is cooked.

4 Divide the fish and star fruit between four to six warmed serving bowls and add a little of the cooking liquid. Garnish with basil leaves and a wedge of lime to squeeze over it. Serve the stew with bowls of steamed rice, which is moistened by spoonfuls of the remaining cooking liquid.

Spicy Fish Curry with Tamarind

The addition of tamarind to this Goan curry gives a slightly sour note to the spicy coconut sauce.

Serves 4
7.5ml/1½ tsp ground turmeric
5ml/1 tsp salt
450g/1lb monkfish fillet, cut into eight pieces
15ml/1 tbsp lemon juice
5ml/1 tsp cumin seeds
5ml/1 tsp coriander seeds
5ml/1 tsp black peppercorns
1 garlic clove, chopped

5cm/2in piece fresh root ginger, finely chopped
25g/1oz tamarind paste
150ml/¼ pint/⅔ cup hot water
30ml/2 tbsp vegetable oil
2 onions, halved and sliced lengthways
400ml/14fl oz/1⅔ cups coconut milk
4 mild green chillies, seeded and cut into thin strips
16 large prawns (shrimp), peeled
30ml/2 tbsp chopped fresh coriander (cilantro) leaves, to garnish

1 Mix together the ground turmeric and salt in a bowl. Place the fish in a shallow dish and sprinkle over the lemon juice, then rub the turmeric mixture over the fish. Cover and chill.

2 Put the cumin and coriander seeds and peppercorns in a blender or food processor and blend to a powder. Add the garlic and ginger and process for a few seconds more.

3 Preheat the oven to 200°C/400°F/Gas 6. Mix the tamarind paste and hot water and set aside. Heat the oil in a frying pan, add the onions and cook for 5–6 minutes, until softened and golden. Transfer the onions to a shallow earthenware dish. Add the fish to pan, and fry over a high heat, turning to seal on all sides. Remove from the pan and place on top of the onions.

4 Fry the ground spice mixture in the pan, stirring constantly, for 1–2 minutes. Stir in the tamarind liquid, coconut milk and chilli strips then bring to the boil. Pour over the fish.

5 Cover the dish and cook in the oven for 10 minutes. Add the prawns, and cook for a further 5 minutes, or until the prawns are pink. Do not overcook them or they will toughen. Check the seasoning, sprinkle with coriander leaves and serve.

Sour Fish Stew Energy 240kcal/1001kJ; Protein 25.9g; Carbohydrate 7.3g, of which sugars 4.7g; Fat 12.1g, of which saturates 1.2g; Cholesterol 0mg; Calcium 27mg; Fibre 1.7g; Sodium 67mg.
Spicy Fish Curry Energy 220kcal/926kJ; Protein 28g; Carbohydrate 12.8g, of which sugars 10.5g; Fat 6.8g, of which saturates 1g; Cholesterol 113mg; Calcium 103mg; Fibre 1.4g; Sodium 720mg.

Spicy Chicken Satay with Chilli Relish

This spicy marinade quickly gives an exotic flavour to tender chicken. The satays can be cooked on a barbecue or under the grill.

Serves 4
4 skinless chicken breast fillets, about 175g/6oz each
60ml/4 tbsp sambal kecap

1 Cut the chicken breast fillets into 2.5cm/1in cubes and place in a bowl with the sambal kecap. Mix thoroughly so the chicken is well coated. Cover and leave in a cool place to marinate for at least 1 hour.

2 Soak eight bamboo skewers in cold water for 30 minutes so they don't burn while cooking the chicken.

3 Pour the chicken and the marinade into a sieve (strainer) placed over a pan and leave to drain for a few minutes. Set the sieve aside.

4 Add 30ml/2 tbsp hot water to the marinade and bring to the boil. Lower the heat and simmer for 2 minutes, then pour into a bowl and leave to cool.

5 Drain the skewers, thread them with the chicken and cook under a grill (broiler) or on a barbecue for about 10 minutes, turning regularly until the chicken is golden brown and cooked through. Serve with the sambal kecap as a dip.

> **Cook's Tip**
> *Sambal kecap is a popular Indonesian sauce. Look for it in Asian food stores or, if unavailable, try making your own version. In a bowl, mix together 30ml/2 tbsp dark soy sauce; juice of ½ a lemon or 1 lime; 2 hot chilli peppers, crushed, or 5ml/1 tsp chilli powder; 2 shallots, sliced very thin; 1 clove of garlic, crushed (optional); 15ml/1 tbsp hot water. Leave to stand for 30 minutes before serving to let the flavours mingle.*

Chicken Satay with Hot Cashew Nut Sambal

Delicious satay skewers are grilled then served with a spicy sambal sauce.

Serves 6
about 1kg/2¼lb skinless chicken breast fillets
30ml/2 tbsp olive oil
5ml/1 tsp ground coriander
2.5ml/½ tsp ground cumin
2.5cm/1in piece of fresh root ginger, finely grated
2 garlic cloves, crushed
5ml/1 tsp caster (superfine) sugar
2.5ml/½ tsp salt

18 long pandanus leaves, each halved to give 21cm/8½in lengths
36 bamboo or wooden skewers

For the hot cashew nut sambal
2 garlic cloves, roughly chopped
4 small fresh hot green chillies (not tiny birdseye chillies), seeded and sliced
50g/2oz/⅓ cup cashew nuts
10ml/2 tsp sugar, preferably palm sugar (jaggery)
75ml/5 tbsp light soy sauce
juice of ½ lime
30ml/2 tbsp coconut cream

1 To make the sambal, grind the garlic and chillies quite finely in a mortar with a pestle. Add the nuts and grind until the mixture is almost smooth, with a bit of texture. Pound in the remaining ingredients, cover and put in a cool place.

2 Soak the bamboo or wooden skewers in water for 30 minutes. Slice the chicken horizontally into thin pieces and then into strips about 2.5cm/1in wide. Toss in the oil. Mix the spices, ginger, garlic, sugar and salt together. Rub this mixture into the chicken. Leave to marinate while you prepare the barbecue.

3 Thread a strip of pandanus leaf and a piece of chicken on to each skewer. Once the flames have died down, rake the coals to one side. Position an oiled grill rack over the coals to heat.

4 When the coals are medium-hot, or with a moderate coating of ash, place the satays meat side down on the rack and cover with a lid or tented heavy-duty foil and cook for 5–7 minutes. Once the meat has seared, move the satays around so that the leaves don't scorch. Serve hot, with the sambal.

Spicy Chicken Satay Energy 265kcal/1120kJ; Protein 55.2g; Carbohydrate 3.5g, of which sugars 2g; Fat 3.4g, of which saturates 1g; Cholesterol 158mg; Calcium 19mg; Fibre 0.6g; Sodium 1204mg.
Chicken Satay Energy 197kcal/835kJ; Protein 42.5g; Carbohydrate 2.4g, of which sugars 2g; Fat 2g, of which saturates 0.5g; Cholesterol 123mg; Calcium 15mg; Fibre 0.4g; Sodium 640mg.

Fragrant Grilled Chicken with Fresh Red Chillies

If you have time, prepare the chicken in advance and leave it to marinate in the refrigerator for several hours – or even overnight – until ready to cook.

Serves 4

450g/1lb chicken breast fillets, with the skin on
30ml/2 tbsp sesame oil
2 garlic cloves, crushed
2 coriander (cilantro) roots, finely chopped
2 small fresh red chillies, seeded and finely chopped

30ml/2 tbsp Thai fish sauce
5ml/1 tsp sugar
cooked rice, to serve
lime wedges, to garnish

For the sauce

90ml/6 tbsp rice vinegar
60ml/4 tbsp sugar
2.5ml/½ tsp salt
2 garlic cloves, crushed
1 small fresh red chilli, seeded and finely chopped
115g/4oz/2 cups fresh coriander (cilantro), finely chopped

1 Lay the chicken breast fillets between two sheets of clear film (plastic wrap), baking parchment or foil and beat with the side of a rolling pin or the flat side of a meat tenderizer until the meat is about half its original thickness. Place in a large, shallow dish or bowl.

2 Mix together the sesame oil, garlic, coriander roots, red chillies, fish sauce and sugar in a bowl. Stir until the sugar has dissolved. Pour over the chicken. Cover with clear film and set aside to marinate in a cool place for at least 20 minutes.

3 Meanwhile, make the sauce. Heat the vinegar in a pan, add the sugar and salt and stir until the mixture begins to thicken. Add the remaining sauce ingredients, stir well, then spoon the sauce into a serving bowl.

4 Preheat the grill (broiler) and cook the chicken for 5 minutes. Turn and baste with the marinade, then cook for a further 5 minutes, or until cooked through and golden brown. Serve with rice and the sauce, garnished with lime wedges.

Chargrilled Chicken with Garlic and Chilli Peppers

An imaginative marinade can make all the difference to chicken. This garlicky marinade, with mustard and chilli, gives tender chicken a real punch.

Serves 4 to 6

1½ chickens, total weight about 2.25kg/5lb, jointed, or 12 chicken pieces
2 or 3 red or green (bell) peppers, quartered and seeded

4 or 5 ripe tomatoes, halved horizontally
lemon wedges, to serve

For the marinade

90ml/6 tbsp extra virgin olive oil
juice of 1 large lemon
5ml/1 tsp French mustard
4 garlic cloves, crushed
2 fresh red or green chillies, seeded and chopped
5ml/1 tsp dried oregano
salt and ground black pepper

1 If you are jointing the chicken yourself, divide the legs into two. Make a couple of slits in the deepest part of the flesh of each piece of chicken, using a small sharp knife. This helps the marinade to be absorbed more efficiently and will also let the chicken cook thoroughly.

2 Mix together all the marinade ingredients in a large bowl. Add the chicken and turn over to coat them thoroughly. Cover with clear film (plastic wrap) and place in the refrigerator for 4–8 hours, turning the pieces over in the marinade occasionally.

3 Prepare the barbecue. When the coals are ready, lift the chicken pieces out of the marinade and place them on the grill rack. Add the pepper quarters and the tomatoes to the marinade and set it aside for 15 minutes. Grill the chicken pieces for 20–25 minutes. Watch them closely and move them away from the area where the heat is most fierce if they start to burn.

4 Turn the chicken pieces over and cook them for 20–25 minutes more. Meanwhile, thread the peppers on two long metal skewers. Add them to the barbecue grill, with the tomatoes, for the last 15 minutes of cooking. Remember to keep an eye on them and turn them over at least once. Serve with the lemon wedges.

Fragrant Chicken Energy 243kcal/1022kJ; Protein 28g; Carbohydrate 17.7g, of which sugars 17.6g; Fat 7.1g, of which saturates 1.2g; Cholesterol 79mg; Calcium 73mg; Fibre 1.5g; Sodium 502mg.
Chargrilled Chicken Energy 760kcal/3,156kJ; Protein 61.7g; Carbohydrate 11.1g, of which sugars 10.8g; Fat 52.2g, of which saturates 13.3g; Cholesterol 313mg; Calcium 40mg; Fibre 3.1g; Sodium 235mg.

Hot Chilli Chicken

Not for the faint-hearted, this delicious fiery, hot curry is made with a spicy chilli masala paste.

Serves 4

30ml/2 tbsp tomato
    purée (paste)
2 garlic cloves, roughly chopped
2 green chillies, roughly chopped
5 dried red chillies
2.5ml/½ tsp salt
1.5ml/¼ tsp sugar
5ml/1 tsp chilli powder
2.5ml/½ tsp paprika
15ml/1 tbsp curry paste

30ml/2 tbsp vegetable oil
2.5ml/½ tsp cumin seeds
1 onion, finely chopped
2 bay leaves
5ml/1 tsp ground coriander
5ml/1 tsp ground cumin
1.5ml/¼ tsp ground turmeric
400g/14oz can chopped
    tomatoes
150ml/¼ pint/⅔ cup water
8 chicken thighs, skinned
5ml/1 tsp garam masala
sliced green chillies, to garnish
chapatis and natural (plain)
    yogurt, to serve

1 Put the tomato purée, garlic, green and dried red chillies, salt, sugar, chilli powder, paprika and curry paste into a food processor or blender and process to a smooth paste. Alternatively, grind all the ingredients together using a mortar and pestle.

2 Heat the oil in a large heavy pan and fry the cumin seeds for 2 minutes. Add the onion and bay leaves and fry for a further 5 minutes.

3 Add the spice paste and fry for 2–3 minutes until it releases a fragrant aroma. Add the remaining ground spices and cook for 2 minutes.

4 Add the chopped tomatoes and the measured water to the pan. Bring the mixture to the boil and simmer for 5 minutes until the sauce thickens.

5 Add the chicken and garam masala to the sauce. Cover the pan and simmer for 25–30 minutes until the chicken is tender. Serve with chapatis and natural yogurt, garnished with sliced green chillies.

Spicy Roast Chicken with Chilli and Lemon Grass

This tasty roasted chicken is stuffed with a spicy paste and infused with lemon grass.

Serves 4 to 6

1 chicken, total weight about
    1.2kg/2½lb
6 lemon grass stalks, bruised
2–3 large sweet potatoes, peeled
    or unpeeled, cut into wedges
40g/1½oz fresh root ginger, cut
    into matchsticks
30–45ml/2–3 tbsp coconut or
    groundnut (peanut) oil
salt and ground black pepper
green papaya salad, to serve

For the paste
90g/3½oz fresh root
    ginger, chopped
2–3 lemon grass stalks, chopped
3 garlic cloves, chopped
90ml/6 tbsp light soy sauce
juice of 1 kalamansi lime or
    1 ordinary lime or lemon
30ml/2 tbsp palm sugar (jaggery)
ground black pepper

For the sweet chilli vinegar
90ml/6 tbsp coconut vinegar
15–30ml/1–2 tbsp granulated
    (white) or soft light brown sugar
2 red chillies, seeded and chopped

1 Preheat the oven to 180°C/350°F/Gas 4. First make the paste. Using a mortar and pestle, grind the ginger, lemon grass and garlic to a coarse paste. Beat in the soy sauce and lime juice. Add the sugar and mix until it dissolves. Season with pepper.

2 Put the chicken on a flat surface and gently massage the skin to loosen it. Make a few incisions in the skin and flesh and rub the paste into the slits and under the skin. Put the chicken in a roasting pan and stuff with four of the lemon grass stalks. Place the sweet potatoes in the pan with the remaining lemon grass stalks and the ginger. Drizzle with oil and season.

3 Roast in the oven for 1–1¼ hours, until the chicken juices run clear. Baste the chicken and potatoes after 50 minutes. Meanwhile, make the chilli vinegar. Mix the vinegar and sugar in a bowl until the sugar dissolves. Stir in the chillies and set aside.

4 When the chicken and potatoes are cooked, serve immediately with the sweet chilli vinegar to splash over it and a green papaya salad.

Hot Chilli Chicken Energy 269kcal/1128kJ; Protein 27g; Carbohydrate 9g, of which sugars 7g; Fat 15g, of which saturates 3g; Cholesterol 120mg; Calcium 68mg; Fibre 1.5g; Sodium 400g.
Spicy Roast Chicken Energy 434kcal/1812kJ; Protein 26.2g; Carbohydrate 28.6g, of which sugars 12.6g; Fat 24.6g, of which saturates 6.5g; Cholesterol 128mg; Calcium 42mg; Fibre 2.5g; Sodium 1209mg.

Stir-fried Chicken with Chillies

This is good, home cooking – simple spicy food that you can enjoy as an everyday meal. There are variations of this dish, using pork or seafood, throughout South-east Asia so this is a good place to start. The essential elements of this dish, as with many dishes from the area, are the fragrant lemon grass and the fire of the chillies, so add as much as you like. Serve with a table salad, rice wrappers and a dipping sauce.

Serves 4
15ml/1 tbsp sugar
30ml/2 tbsp sesame or groundnut (peanut) oil
2 garlic cloves, finely chopped
2–3 green or red Thai chillies, seeded and finely chopped
2 lemon grass stalks, finely sliced
1 onion, finely sliced
350g/12oz skinless chicken breast fillets, cut into bitesize strips
30ml/2 tbsp soy sauce
15ml/1 tbsp Thai fish sauce
1 bunch fresh coriander (cilantro), stalks removed, leaves chopped
salt and ground black pepper
nuoc cham, to serve

1 To make a caramel sauce, put the sugar into a small pan with a few splashes of water, but not enough to soak it. Heat it gently until the sugar has dissolved and turned golden. Set aside.

2 Heat a wok or heavy pan and add the oil. Stir in the garlic, chillies and lemon grass, and cook until they become fragrant. Add the onion and stir-fry for 1 minute, then add the chicken.

3 When the chicken begins to brown a little, add the soy sauce, fish sauce and caramel sauce. Keep the chicken moving around the wok for a minute or two, then season with a little salt and pepper. Toss the fresh coriander into the chicken and serve immediately with nuoc cham to drizzle over it.

Cook's Tip
Nuoc cham is a chilli sauce popular in Vietnam and can be found in Asian food stores. It is used as a condiment and dipping sauce and is usually made from dried red chillies, garlic and sugar, processed with water, fish sauce and lime juice.

Chicken with Basil and Chilli

This easy chicken dish is an excellent introduction to Thai cuisine. Thai basil, which is sometimes known as holy basil, has a unique, pungent flavour that is both spicy and sharp. Deep-frying the leaves adds another dimension to this dish.

Serves 4 to 6
45ml/3 tbsp vegetable oil
4 garlic cloves, thinly sliced
2–4 fresh red chillies, seeded and finely chopped
450g/1lb skinless boneless chicken breast portions, cut into bitesize pieces
45ml/3 tbsp Thai fish sauce
10ml/2 tsp dark soy sauce
5ml/1 tsp sugar
10–12 fresh Thai basil leaves
2 fresh red chillies, seeded and finely chopped, and about 20 deep-fried Thai basil leaves, to garnish

1 Heat the oil in a wok or large frying pan. Add the garlic and chillies and stir-fry for 1–2 minutes until the garlic is golden. Take care not to let the garlic burn, otherwise it will taste bitter.

2 Add the pieces of chicken to the wok or pan, in batches if necessary, and stir-fry until the chicken changes colour.

3 Stir in the fish sauce, soy sauce and sugar. Stir-fry the mixture for 3–4 minutes, or until the chicken is cooked and golden brown.

4 Stir in the fresh Thai basil leaves. Spoon the mixture on to a warm platter. Garnish with the chopped chillies and deep-fried Thai basil and serve immediately.

Cook's Tip
To deep-fry Thai basil leaves, first make sure that the leaves are completely dry or they will splutter when added to the oil. Heat vegetable or groundnut (peanut) oil in a wok or deep-fryer to 190°C/375°F or until a cube of bread, added to the oil, browns in about 45 seconds. Add the leaves and deep-fry them briefly until they are crisp and translucent – this will take only about 30–40 seconds. Lift out the leaves using a slotted spoon or wire basket and leave them to drain on kitchen paper before using.

Stir-fried Chicken Energy 202kcal/847kJ; Protein 22g; Carbohydrate 9g, of which sugars 7g; Fat 9g, of which saturates 1g; Cholesterol 61mg; Calcium 32mg; Fibre 0.6g; Sodium 800mg.
Chicken with Basil Energy 214kcal/899kJ; Protein 28g; Carbohydrate 4g, of which sugars 10g; Fat 10g, of which saturates 1g; Cholesterol 79mg; Calcium 14mg; Fibre 0.1g; Sodium 700mg.

Stir-fried Chicken and Cashews

Although it is not native to South-east Asia, the cashew tree is highly prized in Thailand and the classic partnership of these slightly sweet nuts with chicken is immensely popular both in Thailand and abroad.

Serves 4 to 6
450g/1lb boneless chicken
   breast portions

1 red (bell) pepper
2 garlic cloves
4 dried red chillies
30ml/2 tbsp vegetable oil
30ml/2 tbsp oyster sauce
15ml/1 tbsp soy sauce
pinch of sugar
1 bunch spring onions (scallions),
   cut into 5cm/2in lengths
175g/6oz/1½ cups
   cashews, roasted
coriander (cilantro) leaves,
   to garnish

1 Remove and discard the skin from the chicken breasts and trim off any excess fat. With a sharp knife, cut the chicken into bitesize pieces and set aside.

2 Cut the red pepper in half, scrape out the seeds and the paler membranes and discard, then cut the flesh into 2cm/¾in dice. Peel and thinly slice the garlic and finely chop the dried red chillies.

3 Preheat a wok and then heat the oil. The best way to do this is to drizzle the oil around the inner rim, so that it runs down and coats the entire wok.

4 Add the garlic and dried chillies to the wok and stir-fry over a medium heat until golden. Do not let the garlic burn, otherwise it will taste bitter.

5 Add the chicken to the wok and stir-fry until it is cooked through, then add the red pepper. If the mixture is very dry, add a little water.

6 Stir in the oyster sauce, soy sauce and sugar. Add the spring onions and cashew nuts. Stir-fry for 1–2 minutes more, until heated through. Spoon into a warm dish and serve immediately, garnished with the coriander leaves.

Chicken Marinated in Chilli Paste

Hot, spicy, garlicky and a little sweet, this is a truly tasty dish.

Serves 4
900g/2lb chicken breast fillet or
   boneless thighs
2 round (butterhead) lettuces
vegetable oil
4 spring onions
   (scallions), shredded

For the marinade
60ml/4 tbsp gochujang chilli paste
45ml/3 tbsp mirin or rice wine
15ml/1 tbsp dark soy sauce
4 garlic cloves, crushed
25ml/5 tsp sesame oil
15ml/1 tbsp grated fresh root ginger
2 spring onions (scallions),
   finely chopped
10ml/2 tsp ground black pepper
15ml/1 tbsp lemonade

1 Combine all the marinade ingredients in a large mixing bowl and stir thoroughly so they are well combined.

2 Cut the chicken into bitesize pieces, add to the bowl and stir to coat it with the marinade. Transfer to an airtight container and marinate in the refrigerator for about 3 hours.

3 Remove the outer leaves from the heads of lettuce, keeping them whole. Rinse well and place in a serving dish.

4 Lightly coat a heavy griddle pan or frying pan with vegetable oil and place it over a medium heat (the griddle can be used over charcoal). Griddle the chicken for 15 minutes, or until the meat is cooked and has turned a deep brown. Increase the heat briefly to scorch the chicken and give it a smoky flavour.

5 Serve by wrapping the chicken pieces in lettuce leaves with a few shredded spring onions.

Cook's Tip
Gochujang is a popular savoury condiment throughout Korea. Made from red chilli powder, glutinous rice powder, fermented soya beans, and salt, it was traditionally fermented over years in large earthen pots outdoors. Look for the ready-made paste in jars and bottles available in Asian stores.

Stir-fried Chicken Energy 458kcal/1909kJ; Protein 37.1g; Carbohydrate 17.7g, of which sugars 17.6g; Fat 7.1g, of which saturates 1.2g; Cholesterol 79mg; Calcium 26mg; Fibre 0g; Sodium 447mg.
Chicken Marinated in Chilli Energy 279kcal/1178kJ; Protein 55g; Carbohydrate 2g, of which sugars 2g; Fat 5.7g, of which saturates 1.1g; Cholesterol 158mg; Calcium 39mg; Fibre 0.9g; Sodium 405mg.

Spicy Spanish Chicken

This chicken dish has a spicy red pepper sauce. In the past, the dried choricero pepper – the one that gives chorizos their colour and spice – was used alone, but nowadays the dish is often made with fresh red peppers, spiced with chilli.

Serves 4
675g/1½lb red (bell) peppers
4 free-range chicken portions
10ml/2 tsp paprika
30ml/2 tbsp olive oil
1 large onion, chopped
2 garlic cloves, finely chopped
200g/7oz Serrano or other ham, in one piece, or a gammon chop
200g/7oz can chopped tomatoes
1 dried guindilla or other hot dried chilli, chopped, or 2.5ml/ ½ tsp chilli powder, to taste
salt and ground black pepper
chopped fresh parsley, to garnish
small new potatoes, to serve

1 Preheat the grill (broiler) to high. Put the peppers on a baking sheet and grill (broil) for 8–12 minutes, turning occasionally, until the skins have blistered and blackened. Place the peppers in a bowl, cover with clear film (plastic wrap) and leave to cool.

2 Rub salt and paprika into the chicken portions. Heat the oil in a frying pan and add the chicken, skin side down. Fry over a medium-low heat, turning until golden on all sides.

3 Meanwhile, select a casserole into which the chicken will fit comfortably. Spoon in 45ml/3 tbsp fat from the other pan. Fry the onion and garlic until soft. Dice the ham or gammon and add, stirring occasionally, for a few minutes.

4 Add the chopped tomatoes to the casserole, with the chopped dried chilli or chilli powder. Cook for 4–5 minutes.

5 Peel the skins off the peppers and discard with the seeds. Put the peppers into a blender and strain in the juices. Process, then add the paste to the casserole. Heat through.

6 Add the chicken pieces to the casserole, ensuring they are covered in sauce. Cook, covered, for 15 minutes and check the seasonings, adding more if necessary. Garnish with a little parsley and serve with small new potatoes.

Fiery Chicken Casserole

This warming stew is filled with vegetables and spices. Chillies and gochujang chilli paste supply a vivid red colour and give the chicken a fiery quality.

Serves 4
3 potatoes
1 carrot
2 onions
1 chicken, about 800g/1¾lb
30ml/2 tbsp vegetable oil
2 garlic cloves, crushed
3 green chillies, seeded and sliced
1 red chilli, seeded and sliced
15ml/1 tbsp sesame oil
salt and ground black pepper
2 spring onions (scallions), finely chopped, to garnish

For the marinade
30ml/2 tbsp mirin or rice wine
salt and ground black pepper

For the seasoning
15ml/1 tbsp sesame seeds
10ml/2 tsp light soy sauce
30ml/2 tbsp gochujang chilli paste
45ml/3 tbsp Korean chilli powder

1 Peel the potatoes and cut into bitesize pieces. Soak in cold water for 15–20 minutes and drain. Peel the carrot and onions and cut into medium pieces. Cut the chicken, with skin and bone, into bitesize pieces and mix with the marinade ingredients. Stir to coat and leave for 10 minutes.

2 Heat 15ml/1 tbsp vegetable oil in a frying pan or wok, and quickly stir-fry the crushed garlic. Add the chicken and stir-fry, draining off any fat. When lightly browned, place the chicken on kitchen paper to remove any excess oil.

3 For the seasoning, grind the sesame seeds in a mortar and pestle. Combine the soy sauce, gochujang paste, chilli powder and ground sesame seeds in a bowl.

4 Heat the remaining oil and add the potatoes, carrot and onions. Cook gently, stirring well. Add the chicken. Pour in water to cover two-thirds of the meat and vegetables. Bring to the boil. Add the chilli seasoning. Simmer until the sauce has reduced by a third.

5 Add the sliced chillies and simmer for a little longer until the liquid has thickened slightly. Add the sesame oil, transfer to deep serving bowls and garnish with the chopped spring onion.

Spicy Chicken Energy 332kcal/1396kJ; Protein 47.6g; Carbohydrate 13.8g, of which sugars 12.4g; Fat 10g, of which saturates 2.1g; Cholesterol 134mg; Calcium 33mg; Fibre 3.2g; Sodium 702mg.
Fiery Chicken Casserole Energy 470kcal/1955kJ; Protein 27.4g; Carbohydrate 20.4g, of which sugars 4.7g; Fat 31.5g, of which saturates 7.5g; Cholesterol 128mg; Calcium 56mg; Fibre 2.3g; Sodium 296mg.

Sweet and Spicy Chicken

This deep-fried chicken dish has a spicy kick, mellowed by the sweetness of pineapple and maple syrup.

Serves 3
675g/1½lb chicken breast fillets
   or boneless thighs
175g/6oz/1½ cups
   cornflour (cornstarch)
vegetable oil, for deep-frying
2 green chillies, sliced
2 dried red chillies, seeded
   and sliced
3 walnuts, finely chopped
salt and ground black pepper

For the marinade
15ml/1 tbsp white wine
15ml/1 tbsp dark soy sauce
3 garlic cloves, crushed
¼ onion, finely chopped

For the sauce
15ml/1 tbsp chilli oil
2.5ml/½ tsp gochujang chilli paste
30ml/2 tbsp dark soy sauce
7.5ml/1½ tsp pineapple juice
15 garlic cloves, peeled
30ml/2 tbsp maple syrup
15ml/1 tbsp sugar

1 Slice the chicken into bitesize strips and season with the salt and pepper. Combine all the marinade ingredients in a large bowl. Mix well and add the chicken, rubbing the mixture thoroughly into the meat. Leave to marinate for 20 minutes.

2 Sprinkle the marinated chicken with cornflour, making sure you cover the meat evenly. Fill a wok or medium heavy pan one-third full of oil and heat over high heat to 170°C/340°F, or when a piece of bread dropped in the oil browns in 15 seconds.

3 Add the chicken and deep-fry for 3–5 minutes, or until golden brown. Remove the chicken and drain on kitchen paper to remove any excess oil.

4 Blend all the sauce ingredients together in a large pan, adding the garlic cloves whole, and heat over medium heat.

5 Once the sauce is bubbling, add the fried chicken and stir to coat the meat with the sauce. Leave to simmer until the sauce has formed a sticky glaze over the chicken, and then add the chillies. Stir well and transfer to a shallow serving dish. Garnish with the walnuts before serving.

Chicken with Red-hot Chipotle Sauce

It is important to seek out dried chipotle chillies for this recipe, as they impart a wonderfully rich and smoky flavour to the chicken. The spicy paste can be made ahead of time, making this an ideal recipe to make when entertaining.

Serves 6
6 chipotle chillies
200ml/7fl oz/scant 1 cup
   chicken stock
3 onions
6 boneless chicken breast fillets
45ml/3 tbsp vegetable oil
salt and ground black pepper
fresh oregano, to garnish
boiled rice, to serve

1 Put the dried chillies in a bowl and pour over hot water to cover. Leave for about 30 minutes until soft. Drain, reserving the soaking water in a bowl. Cut off the stalk from each chilli, then slit lengthways and discard the seeds.

2 Preheat the oven to 180°C/350°F/Gas 4. Chop the flesh of the chillies roughly and put in a food processor or blender. Add enough chicken stock to the soaking water to make it up to 400ml/14fl oz/1⅔ cups. Pour into the processor or blender and process at maximum power until smooth.

3 Halve the onions and thinly slice. Remove the skin from the chicken breast fillets, then trim off any stray pieces of fat or membrane. Heat the oil in a large frying pan, add the onions and cook over a medium heat for 5 minutes, or until they have softened but not coloured.

4 Using a slotted spoon, transfer the onion to a casserole that is large enough to hold all the chicken in a single layer. Sprinkle the onion slices with salt and ground black pepper. Arrange the chicken on the onion. Season with salt and black pepper.

5 Pour the chipotle paste over the chicken in the casserole, making sure that each piece is evenly coated.

6 Bake in the preheated oven and bake for 45–60 minutes or until the chicken is cooked through, but is still moist and tender. Garnish with oregano. Serve with boiled white rice.

Sweet and Spicy Chicken Energy 655kcal/2749kJ; Protein 56.4g; Carbohydrate 45.3g, of which sugars 14.4g; Fat 28.8g, of which saturates 3.5g; Cholesterol 158mg; Calcium 34mg; Fibre 0.4g; Sodium 1249mg.
Chicken with Chipotle Energy 229kcal/963kJ; Protein 36.7g; Carbohydrate 4.5g, of which sugars 3.3g; Fat 7.3g, of which saturates 1.1g; Cholesterol 105mg; Calcium 21mg; Fibre 0.8g; Sodium 92mg.

Chicken in Spicy Onions

This is one of the few dishes of India in which onions appear prominently. Chunky onion slices infused with toasted cumin seeds, shredded ginger and green chillies add a delicious contrast to the flavour of the chicken.

Serves 4 to 6
1.3kg/3lb chicken, jointed
   and skinned
2.5ml/½ tsp ground turmeric
2.5ml/½ tsp chilli powder
salt, to taste
60ml/4 tbsp vegetable oil
4 small onions, finely chopped
175g/6oz coriander (cilantro)
   leaves, coarsely chopped
5cm/2in piece fresh root ginger,
   finely shredded
2 green chillies, finely chopped
10ml/2 tsp cumin seeds,
   dry-roasted
75ml/5 tbsp/⅓ cup natural
   (plain) yogurt
75ml/5 tbsp/⅓ cup double
   (heavy) cream
2.5ml/½ tsp cornflour (cornstarch)

1 Rub the chicken joints with the turmeric, chilli powder and salt and leave to marinate for 1 hour.

2 Heat the oil in a frying pan and fry the chicken pieces without overlapping until both sides are sealed. Remove and keep warm.

3 Reheat the oil and fry three of the chopped onions, 150g/5oz of the coriander leaves, half the ginger, the green chillies and the cumin seeds until the onions are beginning to soften and turn translucent.

4 Return the chicken to the pan with any juices and mix well. Cover and cook gently for 15 minutes.

5 Remove the pan from the heat and allow to cool a little. In a bowl, mix together the natural yogurt, cream and cornflour until well combined. Gradually fold the mixture into the chicken pieces, mixing well.

6 Return the pan to the heat and gently cook until the chicken is tender and cooked through. Just before serving, stir in the reserved onion, coriander and ginger. Serve hot.

Baby Chicken in a Chilli Tamarind Sauce

The tamarind in this recipe gives a tasty sweet-and-sour flavour. This balti dish is quite hot.

Serves 4 to 6
60ml/4 tbsp tomato ketchup
15ml/1 tbsp tamarind paste
60ml/4 tbsp water
7.5ml/1½ tsp chilli powder
7.5ml/1½ tsp salt
15ml/1 tbsp sugar
7.5ml/1½ tsp crushed ginger
7.5ml/1½ tsp crushed garlic
30ml/2 tbsp desiccated (dry
   unsweetened shredded) coconut
30ml/2 tbsp sesame seeds
5ml/1 tsp poppy seeds
5ml/1 tsp ground cumin
7.5ml/1½ tsp ground coriander
2 X 450g/1lb baby chickens,
   skinned and cut into
   6–8 pieces each
75ml/5 tbsp corn oil
about 20 curry leaves
2.5ml/½ tsp onion seeds
3 large dried red chillies
2.5ml/½ tsp fenugreek seeds
10–12 cherry tomatoes
45ml/3 tbsp chopped fresh
   coriander (cilantro)
2 fresh green chillies, chopped

1 Put the tomato ketchup, tamarind paste and water into a large mixing bowl and use a fork to blend everything together.

2 Add the chilli powder, salt, sugar, ginger, garlic, coconut, sesame and poppy seeds, ground cumin and ground coriander to the mixture.

3 Add the chicken pieces and stir until they are well coated with the spice mixture. Set to one side.

4 Heat the oil in a deep frying pan or a large karahi. Add the curry leaves, onion seeds, dried red chillies and fenugreek seeds and fry for about 1 minute.

5 Add the chicken pieces to the pan, along with their spice paste, mixing as you go. Simmer gently for about 12–15 minutes, or until the chicken is thoroughly cooked.

6 Add the tomatoes, fresh coriander and green chillies, and serve immediately.

Chicken in Spicy Onions Energy 439kcal/1840kJ; Protein 62.8g; Carbohydrate 7.8g, of which sugars 5.6g; Fat 17.7g, of which saturates 5.9g; Cholesterol 192mg; Calcium 120mg; Fibre 2.4g; Sodium 175mg.
Baby Chicken Energy 268kcal/1120kJ; Protein 26g; Carbohydrate 4.1g, of which sugars 4g; Fat 16.6g, of which saturates 4.5g; Cholesterol 70mg; Calcium 60mg; Fibre 2.2g; Sodium 152mg.

Balti Chicken with Chillied Lentils and Tomatoes

This is rather an unusual combination of flavours, but highly recommended. The mango powder gives a delicious tangy flavour to this spicy dish.

Serves 4 to 6

75g/3oz/½ cup chana dhal
   (split yellow lentils)
60ml/4 tbsp corn oil
2 medium leeks, chopped
6 large dried red chillies
4 curry leaves
5ml/1 tsp mustard seeds
10ml/2 tsp mango powder
2 medium tomatoes, chopped
2.5ml/½ tsp chilli powder
5ml/1 tsp ground coriander
5ml/1 tsp salt
450g/1lb chicken, skinned, boned
   and cubed
15ml/1 tbsp chopped fresh
   coriander (cilantro)

1 Wash the split yellow lentils and remove any stones.

2 Put the lentils into a pan with enough water to cover, and boil for about 10 minutes until they are soft but not mushy. Drain and set aside in a bowl.

3 Heat the oil in a medium karahi or large frying pan. Lower the heat slightly and add the leeks, dried red chillies, curry leaves and mustard seeds to the pan. Stir-fry gently for a few minutes until the leeks soften and the spices are fragrant.

4 Add the mango powder, tomatoes, chilli powder, ground coriander, salt and chicken, and stir-fry for 8–10 minutes.

5 Mix in the cooked lentils and fry for a further 2 minutes, or until you are sure that the chicken is cooked right through.

6 Garnish with fresh coriander and serve with naan or paratha.

> **Cook's Tip**
> Chana dhal, a split yellow lentil, is available from Asian stores. However, split yellow peas are a good substitute.

Chicken Pasanda with Fresh Green Chillies and Coriander

Spicy, creamy and delicious – little wonder that pasanda dishes are firm favourites in Pakistan.

Serves 4

60ml/4 tbsp Greek (US strained
   plain) yogurt
2.5ml/½ tsp black cumin seeds
4 cardamom pods
6 whole black peppercorns
10ml/2 tsp garam masala
2.5cm/1in cinnamon stick
15ml/1 tbsp ground almonds
5ml/1 tsp crushed garlic
5ml/1 tsp crushed ginger
5ml/1 tsp chilli powder
5ml/1 tsp salt
675g/1½lb chicken, skinned,
   boned and cubed
75ml/5 tbsp corn oil
2 medium onions, diced
3 fresh green chillies, chopped
30ml/2 tbsp chopped fresh
   coriander (cilantro)
120ml/4fl oz/½ cup single
   (light) cream

1 Mix the yogurt, cumin seeds, cardamoms, peppercorns, garam masala, cinnamon stick, ground almonds, garlic, ginger, chilli powder and salt in a medium mixing bowl.

2 Add the chicken pieces to the bowl, ensuring they are thoroughly coated in the marinade. Set aside to marinate for about 2 hours.

3 Heat the oil in a large karahi or large frying pan. Add the onions and fry for 2–3 minutes.

4 Pour in the chicken mixture and stir until it is well blended with the onions.

5 Cook over a medium heat for about 12–15 minutes, or until the sauce has thickened and the chicken pieces are tender and cooked through.

6 Add the green chillies and fresh coriander to the pan and mix well. Stir in the cream. Bring to the boil and heat through for a minute or two. Transfer to a serving dish and garnish with more coriander, if you like.

Balti Chicken Energy 196kcal/822kJ; Protein 20.3g; Carbohydrate 9.8g, of which sugars 2.6g; Fat 8.7g, of which saturates 1.2g; Cholesterol 47mg; Calcium 41mg; Fibre 2.5g; Sodium 51mg.
Chicken Pasanda Energy 434kcal/1812kJ; Protein 44.9g; Carbohydrate 13.2g, of which sugars 7.4g; Fat 23g, of which saturates 6g; Cholesterol 135mg; Calcium 107mg; Fibre 1.4g; Sodium 129mg.

Ground Chicken with Green and Red Chillies

Minced chicken is seldom cooked in Indian or Pakistani homes. However it works very well in this delicious spicy dish.

Serves 4

275g/10oz skinless chicken
   breast fillets
2 thick red chillies
3 thick green chillies
45ml/3 tbsp corn oil
6 curry leaves
3 medium onions, sliced
7.5ml/1½ tsp crushed garlic
7.5ml/1½ tsp ground coriander
7.5ml/1½ tsp crushed ginger
5ml/1 tsp chilli powder
5ml/1 tsp salt
15ml/1 tbsp lemon juice
30ml/2 tbsp chopped fresh
   coriander leaves
chapatis and lemon wedges,
   to serve

1 Cut the chicken breast fillets into medium pieces. Add to a pan of boiling water for about 10 minutes until soft and cooked through. Drain.

2 Place the chicken in a food processor to mince (grind), or use a meat mincer if available.

3 Cut the chillies in half lengthways and remove the seeds, if desired. If you want a fiery dish, retain the seeds and add to the pan with the rest of the chillies. Cut the chilli flesh into thin strips.

4 Heat the oil in a non-stick wok or frying pan and fry the curry leaves and onions until the onions are a soft golden brown. Lower the heat and add the crushed garlic, ground coriander, crushed ginger, chilli powder and salt.

5 Add the minced chicken to the pan and stir-fry for about 3–5 minutes until it is beginning to brown.

6 Add the lemon juice, the chilli strips and most of the fresh coriander leaves. Stir for a further 3–5 minutes, then serve, garnished with the remaining coriander leaves and accompanied by chapatis and lemon wedges.

Mild Green Curry of Chicken and Vegetables

Coconut milk creates a rich sauce that is sweet with fruit and fragrant with herbs and spices.

Serves 4

4 garlic cloves, chopped
15ml/1 tbsp chopped fresh
   root ginger
2–3 chillies, chopped
½ bunch fresh coriander (cilantro)
   leaves, roughly chopped
1 onion, chopped
juice of 1 lemon
pinch of cayenne pepper
2.5ml/½ tsp curry powder
2.5ml/½ tsp ground cumin
2–3 pinches of ground cloves
large pinch of ground coriander
3 skinless chicken breast fillets or
   thighs, cut into bitesize pieces
30ml/2 tbsp vegetable oil
2 cinnamon sticks
250ml/8fl oz/1 cup chicken stock
250ml/8fl oz/1 cup coconut milk
15–30ml/1–2 tbsp sugar
1–2 bananas
¼ pineapple, peeled and chopped
handful of sultanas (golden raisins)
handful of raisins or currants
2–3 sprigs of mint, thinly sliced
juice of ¼–½ lemon
salt
flat bread, to serve

1 Purée the garlic, ginger, chillies, fresh coriander, onion, lemon juice, cayenne pepper, curry powder, cumin, cloves, ground coriander and salt in a food processor or blender. Toss together the chicken pieces with about 15–30ml/1–2 tbsp of the spice mixture and set aside.

2 Heat the oil in a wok or frying pan, then add the remaining spice mixture and cook over a medium heat, stirring, for 10 minutes, or until the paste is lightly browned.

3 Stir the cinnamon sticks, stock, coconut milk and sugar into the pan, bring to the boil, then simmer for 10 minutes.

4 Stir the chicken into the sauce and cook for 2 minutes, or until the chicken becomes opaque.

5 Meanwhile, thickly slice the bananas. Stir all the fruit into the pan and cook for 1–2 minutes. Add the mint and lemon juice. Serve immediately, with flat bread.

Ground Chicken Energy 196kcal/819kJ; Protein 18.4g; Carbohydrate 10.2g, of which sugars 7.3g; Fat 9.4g, of which saturates 1.2g; Cholesterol 48mg; Calcium 60mg; Fibre 2.4g; Sodium 49mg.
Mild Green Curry Energy 383kcal/1622kJ; Protein 29.5g; Carbohydrate 11.9g, of which sugars 11.7g; Fat 10.4g, of which saturates 2g; Cholesterol 140mg; Calcium 78mg; Fibre 1.1g; Sodium 462mg.

Red-hot Chicken Curry with Fresh Red Chillies

Bamboo shoots give this fiery curry a crunchy texture.

Serves 4 to 6
1 litre/1¾ pints/4 cups coconut milk
450g/1lb skinless chicken breast
   fillets, diced
30ml/2 tbsp Thai fish sauce
15ml/1 tbsp sugar
1–2 drained canned bamboo
   shoots, total weight about
   225g/8oz, rinsed and sliced
5 kaffir lime leaves, torn
salt and ground black pepper
chopped fresh red chillies and
   kaffir lime leaves, to garnish

For the red curry paste
5ml/1 tsp coriander seeds
2.5ml/½ tsp cumin seeds
12–15 fresh red chillies, seeded
   and coarsely chopped
4 shallots, thinly sliced
2 garlic cloves, chopped
15ml/1 tbsp chopped fresh galangal
2 lemon grass stalks, chopped
3 kaffir lime leaves, chopped
4 fresh coriander (cilantro) roots
10 black peppercorns
good pinch ground cinnamon
5ml/1 tsp ground turmeric
2.5ml/½ tsp shrimp paste
30ml/2 tbsp vegetable oil

1 Make the paste. Dry-fry the coriander and cumin seeds for 1–2 minutes, then put in a mortar or food processor with the remaining ingredients except the oil. Pound or process to a paste. Gradually stir in the oil. Cover and chill until ready to use.

2 Pour half of the coconut milk into a large pan. Bring to the boil, stirring constantly until the milk has separated. Stir in 30ml/2 tbsp of the red curry paste and cook the mixture, stirring, for 2–3 minutes.

3 Add the diced chicken, fish sauce and sugar to the pan. Stir well, then lower the heat and cook gently for 5–6 minutes, stirring until the chicken changes colour and is cooked through. Take care that the curry does not stick to the base of the pan.

4 Add the remaining coconut milk to the pan. Add the bamboo shoots and lime leaves. Bring back to the boil, stirring.

5 To serve, spoon the curry into a warmed serving dish and garnish with the chopped chillies and lime leaves.

Hot Chicken with Spices and Soy Sauce

This spicy dish is an Indonesian favourite, known as *ayam kecap*. Any leftovers taste equally good when reheated the following day.

Serves 4
1.6kg/3½lb chicken, jointed and
   cut into 16 pieces
3 onions, sliced
1 litre/1¾ pints/4 cups water
3 garlic cloves, crushed
3–4 red chillies, seeded and sliced,
   or 15ml/1 tbsp chilli powder
45–60ml/3–4 tbsp vegetable oil
2.5ml/½ tsp ground nutmeg
6 whole cloves
5ml/1 tsp tamarind pulp, soaked
   in 45ml/3 tbsp warm water
30–45ml/2–3 tbsp dark or
   light soy sauce
salt
fresh red chilli shreds, to garnish
boiled rice, to serve

1 Prepare the chicken and place the pieces in a large pan with one of the onions. Pour over enough water to just cover. Bring to the boil and then simmer gently for 20 minutes.

2 Meanwhile, grind the remaining onions, with the garlic and chillies, to a fine paste in a food processor or with a mortar and pestle. Heat a little of the oil in a wok or frying pan and cook the paste to bring out the flavour, but do not allow to brown.

3 Lift the chicken out of the stock in the pan using a slotted spoon and put it straight into the spicy mixture. Toss everything together over a fairly high heat so that the spices permeate the chicken pieces. Reserve 300ml/½ pint/1¼ cups of the chicken stock to add to the pan later.

4 Stir in the nutmeg and cloves. Strain the tamarind and add the tamarind juice and the soy sauce to the chicken. Cook for a further 2–3 minutes, then add the reserved stock.

5 Taste and adjust the seasoning and cook, uncovered, for a further 25–35 minutes, until the chicken pieces are tender.

6 Serve the chicken in a bowl, garnished with shredded chilli, and eat with boiled rice.

Red-hot Chicken Curry Energy 255kcal/1077kJ; Protein 29.5g; Carbohydrate 18g, of which sugars 16.9g; Fat 7.8g; of which saturates 1.5g; Cholesterol 79mg; Calcium 92mg; Fibre 0.9g; Sodium 1104mg.
Hot Chicken with Spices Energy 630kcal/2615kJ; Protein 48.8g; Carbohydrate 13.8g, of which sugars 10.7g; Fat 42.5g; of which saturates 10.6g; Cholesterol 248mg; Calcium 52mg; Fibre 2.6g; Sodium 798mg.

Spiced Guinea Fowl Curry

A traditional spicy curry from Thailand.

Serves 4
1 guinea fowl or similar game bird
15ml/1 tbsp vegetable oil
10ml/2 tsp green curry paste
15ml/1 tbsp Thai fish sauce
2.5cm/1in piece fresh galangal, peeled and finely chopped
15ml/1 tbsp fresh green peppercorns
3 kaffir lime leaves, torn
15ml/1 tbsp whisky, preferably Mekhong
300ml/½ pint/1¼ cups chicken stock
50g/2oz yard-long beans, cut into 2.5cm/1in lengths (about ½ cup)
225g/8oz/3¼ cups chestnut mushrooms, sliced
1 piece drained canned bamboo shoot, about 50g/2oz, shredded
5ml/1 tsp dried chilli flakes, to garnish (optional)

1 Cut up the guinea fowl, remove the skin, then strip the meat off the bones. Chop into bitesize pieces and set aside.

2 Heat the oil in a wok or frying pan and add the paste. Stir-fry over a medium heat for 30 seconds, until it gives off its aroma.

3 Add the fish sauce and the guinea fowl meat and stir-fry until the meat is browned all over. Add the galangal, peppercorns, lime leaves and whisky, then pour in the stock.

4 Bring to the boil. Add the vegetables, return to a simmer and cook gently for 2–3 minutes, until they are just cooked. Spoon into a dish, sprinkle with chilli flakes, if you like, and serve.

> **Cook's Tips**
> • Guinea fowl originated in West Africa and was regarded as a game bird, but has been domesticated in Europe for over 500 years. Their average size is about 1.2kg/2½lb. American readers could substitute two or three Cornish hens, depending on size.
> • Fresh green peppercorns are simply unripe berries. They are sold on the stem. Look for them at Thai and Asian supermarkets. If unavailable, substitute bottled green peppercorns, but rinse well and drain them first.

Hot Sweet and Sour Duck Casserole

This tasty casserole can be made with any game bird. It is a distinctively sweet, sour and hot dish. It is best eaten with boiled rice as an accompaniment.

Serves 4 to 6
1.3kg/3lb duck, jointed and skinned
4 bay leaves
3 tbsp salt
75ml/2½fl oz/⅓ cup
vegetable oil
juice of 5 lemons
8 medium-sized onions, finely chopped
50g/2oz garlic, crushed
50g/2oz chilli powder
300ml/½ pint/1¼ cups pickling vinegar
115g/4oz fresh ginger, finely sliced or shredded
115g/4oz/½ cup sugar
50g/2oz garam masala

1 Place the duck pieces, bay leaves and salt in a large pan and cover with cold water. Bring to the boil, then simmer until the duck is fully cooked.

2 Remove the pieces of duck and keep warm. Reserve the liquid as a base for stock or soups.

3 In a large pan, heat the oil and lemon juice until it reaches smoking point. Add the onions, garlic and chilli powder and fry the onions until they are golden brown.

4 Add the vinegar, ginger and sugar and simmer until the sugar dissolves and the oil has separated from the masala.

5 Return the duck to the pan and add the garam masala. Mix well, then reheat until the masala clings to the pieces of duck and the gravy is thick.

6 Adjust the seasoning if necessary. If you prefer a thinner gravy, add a little of the reserved stock. Serve immediately.

> **Variation**
> Use pieces of rabbit in place of the duck, if you like.

Hot Casserole Energy 383kcal/1607kJ; Protein 26.9g; Carbohydrate 33.2g, of which sugars 25g; Fat 19g, of which saturates 2.8g; Cholesterol 128mg; Calcium 123mg; Fibre 3.6g; Sodium 184mg.
Guinea Fowl Curry Energy 368kcal/1540kJ; Protein 56.8g; Carbohydrate 1.4g, of which sugars 0.9g; Fat 14g, of which saturates 3.2g; Cholesterol 0mg; Calcium 82mg; Fibre 1.1g; Sodium 454mg.

Moghul-style Spicy Roast Lamb

This superb dish is just one of many fine examples of fabulous rich food once enjoyed by Moghul Emperors. Try it as a spicy variation to roast beef.

Serves 4 to 6
4 large onions, chopped
4 garlic cloves
5cm/2in piece fresh root ginger, chopped
45ml/3 tbsp ground almonds
10ml/2 tsp ground cumin
10ml/2 tsp ground coriander
10ml/2 tsp ground turmeric
10ml/2 tsp garam masala
4–6 green chillies
juice of 1 lemon
salt, to taste
300ml/½ pint/1¼ cups natural (plain) yogurt, beaten
1.8kg/4lb leg of lamb
8–10 cloves
4 firm tomatoes, halved and grilled, to serve
15ml/1 tbsp flaked (sliced) almonds, to garnish

1 Place the first 11 ingredients in a food processor and blend to a smooth paste, or grind in a mortar and pestle. Gradually add the yogurt and blend. Grease a large roasting pan and preheat the oven to 190°C/375°F/Gas Mark 5.

2 Remove most of the fat and skin from the lamb. Using a sharp knife, make deep pockets above the bone at each side of the thick end. Make deep diagonal gashes on both sides.

3 Push the cloves into the leg of lamb at random intervals, ensuring they are well embedded.

4 Push some of the spice mixture into the pockets and gashes and spread the remainder evenly all over the meat, working it in with your hands.

5 Place the lamb on the roasting pan and loosely cover the whole pan with foil. Roast for about 2–2½ hours, or until the lamb is cooked, removing the foil for the last 10 minutes of cooking time.

6 Remove the pan from the oven and allow the meat to rest for 10 minutes before carving. Serve with grilled tomatoes and garnish the joint with flaked almonds.

Chilli Lamb Chops

It is best to marinate the chops overnight as this makes them very tender and also helps them to absorb the maximum amount of spicy flavour. Serve with a crisp salad.

Serves 4
8 small lean spring lamb chops
1 large red chilli, seeded
30ml/2 tbsp chopped fresh coriander (cilantro)
15ml/1 tbsp chopped fresh mint
5ml/1 tsp salt
5ml/1 tsp soft light brown sugar
5ml/1 tsp garam masala
5ml/1 tsp crushed garlic
5ml/1 tsp crushed ginger
175ml/6fl oz/⅔ cup natural (plain) low-fat yogurt
10ml/2 tsp corn oil

1 Trim the lamb chops to remove any excess fat. Place them in a large bowl.

2 Finely chop the chilli, then mix with the coriander, mint, salt, brown sugar, garam masala, crushed garlic and crushed ginger.

3 Pour the yogurt into the herb mixture and, using a small whisk or a fork, mix thoroughly.

4 Pour this mixture over the top of the chops and turn them with your fingers to make sure that they are completely covered. Leave to marinate overnight in the refrigerator.

5 Heat the oil in a wok or large frying pan and add the chops. Lower the heat and allow to cook over a medium heat. Turn the chops over then continue frying until they are cooked right through, about 20 minutes, turning again if needed.

6 When the lamb is cooked, place on to warmed plates and serve with a crisp salad.

> **Cook's Tip**
> *These chops can also be cooked under a grill (broiler), and they are great for cooking on a barbecue. Remember to baste the meat with oil before grilling (broiling).*

Spicy Roast Lamb Energy 517kcal/2154kJ; Protein 43.5g; Carbohydrate 20.4g, of which sugars 13.1g; Fat 29.9g, of which saturates 9.7g; Cholesterol 146mg; Calcium 162mg; Fibre 2.3g; Sodium 160mg.
Chilli Lamb Energy 183kcal/764kJ; Protein 15.5g; Carbohydrate 14.1g, of which sugars 9.1g; Fat 7.8g, of which saturates 3.2g; Cholesterol 43mg; Calcium 102mg; Fibre 1.8g; Sodium 77mg.

Lamb Satay with a Chilli Sauce

These tasty spicy skewers are poplar throughout South-east Asia.

Makes 25 to 30 skewers
1kg/2¼lb leg of lamb, boned
3 garlic cloves, crushed
15–30ml/1–2 tbsp chilli sauce or 3–4 fresh chillies, seeded and ground, or 5–10ml/1–2 tsp chilli powder
60–90ml/4–6 tbsp dark soy sauce
juice of 1 lemon

salt and ground black pepper
vegetable oil for brushing
small onion pieces and cucumber wedges, to serve

For the sauce
6 garlic cloves, crushed
15ml/1 tbsp chilli sauce or 2–3 fresh chillies, seeded and ground
90ml/6 tbsp dark soy sauce
25ml/1½ tbsp lemon juice
30ml/2 tbsp boiling water

1 Cut the lamb into thick slices and then into 1cm/½in cubes. Remove any gristle but do not trim off any of the fat because this keeps the satays moist and enhances the flavour.

2 Blend the garlic, the chilli sauce, the ground fresh chillies or chilli powder, soy sauce, lemon juice and seasoning to a paste in a food processor or with a mortar and pestle. Pour over the lamb. Cover and leave for at least an hour. Soak wooden or bamboo skewers in water so they won't burn during cooking.

3 Prepare the sauce. In a bowl, mix the garlic, chilli sauce or chillies, soy sauce, lemon juice and boiling water.

4 Thread the cubed meat on to the skewers. Brush them with oil and cook under the grill (broiler), turning often. Coat each satay with a little sauce and serve hot, with small pieces of onion, cucumber and the remaining sauce.

Variation
Lamb neck fillet is now widely available in supermarkets and can be used instead of boned leg. Brush the lamb fillet with oil before grilling.

Fiery Meat Kebabs

Serve this tasty Indian snack in a bun, as you would a hamburger. Extra chilli sauce will go down a treat for chilli-lovers. Serve with a crisp salad as a main course or unaccompanied as an appetizer.

Serves 4 to 6
2 onions, finely chopped
250g/9oz lean lamb, cut into small cubes
50g/2oz Bengal gram

5ml/1 tsp cumin seeds
5ml/1 tsp garam masala
4–6 green chillies
5cm/2in piece fresh root ginger, crushed
salt, to taste
175ml/6fl oz/¾ cup water
a few coriander (cilantro) and mint leaves, chopped
juice of 1 lemon
15ml/1 tbsp gram flour
2 eggs, beaten
vegetable oil, for shallow-frying
limes, to serve

1 Put the first eight ingredients and the water into a pan and bring to the boil. Reduce the heat and simmer, covered, until the meat and gram are cooked. Cook uncovered to reduce the excess liquid. Cool, and grind to a paste.

2 Place the mixture in a mixing bowl and add the coriander and mint leaves, lemon juice and gram flour. Knead well.

3 Divide the mixture into 10–12 portions and roll each into a ball, then flatten slightly. Chill for about 1 hour. Dip the kebabs in the beaten egg and shallow-fry each side until golden brown. Serve immediately, with lime halves.

Cook's Tips
• Gram flour, also known as besan, is a pale-yellow flour made from ground chickpeas. More aromatic and with less starch content and higher protein than wheat flour, it is used widely in Indian cookery for doughs, batters and for thickening sauces. Look for it in supermarkets or Indian and Asian food stores.
• Bengal gram is a smaller, rusty-coloured variety of chickpea, also known as the black chickpea. It is the most widely grown pulse in India. Use gram flour if unavailable.

Lamb Satay Energy 72kcal/300kJ; Protein 4.2g; Carbohydrate 0.4g, of which sugars 0.3g; Fat 6g, of which saturates 1.2g; Cholesterol 15mg; Calcium 3mg; Fibre 0g; Sodium 342mg.
Fiery Meat Kebabs Energy 219kcal/909kJ; Protein 11.6g; Carbohydrate 8.1g, of which sugars 3.8g; Fat 15.9g, of which saturates 3.6g; Cholesterol 92mg; Calcium 39mg; Fibre 1.3g; Sodium 59mg.

Italian Lamb Meatballs with Chilli Tomato Sauce

Serve these piquant Italian-style meatballs with pasta and a leafy salad. Sprinkle with a little grated Parmesan cheese for that extra Italian touch.

Serves 4
450g/1lb lean minced (ground) lamb
1 large onion, grated
1 garlic clove, crushed
50g/2oz/1 cup fresh white breadcrumbs
15ml/1 tbsp chopped fresh parsley
1 small egg, lightly beaten
30ml/2 tbsp olive oil

salt and ground black pepper
60ml/4 tbsp finely grated Parmesan cheese, pasta and rocket (arugula) leaves, to serve

For the sauce
1 onion, finely chopped
400g/14oz can chopped tomatoes
200ml/7fl oz/scant 1 cup passata (bottled strained tomatoes)
5ml/1 tsp sugar
2 green chillies, seeded and finely chopped
30ml/2 tbsp chopped fresh oregano
salt and ground black pepper

1 Soak a small clay pot in cold water for 15 minutes, then drain. Place the minced lamb, onion, garlic, breadcrumbs, parsley and seasoning in a bowl and mix well. Add the beaten egg and mix to bind the meatball mixture together.

2 Roll the mixture in your hands and shape into about 20 even balls, about the size of walnuts. Wetting your hands slightly will prevent the mixture sticking to them.

3 Heat the olive oil in a frying pan, add the meatballs and cook over a high heat, stirring occasionally, until browned all over.

4 Meanwhile, to make the sauce, mix together the chopped onion, tomatoes, passata, sugar, seeded and chopped chillies and oregano. Season well and pour the sauce into the clay pot.

5 Place the meatballs in the sauce, then cover and place in an unheated oven. Set the oven to 200°C/400°F/Gas 6 and cook for 1 hour, stirring after 30 minutes. Serve over pasta with Parmesan cheese and rocket.

Lamb Stew with Chilli Sauce

The chillies in this stew add depth and richness to the sauce; the potato slices ensure that it is a fairly substantial meal.

Serves 6
6 guajillo chillies, seeded
2 pasilla chillies, seeded
250ml/8fl oz/1 cup hot water
3 garlic cloves, peeled
5ml/1 tsp ground cinnamon
2.5ml/½ tsp ground cloves

2.5ml/½ tsp ground black pepper
15ml/1 tbsp vegetable oil
1kg/2¼lb lean boneless lamb shoulder, cut into 2cm/¾in cubes
400g/14oz potatoes, scrubbed and cut into 1cm/½in thick slices
salt
strips of red pepper and fresh oregano to garnish
cooked rice, to serve

1 Snap or tear the dried chillies into large pieces, put them in a bowl and pour over the hot water. Leave them to soak for 30 minutes, then transfer into a food processor or blender. Add the garlic, cinnamon, cloves and black pepper. Process the mixture to a smooth paste.

2 Heat the oil in a large pan. Add the lamb in batches, stir-fry over a high heat until the cubes are browned on all sides.

3 Return all the lamb cubes to the pan, spread them out, then cover them with a layer of potato slices. Add salt to taste. Put a lid on the pan and cook over a medium heat for about 10 minutes.

4 Pour over the chilli mixture and mix well. Replace the lid then simmer over a low heat for about 1 hour, or until the meat and the potatoes are tender. Serve with a rice dish, and garnish with strips of red pepper and fresh oregano.

Cook's Tip
When frying the lamb, don't be tempted to cook too many cubes at one time, as the meat will steam rather than fry. Cook them in batches, a large handful at a time.

Italian Lamb Meatballs Energy 443kcal/1853kJ; Protein 33.1g; Carbohydrate 22.5g, of which sugars 11.1g; Fat 25.3g, of which saturates 10.3g; Cholesterol 148mg; Calcium 246mg; Fibre 3g; Sodium 389mg
Lamb with Chilli Sauce Energy 367kcal/1536kJ; Protein 34g; Carbohydrate 11.8g, of which sugars 1.9g; Fat 20.8g, of which saturates 9g; Cholesterol 127mg; Calcium 19mg; Fibre 0.9g; Sodium 151mg.

Spanish-style Lamb Stew with Green Olives and Chillies

This spicy dish draws on Spanish culinary tradition; the lamb is first marinated in alcohol so it is tenderized, it is then browned before being braised.

Serves 4

900g/2lb boneless leg or shoulder of lamb, cut into bitesize cubes
45ml/3 tbsp groundnut (peanut) oil
15g/¹⁄₂oz/1 tbsp butter
2 red onions, thickly sliced
8 garlic cloves, crushed whole
2–3 red or green chillies, seeded and sliced
2 red or green (bell) peppers, seeded and sliced
5–10ml/1–2 tsp paprika
15–30ml/1–2 tbsp palm sugar (jaggery) or cane sugar

400g/14oz can plum tomatoes, drained
15–30ml/1–2 tbsp tomato purée (paste)
2–3 bay leaves
225g/8oz green olives
300ml/¹⁄₂ pint/1¹⁄₄ cups water
salt and ground black pepper
1 bunch fresh flat leaf parsley, roughly chopped, to garnish
cooked rice, to serve

For the marinade

250ml/8fl oz/1 cup red wine
250ml/8fl oz/1 cup port
120ml/4fl oz/¹⁄₂ cup coconut or rice vinegar
1 onion, roughly sliced
2 garlic cloves, crushed whole
8 black peppercorns
2–3 bay leaves

1 Mix all the marinade ingredients in a bowl. Add the lamb, mix well, then cover and chill for 6 hours. When ready, transfer the lamb to another bowl. Reserve the marinade.

2 Heat the oil and butter in a large pan. Fry the meat until browned on all sides. Remove and set aside. Add the onions, garlic, chillies and peppers to the pan and fry for 5 minutes. Stir in the paprika and sugar and return the meat to the pan.

3 Add the tomatoes, purée, bay leaves and olives. Pour in the reserved marinade and the water and bring to the boil then simmer, covered, for 2 hours.

4 Season the stew with salt and pepper to taste. Sprinkle with chopped parsley to garnish and serve with rice.

Lamb, New Potato and Red Chilli Curry

This dish makes the most of an economical cut of meat by cooking it slowly until the meat is falling from the bone. Chillies and coconut cream give it lots of flavour.

Serves 4

25g/1oz/2 tbsp butter
4 garlic cloves, crushed
2 onions, sliced into rings
2.5ml/¹⁄₂ tsp each ground cumin, ground coriander, turmeric and cayenne pepper

2–3 red chillies, seeded and finely chopped
300ml/¹⁄₂ pint/1¹⁄₄ cups hot chicken stock
200ml/7fl oz/scant 1 cup coconut cream
4 lamb shanks, all excess fat removed
450g/1lb new potatoes, halved
6 ripe tomatoes, quartered
salt and ground black pepper
coriander (cilantro) leaves, to garnish
spicy rice, to serve

1 Preheat the oven to 160°C/325°F/Gas 3. Melt the butter in a large flameproof casserole, add the garlic and onions and cook over a low heat for 15 minutes, until golden. Stir in the spices and chillies, then cook for a further 2 minutes.

2 Add the hot stock and coconut cream. Place the lamb shanks in the liquid and cover the casserole with foil. Cook in the oven for 2 hours, turning the shanks twice, first after about an hour or so and again about half an hour later.

3 Par-boil the potatoes for 10 minutes, drain and add to the casserole with the tomatoes, then cook uncovered in the oven for a further 35 minutes. Season to taste, garnish with coriander leaves and serve with the spicy rice.

> **Cook's Tip**
> Make this dish a day in advance if possible. Cool and chill overnight, then skim off the excess fat that has risen to the surface. Reheat thoroughly before you serve it.

Spanish-style Stew Energy 654kcal/2722kJ; Protein 47.4g; Carbohydrate 19.2g, of which sugars 16.7g; Fat 43.6g, of which saturates 15.8g; Cholesterol 179mg; Calcium 93mg; Fibre 5.4g; Sodium 1498mg.
Lamb and Chilli Curry Energy 364kcal/1528kJ; Protein 23.5g; Carbohydrate 30.5g, of which sugars 12.1g; Fat 17.4g, of which saturates 8.8g; Cholesterol 89mg; Calcium 58mg; Fibre 3.5g; Sodium 205mg.

Spicy Javanese Curry

This popular spicy goat dish is from Java but there are many variations all over the Indonesian archipelago.

Serves 4
30–60ml/2–4 tbsp palm, coconut
  or groundnut (peanut) oil
10ml/2 tsp shrimp paste
15ml/1 tbsp palm sugar (jaggery)
5ml/1 tsp coriander seeds
5ml/1 tsp cumin seeds
2.5ml/½ tsp grated nutmeg
2.5ml/½ tsp ground black pepper
2–3 lemon grass stalks, halved
  and bruised
700g/1lb 9oz boneless shoulder
  or leg of goat, or lamb, cut into
  bitesize pieces

400g/14oz can coconut milk
200ml/7fl oz/scant 1 cup water
  (if necessary)
12 yard-long beans
1 bunch fresh coriander (cilantro)
  leaves, roughly chopped
cooked rice and 2–3 chillies,
  seeded and finely chopped,
  to serve

For the spice paste
2–3 shallots, chopped
2–3 garlic cloves, chopped
3–4 chillies, seeded and chopped
25g/1oz galangal, chopped
40g/1½oz fresh turmeric, chopped,
  or 10ml/2 tsp ground turmeric
1 lemon grass stalk, chopped
2–3 candlenuts, finely ground

1 Using a mortar and pestle or food processor, grind all the spice paste ingredients together. Heat 15–30ml/1–2 tbsp of the oil in a heavy pan. Fry the paste until fragrant. Add the shrimp paste and sugar and stir-fry for 2 minutes.

2 Heat the remaining oil in a large pan. Stir in the coriander seeds, cumin seeds, nutmeg and black pepper, then add the paste and lemon grass. Stir-fry for 2–3 minutes, until dark and fragrant.

3 Stir the meat into the pan, making sure that it is well coated in the paste. Pour in the coconut milk and water, bring to the boil, then cover and simmer for about 3 hours, until the meat is tender.

4 Add the beans and cook for 10–15 minutes. Check the meat occasionally and add the water if the curry is too dry.

5 Toss a few coriander leaves into the curry and season to taste. Transfer the curry into a warmed serving dish and garnish with the remaining coriander. Serve with rice and chillies.

Spiced Lamb with Chillies

This is a fairly hot stir-fry dish, although you can, of course, make it less so by reducing the amount of chilli you use.

Serves 4
225g/8oz lean lamb fillet
120ml/4fl oz/½ cup natural
  (plain) low-fat yogurt
1.5ml/¼ tsp ground cardamom
5ml/1 tsp crushed ginger
5ml/1 tsp crushed garlic

5ml/1 tsp chilli powder
5ml/1 tsp garam masala
5ml/1 tsp salt
15ml/1 tbsp corn oil
2 medium onions, chopped
1 bay leaf
300ml/½ pint/1¼ cups water
2 red chillies, seeded and
  sliced lengthways
2 green chillies, seeded and
  sliced lengthways
30ml/2 tbsp fresh coriander
  (cilantro) leaves

1 Using a sharp knife, cut the lamb into even strips. Mix together the yogurt, cardamom, ginger, garlic, chilli powder, garam masala and salt. Add the lamb, mix well, and leave for 1 hour to marinate.

2 Heat the oil in a non-stick wok or frying pan and fry the onions for 3–5 minutes, or until golden brown.

3 Add the bay leaf, then add the lamb with the yogurt and spices and stir-fry for 2–3 minutes over a medium heat.

4 Pour over the water, cover and cook for 15–20 minutes over a low heat, checking occasionally. Once the water has evaporated, stir-fry the mixture for 1 minute more.

5 Add the red and green chillies and the fresh coriander, and stir well. Serve immediately.

Cook's Tip
Garam masala, meaning 'warm spice', is a blend of ground spices commonly used in Indian cuisine. Typically it will contain black pepper, black cumin, cinnamon, cloves, mace, cardamom, coriander seed, nutmeg, fennel and bay leaf, all dry-fried or roasted then dried and ground.

Spicy Javanese Curry Energy 450kcal/1877kJ; Protein 37.9g; Carbohydrate 10.8g, of which sugars 9.1g; Fat 28.7g, of which saturates 10.3g; Cholesterol 146mg; Calcium 129mg; Fibre 2.4g; Sodium 375mg.
Spiced Lamb Energy 183kcal/764kJ; Protein 15.5g; Carbohydrate 14.1g, of which sugars 9.1g; Fat 7.8g, of which saturates 3.2g; Cholesterol 43mg; Calcium 102mg; Fibre 1.8g; Sodium 77mg.

Lamb Dhansak with Green Chillies

This is a Parsee dish with a hot, sweet and sour flavour, often eaten for Sunday lunch.

Serves 4 to 6
90ml/6 tbsp vegetable oil
5 green chillies, chopped
2.5cm/1in piece fresh root
  ginger, crushed
3 garlic cloves, crushed
1 clove garlic, sliced
2 bay leaves
5cm/2in cinnamon stick
900g/2lb lean lamb, cubed
600ml/1 pint/2½ cups water
175g/6oz red gram
50g/2oz each bengal gram,
  husked moong and red lentils

2 potatoes, chopped
1 aubergine (eggplant), chopped
4 onions, finely sliced, deep-fried
  and drained
50g/2oz fresh spinach, trimmed,
  washed and chopped
25g/1oz fresh fenugreek leaves
115g/4oz carrots, or pumpkin
115g/4oz fresh coriander
  (cilantro) leaves, chopped
50g/2oz mint leaves, chopped
30ml/2 tbsp dhansak masala
30ml/2 tbsp sambhar masala
salt, to taste
10ml/2 tsp soft light brown sugar
60ml/4 tbsp tamarind juice

1 Heat 45ml/3 tbsp of oil in a frying pan. Cook the chillies, ginger and crushed garlic for 2 minutes. Add the bay leaves, cinnamon, lamb and water. Boil, then simmer until the lamb is half cooked.

2 Drain the water into another pan and put the lamb aside. Add the gram and lentils to the water and cook until they are tender. Mash with the back of a spoon.

3 Add the aubergine and potatoes to the lentils with three of the deep-fried onions, the spinach, fenugreek and carrot or pumpkin. When the vegetables are tender, mash coarsely.

4 Heat 15ml/1 tbsp of the oil and fry the coriander and mint leaves, saving a little to garnish, with the dhansak and sambhar masala, salt and sugar. Add the lamb and fry for 5 minutes. Stir into the vegetable mixture. Heat gently until the lamb is cooked.

5 Add the tamarind juice. Heat the remaining oil. Fry the sliced garlic until golden. Pour over the dhansak. Garnish with the remaining deep-fried onion and reserved coriander and mint.

Fiery Dry Lamb Curry

This dish is nearly as hot as a *phaal*, the dish renowned as India's hottest curry. Although fiery, the spices can still be distinguished above the chilli.

Serves 4 to 6
30ml/2 tbsp vegetable oil
1 large onion, finely sliced
5cm/2in piece fresh root
  ginger, crushed
4 garlic cloves, crushed
6–8 curry leaves

45ml/3 tbsp extra hot curry
  paste, or 60ml/4 tbsp hot
  curry powder
15ml/1 tbsp chilli powder
5ml/1 tsp five-spice powder
5ml/1 tsp ground turmeric
900g/2lb lean lamb, beef or
  pork, cubed
175ml/6fl oz/¾ cup thick
  coconut milk
salt, to taste
2 large tomatoes, finely chopped,
  to garnish

1 Heat the oil in a large frying pan and fry the onion, ginger, garlic and curry leaves until the onion is soft and turning translucent. Add the curry paste, chilli and five-spice powder, turmeric and salt. Stir-fry for 1–2 minutes until the spices release their fragrances.

2 Add the meat and stir well over a medium heat to seal and evenly brown the meat pieces. Keep stirring until the oil separates. Cover and cook for about 20 minutes.

3 Add the coconut milk, mix well and simmer until the meat is cooked. Towards the end of cooking, uncover the pan to reduce the excess liquid. Garnish and serve immediately.

> **Cook's Tip**
> *Hotter even than a vindaloo, the phaal has achieved notoriety as the hottest curry dish, often with up to 12 chillies per serving. If the above dish is still not quite hot enough for you seek out a phaal in an Indian restaurant. However, such is the reputed heat in a phaal that many curry houses will not actually have it listed on their menu so you may need to specifically ask for it.*

Lamb Dhansak Energy 627kcal/2626kJ; Protein 43.6g; Carbohydrate 48.6g, of which sugars 12g; Fat 30.3g, of which saturates 9.4g; Cholesterol 114mg; Calcium 141mg; Fibre 6.5g; Sodium 177mg.
Lamb Curry Energy 559kcal/2343kJ; Protein 54.4g; Carbohydrate 20.5g, of which sugars 18.8g; Fat 29.6g, of which saturates 13.5g; Cholesterol 191mg; Calcium 139mg; Fibre 4.6g; Sodium 278mg.

Balti Lamb with Cauliflower

Cauliflower and lamb go beautifully together. This curry is given a final *tarka* – an Indian garnish – of cumin seeds and curry leaves, which enhances the flavour.

Serves 4
10ml/2 tsp corn oil
2 medium onions, sliced
7.5ml/1½ tsp crushed ginger
5ml/1 tsp chilli powder
5ml/1 tsp crushed garlic
1.5ml/¼ tsp ground turmeric
2.5ml/½ tsp ground coriander

30ml/2 tbsp fresh fenugreek leaves
275g/10oz boned lean spring lamb, cut into strips
1 small cauliflower, cut into small florets
300ml/½ pint/1¼ cups water
30ml/2 tbsp fresh coriander (cilantro) leaves
½ red (bell) pepper, sliced
15ml/1 tbsp lemon juice

For the tarka
10ml/2 tsp corn oil
2.5ml/½ tsp white cumin seeds
4–6 curry leaves

1 Heat the oil in a non-stick wok or frying pan and fry the onions until golden brown. Lower the heat and add the crushed ginger, chilli powder, crushed garlic, turmeric and ground coriander, followed by the fenugreek.

2 Add the lamb strips to the wok and stir-fry until the lamb is completely coated with the spices. Add half the cauliflower florets and stir the mixture well.

3 Pour in the water, cover the wok, and simmer for 5–7 minutes until the cauliflower and lamb are almost cooked through.

4 Add the remaining cauliflower, half the fresh coriander, the red pepper and lemon juice and stir-fry for about 5 minutes, making sure that the sauce does not catch on the bottom of the wok.

5 Check that the lamb is completely cooked, then remove from the heat and set aside.

6 To make the tarka, heat the oil and fry the seeds and curry leaves for about 30 seconds. While it is still hot, pour the seasoned oil over the cauliflower and lamb and serve garnished with the remaining fresh coriander leaves.

Keema Lamb with Curry Leaves and Green Chillies

This delicious dry curry is made by cooking minced lamb in its own juices with a few spices and herbs, but no other liquid.

Serves 4
10ml/2 tsp corn oil
2 medium onions, chopped
10 curry leaves
6 green chillies

350g/12oz lean minced (ground) lamb
5ml/1 tsp crushed garlic
5ml/1 tsp crushed ginger
5ml/1 tsp chilli powder
1.5ml/¼ tsp ground turmeric
5ml/1 tsp salt
2 tomatoes, skinned and quartered
15ml/1 tbsp chopped fresh coriander (cilantro)

1 Heat the oil in a non-stick wok or frying pan. Stir-fry the onions together with the curry leaves and three of the whole green chillies for 3–4 minutes, until the onions begin to soften and turn translucent.

2 Put the lamb into a mixing bowl and add the garlic and crushed ginger, chilli powder, turmeric and salt. Blend everything together thoroughly.

3 Add the lamb mixture to the pan with the onions and stir-fry for about 7–10 minutes, lowering the heat to medium if necessary.

4 Add the tomatoes and coriander to the pan. Stir in the remaining whole green chillies. Continue to stir-fry for a further 2 minutes before serving.

Cook's Tip
• This curry also makes a terrific brunch. Serve with fried eggs and light Indian breads such as pooris or chapatis.
• This curry would make an ideal filling for samosas, the spicy Indian snacks. Cook as above but ensure that all the ingredients are finely chopped before using.

Balti Lamb Energy 277kcals/1154kJ; Protein 18.7g; Carbohydrate 14.4g, of which sugars 9g; Fat 16.7g, of which saturates 4.7g; Cholesterol 52mg; Calcium 62mg; Fibre 3.2g; Sodium 73mg.
Keema Lamb Energy 239kcal/998kJ; Protein 19.7g; Carbohydrate 13.5g, of which sugars 9.3g; Fat 12.3g, of which saturates 4.9g; Cholesterol 67mg; Calcium 50mg; Fibre 2.5g; Sodium 578mg.

Stir-fried Pork with Peanuts, Chillies and Lime

Pork or chicken stir-fried with nuts and herbs, with a splash of citrus flavour or fish sauce, is everyday home cooking in Vietnam. The combination of chilli, lime, basil and mint in this recipe makes it particularly refreshing and tasty. Serve with steamed or sticky rice, or with rice wrappers, salad and a dipping sauce.

Serves 4

45ml/3 tbsp vegetable or
  groundnut (peanut) oil
450g/1lb pork tenderloin, cut into
  fine strips
4 spring onions (scallions), chopped
4 garlic cloves, finely chopped
4cm/1½in fresh root ginger,
  finely chopped
2 green or red Thai chillies,
  seeded and finely chopped
100g/3½oz/generous ½ cup
  shelled, unsalted peanuts
grated rind and juice of 2 limes
30ml/2 tbsp nuoc mam
30ml/2 tbsp grated fresh coconut
25g/1oz/½ cup chopped fresh
  mint leaves
25g/1oz/½ cup chopped fresh
  basil leaves
25g/1oz/½ cup chopped fresh
  coriander (cilantro) leaves

1 Heat a wok or heavy pan and pour in 30ml/2 tbsp of the oil. Add the pork and sear over a high heat, until browned. Transfer the meat and juices on to a plate and set aside.

2 Heat the remaining oil and add the spring onions, garlic, ginger and chillies. When the aromas begin to rise from the pan, add the peanuts and stir-fry for 1–2 minutes.

3 Add the meat back into the wok. Stir in the lime rind and juice, and the nuoc mam. Add the coconut and herbs, and serve.

> **Cook's Tip**
> Nuoc mam is a Vietnamese fish sauce, which is used in moderation because it is so intensely flavoured. It is traditionally made by fermenting anchovies with salt in wooden boxes. The fish are then slowly pressed, yielding the salty, fishy liquid.

Spicy Pork Stir-fry

This simple dish is quick to prepare and makes thinly sliced pork fabulously spicy. The potent flavour of gochujang chilli paste predominates in the seasoning for the pork and will set the tastebuds aflame. Serve with rice to help counterbalance the fiery character of the dish.

Serves 2

400g/14oz pork shoulder
1 onion
½ carrot
2 spring onions (scallions)
15ml/1 tbsp vegetable oil
½ red chilli, finely sliced
½ green chilli, finely sliced
steamed rice and miso soup,
  to serve

For the seasoning

30ml/2 tbsp dark soy sauce
30ml/2 tbsp gochujang chilli paste
30ml/2 tbsp mirin or rice wine
15ml/1 tbsp Korean chilli powder
1 garlic clove, finely chopped
1 spring onion (scallion),
  finely chopped
15ml/1 tbsp grated fresh root ginger
15ml/1 tbsp sesame oil
30ml/2 tbsp sugar
ground black pepper

1 Freeze the pork shoulder for 30 minutes, to make slicing easier, and then slice it thinly, to about 5mm/¼in thick. Cut the onion and carrot into thin strips, and slice the spring onions into lengthways strips.

2 To make the seasoning, combine the seasoning ingredients in a large bowl, mixing together thoroughly to form a paste. If the mixture is too dry, add a splash of water.

3 Heat a wok or large frying pan, and add the vegetable oil. Once the oil is smoking, add the pork, onion, carrot, spring onions and chillies. Stir-fry the ingredients, ensuring that they are kept moving all the time in the pan.

4 Once the pork has lightly browned, add the seasoning, and thoroughly coat the meat and vegetables. Stir-fry for 2 minutes more, or until the pork is cooked through.

5 Serve immediately with rice and a bowl of miso soup to help balance the spicy flavours of the dish.

Stir-fried Pork Energy 401kcal/1668kJ; Protein 32g; Carbohydrate 7g, of which sugars 3g; Fat 27g, of which saturates 5g; Cholesterol 71mg; Calcium 42mg; Fibre 1.8g; Sodium 400mg.
Spicy Pork Stir-fry Energy 430kcal/1799kJ; Protein 44.1g; Carbohydrate 21.3g, of which sugars 20.4g; Fat 19.2g, of which saturates 4.3g; Cholesterol 126mg; Calcium 44mg; Fibre 1.2g; Sodium 1216mg.

Lemon Grass Pork with Chillies and Garlic

Chillies and lemon grass flavour this simple stir-fry, while peanuts add an interesting contrast in texture and the chillies add a satisfying kick. Look for jars of chopped lemon grass, which are handy when the fresh variety isn't available.

Serves 4
675g/1½lb boneless pork loin
2 lemon grass stalks,
    finely chopped
4 spring onions (scallions),
    thinly sliced
5ml/1 tsp salt
12 black peppercorns,
    coarsely crushed
30ml/2 tbsp groundnut
    (peanut) oil
2 garlic cloves, chopped
2 fresh red chillies, seeded
    and chopped
5ml/1 tsp soft light brown sugar
30ml/2 tbsp Thai fish sauce
25g/1oz/¼ cup roasted unsalted
    peanuts, chopped
ground black pepper
cooked rice noodles, to serve
coarsely torn coriander (cilantro)
    leaves, to garnish

1 Trim any excess fat from the pork. Cut the meat across into 5mm/¼in thick slices, then cut each slice into 5mm/¼in strips.

2 Put the pork into a large bowl with the lemon grass, spring onions, salt and crushed peppercorns; mix well. Cover the bowl with clear film (plastic wrap) and leave to marinate in a cool place for 30 minutes.

3 Preheat a wok, add the oil and swirl it around. Add the pork mixture and stir-fry over a medium heat for about 3 minutes, until browned all over.

4 Add the garlic and red chillies and stir-fry for a further 5–8 minutes over a medium heat, until the pork is cooked through and tender.

5 Add the sugar, fish sauce and chopped peanuts and toss to mix, then season to taste with black pepper. Serve immediately on a bed of rice noodles, garnished with the coarsely torn coriander leaves.

Pork Chops with Field Mushrooms and Chilli Sauce

In Thailand, meat is frequently cooked over a brazier or open fire, so it isn't surprising that many tasty barbecue-style dishes come from there. These fabulous pork chops in a spicy sauce are great favourites with everyone.

Serves 4
4 pork chops
4 large mushrooms
45ml/3 tbsp vegetable oil
4 fresh red chillies, seeded and
    thinly sliced
45ml/3 tbsp Thai fish sauce
90ml/6 tbsp fresh lime juice
4 shallots, chopped
5ml/1 tsp roasted ground rice
30ml/2 tbsp spring onions
    (scallions), chopped, plus
    shredded spring onions to garnish
tagliatelle, to serve

For the marinade
2 garlic cloves, chopped
15ml/1 tbsp granulated
    (white) sugar
15ml/1 tbsp Thai fish sauce
30ml/2 tbsp soy sauce
15ml/1 tbsp sesame oil
15ml/1 tbsp whisky or dry sherry
2 lemon grass stalks, finely chopped
2 spring onions (scallions), chopped

1 Make the marinade. Combine the garlic, sugar, sauces, oil and whisky or sherry in a large, shallow dish. Stir in the lemon grass and spring onions.

2 Add the pork chops, turning to coat them in the marinade. Cover and leave to marinate for 1–2 hours.

3 Lift the chops out of the marinade and place them on a barbecue grill over hot coals or on a grill (broiler) rack. Add the mushrooms and brush them with 15ml/1 tbsp of the oil. Cook the pork chops for 5–7 minutes on each side and the mushrooms for about 2 minutes. Brush both with the marinade while cooking.

4 Heat the remaining oil in a wok or small frying pan, then remove the pan from the heat and stir in the chillies, fish sauce, lime juice, shallots, ground rice and spring onions. Serve the pork chops and mushrooms and spoon over the sauce. Garnish with the shredded spring onion and serve with the tagliatelle.

Lemon Grass Pork Energy 12kcal/49kJ; Protein 1.5g; Carbohydrate 0.1g, of which sugars 0.1g; Fat 0.6g, of which saturates 0.2g; Cholesterol 4mg; Calcium 1mg; Fibre 0g; Sodium 34mg.
Pork Chops Energy 339kcal/1418kJ; Protein 39.7g; Carbohydrate 2.3g, of which sugars 1g; Fat 19.1g, of which saturates 4.1g; Cholesterol 90mg; Calcium 26mg; Fibre 1g; Sodium 678mg.

Curried Meat with Spicy Peas

This spicy dish can be served as a main course, or try mixing it with fried or scrambled eggs for a delicious brunch. It also makes a good pizza topping, and can be used as a filling for samosas.

Serves 4 to 6
5ml/1 tsp vegetable oil
1 large onion, finely chopped
2 garlic cloves, crushed
5cm/2in piece fresh root
  ginger, crushed
4 green chillies, chopped
30ml/2 tbsp curry powder
450g/1lb lean minced (ground)
  pork, beef, or lamb
225g/8oz frozen peas, thawed
salt, to taste
juice of 1 lemon
a few coriander (cilantro)
  leaves, chopped

1 Heat the vegetable oil in a wok or large frying pan. Add the chopped onion and cook for 2–3 minutes until it is just beginning to soften.

2 Add the garlic, ginger and chillies to the pan and cook, stirring constantly, for 4–5 minutes until the onion has turned translucent.

3 Turn the heat down to low, add the curry powder to the pan and mix well. Cook for a minute until the curry powder releases its fragrances.

4 Add the meat to the pan and stir well, pressing the meat down with the back of a spoon. Cook, stirring frequently, for 8–10 minutes until the meat is just cooked through and evenly browned all over.

5 Add the peas, salt and lemon juice to the pan, mix well, cover and simmer for 4–5 minutes until the peas are tender. Mix in the fresh coriander. Serve immediately.

> **Variation**
> *This dish is equally delicious if made with minced lean lamb or pork. Simply substitute the same amount of lamb or pork for the minced beef. Or try using half pork and half beef.*

Pork Satays with Peanut and Chilli

These satays are made by marinating pork, then cooking it on skewers on the barbecue, and serving with a spicy nutty sauce. Beef or lamb could be used for these satays instead.

Makes 12 to 16 skewers
500g/1¼lb pork fillet (tenderloin)
lime wedges and fried onions, to
  serve

For the marinade
150ml/¼ pint/⅔ cup dark
  soy sauce

3–4 garlic cloves, crushed
45ml/3 tbsp groundnut
  (peanut) oil
50g/2oz peanuts, finely crushed
salt and ground pepper

For the sauce
1 onion, finely chopped
2–3 fresh red chillies, seeded
  and ground, or 15ml/1 tbsp
  chilli sauce
75ml/3fl oz/⅓ cup dark
  soy sauce
60–90ml/4–6 tbsp water
juice of 1–2 limes or 1 large lemon
50g/2oz peanuts, coarsely ground

1 Wipe and trim the meat. Cut the pork into 2.5cm/1in cubes or into thin strips about 1cm/½in wide by 5cm/2in long.

2 Blend the dark soy sauce, garlic and oil together with the seasoning and the crushed peanuts. Pour over the meat and allow to marinate for at least 1 hour.

3 If using wooden or bamboo skewers, soak them in water for at least 1 hour so that they don't burn when the satays are being cooked. Then thread three or four pieces of meat on to one end of each of the skewers.

4 Make the sauce. Put the onion, chillies or chilli sauce, soy sauce and water in a pan. Bring to the boil, and simmer for 4–5 minutes. Cool, then add the lime or lemon juice. Add the crushed peanuts just before serving. Preheat the grill (broiler) or barbecue.

5 Cook the satays for about 5–8 minutes, turning frequently, until they are tender. Place on a large platter. Garnish with lime or lemon wedges and fried onions and serve with the sauce.

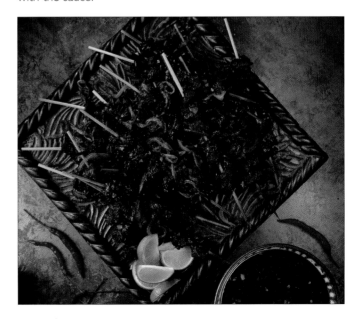

Curried Meat with Peas Energy 199kcal/827kJ; Protein 17.5g; Carbohydrate 7.3g, of which sugars 2.7g; Fat 11.3g, of which saturates 4.8g; Cholesterol 58mg; Calcium 40mg; Fibre 2.6g; Sodium 61mg.
Pork Satays Energy 189kcal/784kJ; Protein 14.5g; Carbohydrate 2.9g, of which sugars 2.2g; Fat 13.3g, of which saturates 5.8g; Cholesterol 35mg; Calcium 25mg; Fibre 0.9g; Sodium 70mg.

Pork Belly with Sesame Dip and Chilli Sauce

Thinly sliced pork belly is griddled until the outside is crisp, leaving a smooth texture at the centre. The meat is then immersed in a salty sesame dip, before being wrapped in lettuce leaves with a spoonful of red chilli paste.

Serves 3
675g/1½lb pork belly
2 round (butterhead) lettuces

For the dip
45ml/3 tbsp sesame oil
10ml/2 tsp salt
ground black pepper

For the sauce
45ml/3 tbsp gochujang chilli paste
75ml/5 tbsp doenjang soya
   bean paste
2 garlic cloves, crushed
1 spring onion (scallion),
   finely chopped
5ml/1 tsp sesame oil

Hot Portuguese Pork

This deliciously fiery dish displays the influence of Portuguese cooking on Indian cuisine.

Serves 4 to 6
30ml/2 tbsp vegetable oil
1 onion
4 fresh red chillies, seeded and
   finely chopped or 5ml/1 tsp
   chilli powder
60ml/4 tbsp vindaloo
   masala paste
90ml/6 tbsp white wine vinegar
90ml/6 tbsp tomato
   purée (paste)
2.5ml/½ tsp fenugreek seeds
5ml/1 tsp ground turmeric
5ml/1 tsp crushed mustard
   seeds, or 2.5ml/½ tsp
   mustard powder
7.5ml/1½ tsp sugar
900g/2lb boneless
   pork spareribs
250ml/8fl oz/1 cup water
salt, to taste
plain boiled rice, to serve

1 Heat the oil in a wok or large frying pan. Finely chop the onion and add to the pan. Cook for 2–3 minutes until beginning to soften.

2 Add the fresh chilli or chilli powder and stir-fry for 2 minutes. Add the vindaloo paste and fry for a minute, stirring constantly until it releases its fragrances.

3 Pour in the white wine vinegar, mixing well. Add the tomato purée, fenugreek seeds, turmeric and mustard seeds or mustard powder. Season with salt, to taste, and add the sugar. Mix well until all the ingredients are throughly combined. Remove from the heat and leave to cool slightly.

4 Cut the pork spareribs into bitesize cubes and add to the pan, ensuring that it is thoroughly coated in the sauce. Set aside to marinate for 2 hours.

5 Add the water to the pan and mix with the other ingredients. Bring to the boil and then simmer gently for about 2 hours. Taste the sauce and adjust the seasoning if necessary.

6 Transfer the meat and the sauce to a large serving dish. Serve immediately with the plain boiled rice.

1 Freeze the pork belly for 30 minutes and then slice it very thinly, to about 3mm/⅛in thick. (You could ask the butcher to do this, or buy the meat pre-sliced at an Asian store.)

2 To make the dip, combine the sesame oil, salt and pepper in a small serving bowl.

3 To make the sauce, blend the chilli paste, doenjang soya bean paste, garlic, spring onion and sesame oil in a bowl, mixing the oil thoroughly into the paste. Transfer to a serving bowl.

4 Remove the outer leaves from the heads of lettuce, keeping them whole. Rinse well and place in a serving dish.

5 Heat a griddle pan or heavy frying pan over high heat (the griddle can be used over charcoal). Add the pork to the pan and cook until the surface is crisp and golden brown.

6 Serve the pork with the accompanying dishes of lettuce, sesame dip and chilli sauce. To eat, take a strip of pork and dip it into the sesame dip. Then place the meat in the middle of a lettuce leaf and add a small spoonful of the chilli sauce. Fold the sides of the leaf inwards and roll up into a parcel.

Hot Portuguese Pork Energy 267kcal/1119kJ; Protein 34.6g; Carbohydrate 11.3g, of which sugars 7.3g; Fat 9.6g, of which saturates 2.5g; Cholesterol 95mg; Calcium 68mg; Fibre 2.2g; Sodium 166mg.
Pork Belly Energy 991kcal/4093kJ; Protein 37g; Carbohydrate 1.1g, of which sugars 0.6g; Fat 93.1g, of which saturates 31.4g; Cholesterol 162mg; Calcium 37mg; Fibre 1.2g; Sodium 1475mg.

Cabbage Leaves with Spicy Pork

In South-east Asia, spicy pork or shellfish mixtures are often wrapped in leaves and steamed, or stuffed into bamboo stems and smoked over open fires.

Serves 4 to 6
1 leafy green cabbage
15–30ml/1–2 tbsp palm or
   groundnut (peanut) oil
10ml/2 tsp coriander seeds
2 shallots, finely chopped
2 garlic cloves, finely chopped
2–3 red chillies, seeded and
   finely chopped
25g/1oz galangal, finely chopped
2–3 spring onions (scallions),
   finely chopped
10ml/2 tsp palm sugar (jaggery)
2–3 tomatoes, skinned, seeded
   and finely chopped
30ml/2 tbsp coconut cream
1 small bunch fresh coriander
   (cilantro) leaves, finely chopped
225g/8oz minced (ground) pork
50g/2oz pig's liver, finely chopped
50g/2oz pig's heart, finely chopped
salt and ground black pepper
kecap manis, for dipping

1 Prepare the cabbage. Pull the cabbage apart so that you have about 20 leaves. Steam or blanch the leaves to soften, drain and refresh under cold water. Cut off any thick stems and set aside.

2 Heat the oil in a wok or heavy pan, stir in the coriander seeds and fry for 1 minute. Add the chopped shallots, garlic, the finely chopped chillies, galangal, spring onions and sugar and stir-fry until they begin to colour. Stir in the tomatoes, coconut cream and coriander leaves and cook for 5 minutes until the mixture resembles a thick sauce. Season with salt and pepper and transfer to a bowl to cool.

3 Add the minced pork and liver and, using your hand or a fork, mix well together. Place a cabbage leaf on a flat surface in front of you and place a spoonful of the mixture in the centre. Fold in the sides of the leaf and roll it up into a log, making sure that all of the meat is enclosed. Repeat the process with the remaining leaves.

4 Place the stuffed leaves in a steamer, seam side down, and steam for 25–30 minutes, until the meat is cooked. Serve hot with kecap manis for dipping.

Jamaican Jerk Pork with Red Chillies

This is a Jamaican way of spicing meat or poultry before roasting in the oven or over a fire.

Serves 4
15ml/1 tbsp oil
2 onions, finely chopped
2 fresh red chillies, seeded and
   finely chopped
1 garlic clove, crushed
2.5cm/1in piece fresh root
   ginger, grated
5ml/1 tsp dried thyme
5ml/1 tsp ground allspice
5ml/1 tsp hot pepper sauce
30ml/2 tbsp rum
grated rind and juice of 1 lime
4 pork chops
salt and ground black pepper
fresh thyme, small red chillies and
   lime wedges, to garnish

1 Heat the oil in a frying pan. Add the onions and cook for 10 minutes until soft and translucent.

2 Add the chillies, garlic, ginger, thyme and allspice and fry for 2 minutes. Stir in the hot pepper sauce, rum, lime rind and juice.

3 Lower the heat and simmer gently until the mixture has formed a dark paste. Season with salt and pepper to taste, and set aside to cool.

4 Rub the paste all over the chops, ensuring they are well covered. Place them in a shallow dish, cover and marinate overnight in the refrigerator.

5 Preheat the oven to 190°C/375°F/Gas 5. Place the chops on a rack in a roasting pan and roast in the oven for 30 minutes until fully cooked.

6 Serve garnished with thyme, chillies and lime wedges.

> **Variation**
> Chicken joints or even a whole chicken can also be coated with this delicious spicy paste before roasting.

Jerk Pork Energy 271kcal/1134kJ; Protein 33.9g; Carbohydrate 9.2g, of which sugars 5.6g; Fat 9.4g, of which saturates 2.5g; Cholesterol 95mg; Calcium 42mg; Fibre 1.4g; Sodium 109mg.
Cabbage Leaves Energy 183kcal/764kJ; Protein 12.6g; Carbohydrate 7.3g, of which sugars 7g; Fat 11.8g, of which saturates 5g; Cholesterol 56mg; Calcium 55mg; Fibre 2.2g; Sodium 53mg.

Chilli Pork in Chinese Leaves

Meltingly tender pork, imbued with the flavours of Korean doenjang soya bean paste and garlic, is combined with a refreshingly zesty mooli stuffing and wrapped in parcels of Chinese leaves.

Serves 3 to 4

I head Chinese leaves
(Chinese cabbage)
5 garlic cloves, roughly chopped
1/2 onion, roughly chopped
I leek, roughly chopped
15ml/1 tbsp doenjang soya
bean paste
100ml/3 1/2fl oz/scant 1/2 cup sake
or rice wine

675g/1 1/2lb pork neck
salt
sugar

For the stuffing

500g/1 1/4lb mooli (daikon), peeled
and thinly sliced
3 chestnuts, sliced
1/2 Asian pear, sliced
65g/2 1/2oz watercress, or rocket
(arugula), chopped
45ml/3 tbsp Korean chilli powder
5ml/1 tsp Thai fish sauce
2 garlic cloves, crushed
2.5ml/1/2 tsp grated fresh
root ginger
5ml/1 tsp honey
5ml/1 tsp sesame seeds

1 Soak the whole head of Chinese leaves in salty water (using 50g/2oz/1/4 cup of salt) for about I hour, or until softened.

2 Make the stuffing. Put the mooli into a colander and sprinkle with salt. Leave to stand for 10 minutes, then rinse well and transfer to a large bowl. Add the chestnuts, pear and chopped watercress or rocket to the bowl and mix well. Add all the other stuffing ingredients, with salt to taste, and mix well.

3 Prepare the poaching liquid. Put the garlic, onion and leek in a large pan. Mix in the doenjang paste and sake or rice wine, and add the pork. Add water to cover then bring to the boil. Cook the pork for 30–40 minutes, until tender.

4 Drain the Chinese leaves and tear off whole leaves and place on a serving plate. Transfer the stuffing mixture to a serving dish. Slice the pork into bitesize pieces.

5 Place a slice of pork on a Chinese leaf. Spoon stuffing on to the meat, and wrap it into a parcel before eating it.

Braised Beef Strips with Jalapeño Chillies, Soy and Ginger

Fine strips of braised beef are enhanced by a rich, dark soy and garlic sauce, with a piquant kick of root ginger. Muscovado sugar adds an almost imperceptible sweetness, complemented by hot jalapeño chillies. This dish makes an excellent side serving to accompany a larger stew or noodle dish.

Serves 2 to 3

450g/1lb beef frying (flank) steak
25g/1oz fresh root ginger, peeled
100ml/3 1/2 fl oz/scant 1/2 cup
dark soy sauce
75g/3oz light muscovado
(brown) sugar
12 garlic cloves, peeled
6 jalapeño chillies

1 Bring a large pan of water to the boil and add the beef. Cook for around 40 minutes until tender. Drain the meat and rinse it in warm water. Leave the beef to cool, then roughly slice it into strips about 5cm/2in long.

2 Place the peeled root ginger in a large pan with the beef and add 300ml/1/2 pint/1 1/4 cups water. Bring to the boil, cover, then reduce the heat and simmer for 30 minutes. Skim the fat from the surface of the liquid as the meat cooks. The liquid should have reduced to half its initial volume.

3 Add the soy sauce, muscovado sugar and garlic, and simmer for a further 20 minutes. Then add the jalapeño chillies, and cook for a further 5 minutes.

4 Discard the root ginger from the pan, and serve the beef strips in warmed bowls with generous quantities of the garlic cloves and chillies.

> **Cook's Tip**
> If you're using any beef cut other than frying steak, the meat should be cut into thin strips or torn by hand to ensure that it is tender when cooked.

Chilli Pork Energy 332kcal/1391kJ; Protein 40.2g; Carbohydrate 18.7g, of which sugars 14.9g; Fat 7.9g, of which saturates 2.6g; Cholesterol 106mg; Calcium 136mg; Fibre 5.9g; Sodium 507mg.
Braised Beef Strips Energy 408kcal/1713kJ; Protein 37.8g; Carbohydrate 34.3g, of which sugars 29.1g; Fat 14.2g, of which saturates 5.7g; Cholesterol 87mg; Calcium 33mg; Fibre 1.4g; Sodium 2472mg.

Kneaded Sirloin Steak in a Spring Onion and Chilli Marinade

The marinade does not contain any complex ingredients, rather the recipe relies on the taste of high quality sirloin steak. Kneading the meat with salt makes it deliciously tender, and the simple seasoning provides a delicate garlic flavour. Accompanied by a bowl of doenjang soup, this dish is without equal.

Serves 4
450g/1lb beef sirloin
2 round (butterhead) lettuces

For the marinade
8 garlic cloves, chopped
75g/3oz oyster mushrooms, sliced
3 spring onions (scallions), finely chopped
20ml/4 tsp mirin or rice wine
10ml/2 tsp salt
ground black pepper

For the spring onion mixture
8 shredded spring onions (scallions)
20ml/4 tsp rice vinegar
20ml/4 tsp Korean chilli powder
10ml/2 tsp sugar
10ml/2 tsp sesame oil

1 Slice the beef into thin bitesize strips and place in a bowl. Add the garlic, mushrooms and spring onions and mix well.

2 Pour the mirin or rice wine into the bowl with the beef mixture and add the salt and several twists of black pepper.

3 Mix the marinade together, making sure that the beef strips are evenly coated. Knead the meat well to tenderize. Chill, and leave for at least 2 hours.

4 Make the spring onion mixture. In a bowl, mix all the ingredients together until well combined.

5 Remove the outer leaves from the lettuce and rinse well.

6 Place a griddle pan over medium heat, and add the marinated beef. Cook gently until the meat has darkened, and then remove.

7 Serve by wrapping the meat in a lettuce leaf with a chopstick pinch of the seasoned shredded spring onion mixture.

Spicy Mexican Pie

Spiced beef is mixed with rice and layered between tortillas, with a hot salsa sauce.

Serves 4
1 onion, chopped
2 garlic cloves, crushed
1 fresh red chilli, seeded and sliced
350g/12oz rump (round) steak, cut into small cubes
15ml/1 tbsp oil
225g/8oz/2 cups cooked rice
beef stock, to moisten
3 large wheat tortillas

For the salsa picante
2 X 400g/14oz cans chopped tomatoes

2 garlic cloves, halved
1 onion, quartered
1–2 fresh red chillies, seeded and roughly chopped
5ml/1 tsp ground cumin
2.5–5ml/½–1 tsp cayenne pepper
5ml/1 tsp fresh oregano or 2.5ml/½ tsp dried oregano
tomato juice or water, if required

For the cheese sauce
50g/2oz/4 tbsp butter
50g/2oz/½ cup plain (all-purpose) flour
600ml/1 pint/2½ cups milk
115g/4oz/1 cup grated Cheddar cheese
salt and ground black pepper

1 Preheat the oven to 180°C/350°F/Gas 4. Make the salsa picante. Place the tomatoes, garlic, onion and chillies in a blender or food processor and process until smooth. Pour into a small pan, add the spices and oregano and season with salt. Bring to the boil, stirring occasionally. Boil for 1–2 minutes, then cover and simmer for 15 minutes.

2 Make the cheese sauce. Melt the butter and stir in the flour. Cook for 1 minute. Add the milk and cook until the sauce thickens. Stir in all but 30ml/2 tbsp of the cheese and season. Set aside.

3 Mix the onion, garlic and chilli in a bowl. Add the beef and mix well. Heat the oil in a frying pan and stir-fry the mixture for 10 minutes. Stir in the rice and beef stock to moisten. Season to taste. Pour a quarter of the cheese sauce into an ovenproof dish. Add a tortilla. Spread over half the salsa, then half the meat.

4 Repeat these layers, then add half the remaining cheese sauce and the last tortilla. Pour over the last of the sauce and sprinkle the reserved cheese on top. Bake for 15–20 minutes until golden.

Kneaded Sirloin Steak Energy 188kcal/786kJ; Protein 27.6g; Carbohydrate 4g, of which sugars 3.9g; Fat 6.9g, of which saturates 2.6g; Cholesterol 57mg; Calcium 26mg; Fibre 0.9g; Sodium 83mg.
Mexican Pie Energy 595kcal/2516kJ; Protein 30.3g; Carbohydrate 91.2g, of which sugars 11.3g; Fat 14.7g, of which saturates 4.7g; Cholesterol 53mg; Calcium 153mg; Fibre 4.0g; Sodium 379mg.

Beef Enchiladas with Chilli Sauce

Enchiladas are usually made with corn tortillas, although in parts of northern Mexico flour tortillas may be used. The chilli sauce gives this dish a satisfying kick.

Serves 3 to 4
500g/1¼lb rump (round) steak, cut into 5cm/2in cubes

2 ancho chillies, seeded
2 pasilla chillies, seeded
2 garlic cloves, crushed
10ml/2 tsp dried oregano
2.5ml/½ tsp ground cumin
30ml/2 tbsp vegetable oil
7 fresh corn tortillas
shredded onion and flat-leaved parsley, to garnish
salsa, to serve

1 Put the steak in a deep frying pan and cover with water. Bring to the boil, then lower the heat and simmer the meat for 1–1½ hours, or until very tender.

2 Meanwhile, put the dried chillies in a small bowl and just cover with hot water. Leave to soak for 30 minutes, then transfer the chillies to a blender and blend, gradually adding some of the soaking water to make a smooth paste.

3 Drain the steak and leave to cool, reserving 250ml/8fl oz/1 cup of the cooking liquid. Meanwhile, fry the garlic, oregano and cumin in the oil for 2 minutes.

4 Stir in the chilli paste and the reserved cooking liquid from the beef. Tear one of the tortillas into small pieces and add it to the mixture. Bring to the boil, then lower the heat. Simmer for 10 minutes, stirring occasionally, until the sauce has thickened. Shred the steak, using two forks, and stir it into the sauce. Heat through for a few minutes.

5 Wrap the tortillas in foil and steam them on a plate over boiling water until pliable.

6 Spoon some of the meat mixture on to each tortilla and roll it up to make an enchilada. Keep the enchiladas in a warmed dish until you have rolled them all. Garnish with shreds of onion and fresh flat-leaved parsley and then serve immediately with the salsa.

Oxtail in Hot Tangy Sauce

Considered a delicacy in some parts of South-east Asia, oxtail and the tails of water buffalo are generally cooked for special feasts and celebrations. In Malaysia and Singapore, oxtail is occasionally cooked in European-style stews but the many Malays and Indonesians prefer to cook it slowly in a hot, tangy sauce. Served with steamed rice, or chunks of fresh, crusty bread, it makes a very tasty supper dish.

Serves 4 to 6
8 shallots, chopped
8 garlic cloves, chopped
6 red chillies, seeded and chopped

25g/1oz fresh galangal, chopped
30ml/2 tbsp rice flour or plain (all-purpose) flour
15ml/1 tbsp ground turmeric
8–12 oxtail joints, cut to roughly the same size and trimmed of fat
45ml/3 tbsp vegetable oil
400g/14oz can plum tomatoes, drained
2 lemon grass stalks, halved and bruised
a handful of fresh kaffir lime leaves
225g/8oz tamarind pulp, soaked in 600ml/1 pint/2½ cups water, squeezed and strained
30–45ml/2–3 tbsp sugar
salt and ground black pepper
fresh coriander (cilantro) leaves, roughly chopped

1 Using a mortar and pestle or food processor, grind the shallots, garlic, chillies and galangal to a coarse paste. Mix the flour with the ground turmeric and spread it on a flat surface. Roll the oxtail in the flour and set aside.

2 Heat the oil in a heavy pan or earthenware pot. Stir in the spice paste and cook until fragrant and golden. Add the oxtail joints and brown on all sides. Add the tomatoes, lemon grass stalks, lime leaves and tamarind juice. Add enough water to cover the oxtail, and bring it to the boil. Skim off any fat from the surface. Reduce the heat, put the lid on the pan and simmer the oxtail for 2 hours.

3 Stir in the sugar, season with salt and pepper and continue to cook, uncovered, for a further 30–40 minutes, until the meat is very tender. Garnish with the chopped coriander and serve straight from the pan.

Beef Enchiladas Energy 503kcal/2121kJ; Protein 43g; Carbohydrate 51.9g, of which sugars 2.9g; Fat 15.1g, of which saturates 3.7g; Cholesterol 98mg; Calcium 101mg; Fibre 2.5g; Sodium 335mg.
Oxtail in Tangy Sauce Energy 386kcal/1611kJ; Protein 34.5g; Carbohydrate 11.3g, of which sugars 6.6g; Fat 22.6g, of which saturates 7.7g; Cholesterol 125mg; Calcium 31mg; Fibre 1.2g; Sodium 191mg.

Spicy Meat Loaf

This mouthwatering meat loaf has a deliciously fiery kick from the fresh green chillies. It is simply baked in the oven and will provide a hearty lunch on cold days, or a tasty mid-week meal.

Serves 4 to 6

5 eggs
450g/1lb lean minced
   (ground) beef
30ml/2 tbsp ground ginger
30ml/2 tbsp ground garlic
6 green chillies, seeded
   and chopped
2 small onions, finely chopped
2.5ml/½ tsp ground turmeric
50g/2oz coriander (cilantro)
   leaves, chopped
175g/6oz potato, grated
salt, to taste

1 Preheat the oven to 180°C/350°F/Gas Mark 4. Grease a small baking tray. Beat two eggs in a bowl until fluffy and pour into the greased baking tray.

2 In a large mixing bowl, knead the meat, ginger and garlic, four of the green chillies, half the chopped onion, one beaten egg, the turmeric, coriander leaves, potato and salt.

3 Pack the meat mixture into the baking tray and smooth the surface with a metal spatula. Put the tray in the preheated oven and cook for 45 minutes.

4 Beat the remaining eggs in a bowl and fold in the remaining green chillies and onion. Remove the baking tray from the oven and pour the mixture all over the meat. Return to the oven and cook until the eggs have set.

5 Carefully transfer the meat loaf on to a serving plate and serve immediately, cut up into slices.

> **Cook's Tip**
> Meat loaf is great for all the family, but reduce the amount of chillies in this version if serving to children.

Beef Satay with a Chilli and Peanut Sauce

The spicy peanut paste, satay, is a great favourite in South-east Asia. Although it is more associated with Thai cooking, it is thought to have originated in India. In southern Vietnam, it is used for grilling and stir-frying meats, as well as for dressing noodles and spiking marinades. This is a great barbecue dish that works with pork, chicken, prawns or shrimp. Jars of satay are available to buy but they taste nothing like the home-made paste, which you can pep up with as much garlic and chilli as you like.

Serves 4 to 6

500g/1¼lb beef sirloin,
   sliced against the grain
   in bitesize pieces
15ml/1 tbsp groundnut
   (peanut) oil
1 bunch each of fresh coriander
   (cilantro) and mint,
   stalks removed

For the satay

60ml/4 tbsp groundnut (peanut)
   or vegetable oil
4–5 garlic cloves, crushed
4–5 dried Serrano chillies, seeded
   and ground
5–10ml/1–2 tsp curry powder
50g/2oz/⅓ cup roasted peanuts,
   finely ground

1 To make the satay, heat the oil in a heavy pan and stir in the garlic until it begins to colour. Add the chillies, curry powder and peanuts and stir over a gentle heat until the mixture forms a paste. Remove from the heat and leave to cool.

2 Put the beef into a bowl. Beat the groundnut oil into the satay and tip the mixture on to the beef. Mix well, so that the beef is evenly coated. Soak four to six wooden skewers in water for 30 minutes. Prepare a barbecue. Thread the meat on to the skewers and cook for 2–3 minutes on each side. Serve the meat with the herb leaves for wrapping.

> **Cook's Tip**
> The beef is also delicious served with a salad, rice wrappers and a light dipping sauce.

Spicy Meat Loaf Energy 272kcal/1133kJ; Protein 22.1g; Carbohydrate 7.3g, of which sugars 2g; Fat 17.6g, of which saturates 6.6g; Cholesterol 204mg; Calcium 73mg; Fibre 1.5g; Sodium 129mg.
Beef Satay Energy 433kcal/1798kJ; Protein 34g; Carbohydrate 4g, of which sugars 1g; Fat 31g, of which saturates 7g; Cholesterol 64mg; Calcium 68mg; Fibre 1.5g; Sodium 100mg.

Beef and Aubergine Curry with Fresh Red Chillies

Serves 6

120ml/4fl oz/½ cup sunflower oil
2 onions, thinly sliced
2.5cm/1in fresh root ginger, sliced
  and cut in matchsticks
1 garlic clove, crushed
2 fresh red chillies, seeded and
  very finely sliced
2.5cm/1in fresh turmeric, peeled
  and crushed, or 5ml/1 tsp
  ground turmeric
1 lemon grass stem, lower part
  sliced finely, top bruised

675g/1½ lb braising steak, cut in
  even-size strips
400ml/14fl oz can coconut milk
300ml/½ pint/1¼ cups water
1 aubergine, sliced and patted dry
5ml/1 tsp tamarind pulp, soaked
  in 60ml/4 tbsp warm water
salt and ground black pepper
finely sliced chilli, (optional) and
  fried onions, to garnish
boiled rice, to serve

1 Heat half the oil and fry the onions, ginger and garlic until they give off a rich aroma. Add the chillies, turmeric and the lower part of the lemon grass. Push to one side and then turn up the heat and add the steak, stirring until the meat changes colour.

2 Add the coconut milk, water, lemon grass top and seasoning to taste. Cover and simmer gently for 1½ hours, or until the meat is tender.

3 Towards the end of the cooking time heat the remaining oil in a frying pan. Fry the aubergine slices until brown on both sides.

4 Add the browned aubergine slices to the beef curry and cook for a further 15 minutes. Stir gently from time to time. Strain the tamarind and stir the juice into the curry. Taste and adjust the seasoning. Put into a warm serving dish. Garnish with the sliced chilli, if using, and fried onions, and serve with boiled rice.

> **Cook's Tip**
> If you want to make this curry ahead, follow the above method to the end of step 2 and finish later.

Chilli Beef and Tomato Curry

When served with boiled yam or rice, this delicious curry makes a hearty dish, certain to be popular with anybody who likes their food spicy.

Serves 4

450g/1lb stewing beef
5ml/1 tsp dried thyme
45ml/3 tbsp palm or vegetable oil
1 large onion, finely chopped
2 garlic cloves, crushed

4 canned plum tomatoes,
  chopped, plus 60ml/4 tbsp
  of the juice
15ml/1 tbsp tomato
  purée (paste)
2.5ml/½ tsp mixed spice
1 fresh red chilli, seeded
  and chopped
900ml/1½ pints/3¾ cups
  chicken stock or water
1 large aubergine (eggplant),
  about 350g/12oz
salt and ground black pepper

1 Cut the beef into cubes and season with 2.5ml/½ tsp of the thyme and salt and pepper.

2 Heat 15ml/1 tbsp of the oil in a large pan and fry the meat, in batches if necessary, for 8–10 minutes, stirring constantly, until evenly browned all over. Transfer to a bowl using a slotted spoon and set aside.

3 Heat the remaining oil in the pan and fry the onion and garlic for a few minutes until the onion begins to soften.

4 Add the tomatoes and tomato juice to the pan and simmer for a further 8–10 minutes, stirring occasionally.

5 Add the tomato purée, mixed spice, chilli and remaining thyme to the pan and stir well.

6 Add the cubed beef and the chicken stock or water to the pan. Bring to the boil, reduce the heat, cover the pan and simmer gently for 30 minutes.

7 Cut the aubergine into 1cm/½in dice. Stir into the beef mixture and cook, covered, for a further 30 minutes until the beef is completely tender. Taste the sauce, adjust the seasoning if necessary and serve immediately.

Beef and Aubergine Curry Energy 394kcal/1638kJ; Protein 26g; Carbohydrate 12g, of which sugars 10g; Fat 27g, of which saturates 5g; Cholesterol 71mg; Calcium 54mg; Fibre 203g; Sodium 700mg.
Chilli Beef Curry Energy 251kcal/1050kJ; Protein 27.2g; Carbohydrate 7.2g, of which sugars 6.2g; Fat 12.8g, of which saturates 2.9g; Cholesterol 75mg; Calcium 29mg; Fibre 3g; Sodium 87mg.

Thick Beef Curry in Sweet Peanut and Chilli Sauce

This curry is deliciously rich and thicker than most other Thai curries.

Serves 4 to 6

600ml/1 pint/2½ cups coconut milk
45ml/3 tbsp Thai red curry paste
45ml/3 tbsp Thai fish sauce
30ml/2 tbsp palm sugar (jaggery) or
    light muscovado (brown) sugar

2 lemon grass stalks, bruised
450g/1lb rump (round) steak, cut
    into thin strips
75g/3oz/¾ cup roasted
    peanuts, ground
2 fresh red chillies, sliced
5 kaffir lime leaves, torn
salt and ground black pepper
2 salted eggs, cut in wedges, and
    15 Thai basil leaves, to garnish

1 Pour half the coconut milk into a large, heavy pan. Place over a medium heat and bring to the boil, stirring constantly until the milk separates.

2 Stir the red curry paste into the pan and cook for about 2–3 minutes until the mixture is fragrant and thoroughly blended. Add the fish sauce, sugar and bruised lemon grass stalks. Mix well.

3 Continue to cook until the colour deepens. Gradually add the remaining coconut milk, stirring constantly. Bring the mixture back to the boil.

4 Add the beef and peanuts to the pan. Cook, stirring constantly, for 8–10 minutes, or until most of the liquid has evaporated. Add the chillies and lime leaves. Season to taste with salt and black pepper. Serve immediately, garnished with wedges of salted eggs and Thai basil leaves.

> **Cook's Tip**
> If you don't have the time to make your own red curry paste, you can buy ready-made jars of Thai curry paste, which are great time-savers. There is a wide range available in most Asian food stores and large supermarkets.

Dry Beef Curry with Peanut and Lime

This spicy dry curry can be served with a moist dish such as a vegetable curry.

Serves 4 to 6

400g/14oz can coconut milk
900g/2lb stewing steak, cubed
300ml/½ pint/1¼ cups beef stock
30ml/2 tbsp crunchy peanut butter
juice of 2 limes, plus lime slices,
    chopped coriander (cilantro)
    and chilli slices, to garnish
boiled rice, to serve

For the red curry paste

30ml/2 tbsp coriander seeds
5ml/1 tsp cumin seeds
seeds from 6 cardamom pods
2.5ml/½ tsp grated nutmeg

1.5ml/¼ tsp ground cloves
2.5ml/½ tsp ground cinnamon
20ml/4 tsp paprika
pared rind of 1 mandarin orange,
    finely chopped
4–5 small fresh red chillies,
    seeded and finely chopped
25ml/5 tsp sugar
2.5ml/½ tsp salt
1 piece lemon grass, shredded
3 garlic cloves, crushed
2cm/¾in piece fresh galangal,
    peeled and finely chopped
4 red shallots, finely chopped
2cm/¾in piece shrimp paste
50g/2oz coriander (cilantro) root
    or stem, chopped
juice of ½ lime
30ml/2 tbsp vegetable oil

1 Strain the coconut milk into a bowl, retaining the thicker coconut milk in the sieve (strainer). Pour the thin milk into a large pan, then scrape in half the residue from the sieve. Reserve the remaining thick milk. Add the steak and the stock and bring to the boil, then simmer, covered, for 50 minutes.

2 Make the paste. Dry-fry all the seeds for 1–2 minutes. Transfer into a bowl and add the nutmeg, cloves, cinnamon, paprika and orange rind. Pound the chillies with the sugar and salt. Add the spice mixture, lemon grass, garlic, galangal, shallots and shrimp paste and pound. Mix in the coriander, lime juice and oil.

3 Strain the beef, and place a cupful of the cooking liquid in a wok. Stir in 30–45ml/2–3 tbsp of the paste. Boil until the liquid has evaporated. Stir in the reserved thick coconut milk, the peanut butter and beef. Simmer, uncovered, for 15–20 minutes.

4 Before serving, stir in the lime juice. Serve in bowls over rice, garnished with the lime slices, coriander and sliced red chillies.

Thick Beef Curry Energy kcal310/1296kJ; Protein 29.1g; Carbohydrate 9.7g, of which sugars 8.5g; Fat 17.4g, of which saturates 5.3g; Cholesterol 69mg; Calcium 59mg; Fibre 1.2g; Sodium 215mg.
Dry Beef Curry Energy 406kcal/1703kJ; Protein 55.4g; Carbohydrate 6.4g, of which sugars 5.9g; Fat 18g, of which saturates 5.1g; Cholesterol 170mg; Calcium 92mg; Fibre 0.6g; Sodium 812mg.

Aubergine and Sweet Potato Stew

Scented with fragrant lemon grass, ginger, chilli and lots of garlic, this is a particularly tasty combination of flavours.

Serves 6

400g/14oz baby aubergines (eggplants) or 2 large aubergines
60ml/4 tbsp groundnut (peanut) oil
225g/8oz Thai red shallots or other shallots or pickling onions
5ml/1 tsp fennel seeds, crushed
4–5 garlic cloves, thinly sliced
25ml/1½ tbsp finely chopped fresh root ginger
475ml/16fl oz/2 cups stock
2 lemon grass stalks, outer layers discarded, finely chopped
15g/½oz coriander (cilantro), stalks and leaves chopped separately
3 kaffir lime leaves, lightly bruised
2–3 small fresh red chillies
60ml/4 tbsp Thai green curry paste
675g/1½lb sweet potatoes, peeled and cut into chunks
400ml/14fl oz coconut milk
5ml/1 tsp palm sugar (jaggery)
250g/9oz mushrooms, thickly sliced
juice of 1 lime, to taste
salt and ground black pepper
boiled rice and 18 fresh Thai basil or ordinary basil leaves, to serve

1 Slice baby aubergines in half. Cut large aubergines into chunks. Heat half the oil in a frying pan. Add the aubergines and cook, stirring occasionally, until lightly browned on all sides. Set aside.

2 Slice 4–5 of the shallots. Cook the whole shallots in the oil left in the pan until lightly browned. Set aside. Add the remaining oil and cook the sliced shallots, fennel seeds, garlic and ginger over a low heat for 5 minutes.

3 Pour in the stock, then add the lemon grass, coriander stalks, lime leaves and whole chillies. Cover and simmer for 5 minutes.

4 Stir in 30ml/2 tbsp of the curry paste and the sweet potatoes. Simmer for about 10 minutes, then return the aubergines and shallots to the pan and cook for a further 5 minutes.

5 Stir in the coconut milk and the sugar. Season to taste, then stir in the mushrooms and simmer for 5 minutes, or until all the vegetables are cooked and tender.

6 Stir in lime juice to taste, followed by the coriander leaves. Sprinkle basil leaves over and serve immediately with rice.

Vietnamese Vegetable Curry with Thai Chillies

Variations of this fiery, flavoursome vegetable curry are found all over southern Vietnam. A favourite with the Buddhist monks and often sold from countryside stalls, it can be served with plain rice or noodles, or chunks of crusty bread.

Serves 4

30ml/2 tbsp vegetable oil
2 onions, roughly chopped
2 lemon grass stalks, roughly chopped and bruised
4 green Thai chillies, seeded and finely sliced
4cm/1½in galangal or fresh root ginger, peeled and chopped
3 carrots, peeled, halved lengthways and sliced
115g/4oz yard-long beans
grated rind of 1 lime
10ml/2 tsp soy sauce
15ml/1 tbsp rice vinegar
10ml/2 tsp Thai fish sauce
5ml/1 tsp black peppercorns, crushed
15ml/1 tbsp sugar
10ml/2 tsp ground turmeric
115g/4oz canned bamboo shoots
75g/3oz spinach, steamed and roughly chopped
150ml/¼ pint/⅔ cup coconut milk
salt
chopped fresh coriander (cilantro) and mint leaves, to garnish

1 Heat a wok or heavy pan and add the oil. Once hot, stir in the onions, lemon grass, chillies and galangal or ginger. Add the carrots and beans with the lime rind and stir-fry for 1–2 minutes.

2 Stir in the soy sauce, rice vinegar and fish sauce. Add the crushed peppercorns, sugar and turmeric, then stir in the bamboo shoots and the chopped spinach.

3 Stir in the coconut milk and simmer for 10 minutes, until the vegetables are tender. Season with salt and serve immediately, garnished with fresh coriander and mint.

Cook's Tip
This curry should be fiery, almost dominated by the chilli. In Vietnam it is eaten for breakfast as a great pick-me-up.

Aubergine Stew Energy 236kcal/992kJ; Protein 3.5g; Carbohydrate 30.2g, of which sugars 12.4g; Fat 12.2g, of which saturates 2.2g; Cholesterol 0mg; Calcium 65mg; Fibre 1.3g; Sodium 210mg.
Vietnamese Vegetable Curry Energy 159kcal/660kJ; Protein 3g; Carbohydrate 19g, of which sugars 16g; Fat 8g, of which saturates 1g; Cholesterol 0mg; Calcium 68mg; Fibre 3.7g; Sodium 200mg.

Spicy Chickpeas with Potato Cakes and Green Chillies

The potato cakes in this recipe are given a slightly sour-sweet flavour by the addition of amchur, a powder that is made from unripe or green mangos.

Makes 10 to 12
30ml/2 tbsp vegetable oil
30ml/2 tbsp ground coriander
30ml/2 tbsp ground cumin
2.5ml/½ tsp ground turmeric
2.5ml/½ tsp salt
2.5ml/½ tsp sugar
30ml/2 tbsp flour paste
450g/1lb boiled chickpeas, drained
2 fresh green chillies, chopped
1 piece fresh ginger, 5cm/2in long, finely crushed
85g/3oz fresh coriander (cilantro) leaves, chopped
2 firm tomatoes, chopped

For the potato cakes
450g/1lb potatoes, boiled and coarsely mashed
4 green chillies, finely chopped
50g/2oz coriander (cilantro) leaves, finely chopped
7.5ml/1½ tsp ground cumin
5ml/1 tsp amchur (dry mango powder)
salt, to taste
vegetable oil, for shallow-frying

1 Make the spicy chickpeas. Heat the oil in a pan and fry the coriander, cumin, turmeric, salt, sugar and flour paste until the water has evaporated and the oil separated.

2 Add the chickpeas, chillies, ginger, fresh coriander and tomatoes. Mix well and simmer for 5 minutes. Transfer to a serving dish and keep warm.

3 To make the potato cakes, mix the mashed potato in a large bowl with the green chillies, coriander, ground cumin, amchur and salt, to taste. Mix well until all the ingredients are thoroughly blended.

4 Using your hands, shape the potato mixture into little cakes. Heat the oil in a shallow frying pan or griddle and fry them on both sides until golden brown. Transfer to a serving dish and serve with the spicy chickpeas.

Curried Spinach and Potato with Mixed Chillies

This delicious curry, suitable for vegetarians, is mildly spiced with a warming flavour from the fresh and dried chillies.

Serves 4 to 6
60ml/4 tbsp vegetable oil
225g/8oz potato
2.5cm/1in piece fresh root ginger, crushed
4 garlic cloves, crushed
1 onion, coarsely chopped
2 green chillies, chopped
2 whole dried red chillies, coarsely broken
5ml/1 tsp cumin seeds
225g/8oz fresh spinach, trimmed, washed and chopped or 225g/8oz frozen spinach, thawed and drained
salt
2 firm tomatoes, coarsely chopped, to garnish

1 Wash the potatoes and cut into quarters. If using small new potatoes, leave them whole. Heat the oil in a frying pan and fry the potatoes until brown on all sides. Remove and set aside.

2 Remove the excess oil leaving 15ml/1 tbsp in the pan. Fry the ginger, garlic, onion, green chillies, dried chillies and cumin seeds until the onion is golden brown.

3 Add the potatoes and salt to the pan and stir well. Cover the pan and cook gently until the potatoes are tender and can be easily pierced with a sharp knife.

4 Add the spinach and stir well. Cook with the pan uncovered until the spinach is tender and all the excess fluids in the pan have evaporated. Transfer the curry to a serving plate, garnish with the chopped tomatoes and serve immediately.

Cook's Tip
India is blessed with over 18 varieties of spinach. If you have access to an Indian or Chinese grocer, look out for some of the more unusual varieties.

Spicy Chickpeas Energy 163kcal/684kJ; Protein 5.2g; Carbohydrate 17.3g, of which sugars 1.6g; Fat 8.8g, of which saturates 1.1g; Cholesterol 0mg; Calcium 68mg; Fibre 3g; Sodium 96mg.
Curried Spinach Energy 135kcal/560kJ; Protein 3g; Carbohydrate 13.5g, of which sugars 5.9g; Fat 8g, of which saturates 1g; Cholesterol 0mg; Calcium 86mg; Fibre 2.6g; Sodium 62mg.

Curried Mushrooms, Peas and Paneer with Green Chillies

Paneer is a traditional cheese made from rich milk and is most popular with northern Indians. This makes a great dish for lunch when eaten with thick parathas.

Serves 4 to 6
90ml/6 tbsp ghee or vegetable oil
225g/8oz paneer, cubed
1 onion, finely chopped
a few mint leaves, chopped
50g/2oz coriander (cilantro)
    leaves, chopped
3 green chillies, chopped
3 garlic cloves
2.5cm/1in piece fresh root

ginger, sliced
5ml/1 tsp ground turmeric
5ml/1 tsp chilli powder (optional)
5ml/1 tsp garam masala
225g/8oz tiny button (white)
    mushrooms, washed
225g/8oz frozen peas, thawed
    and drained
175ml/6fl oz/³/₄ cup natural
    (plain) yogurt, mixed with
    5ml/1 tsp cornflour
    (cornstarch)
salt
tomatoes and coriander (cilantro)
    leaves, to garnish

1 Heat the ghee or oil in a frying pan and fry the paneer cubes until they are golden brown on all sides. Remove and drain on kitchen paper.

2 Grind the onion, mint, coriander, chillies, garlic and ginger in a mortar and pestle or food processor to a fairly smooth paste.

3 Transfer the paste to a bowl and mix in the turmeric, chilli powder, if using, garam masala and salt.

4 Remove any excess ghee or oil from the pan, leaving about 15ml/1 tbsp. Heat the oil and fry the paste until the raw onion smell disappears and the oil separates.

5 Add the mushrooms, peas and paneer to the pan. Mix well. Cool the mixture slightly and gradually fold in the yogurt. Simmer for about 10 minutes.

6 Garnish with tomatoes and coriander and serve immediately.

Yard-long Bean Stew with Chillies

The southern Luzon peninsula in the Philippines is renowned for its fiery food, laced with hot chillies and coconut milk. In typical style, this rich, pungent dish is hot and, believe it or not, it is served with extra chillies to chew on.

Serves 3 to 4
30–45ml/2–3 tbsp coconut or
    groundnut (peanut) oil
1 onion, finely chopped
2–3 garlic cloves, finely chopped
40g/1¹/₂oz fresh root ginger,
    finely chopped
1 lemon grass stalk, bruised and
    finely chopped

4–5 red chillies, seeded and
    finely chopped
15ml/1 tbsp shrimp paste
15–30ml/1–2 tbsp tamarind paste
15–30ml/1–2 tbsp palm
    sugar (jaggery)
2 X 400g/14oz cans
    unsweetened coconut milk
4 kaffir lime leaves
500g/1¹/₄lb yard-long beans
salt and ground black pepper
1 bunch of fresh coriander
    (cilantro) leaves, roughly
    chopped, to garnish

To serve
cooked rice
raw chillies

1 Heat the oil in a wok or large, heavy frying pan that has a lid. Stir in the onion, garlic, ginger, lemon grass and chillies and fry until fragrant and beginning to colour. Add the shrimp paste, tamarind paste and sugar and mix well. Stir in the coconut milk and the lime leaves.

2 Bring the mixture to the boil, reduce the heat and toss in the whole yard-long beans. Partially cover the pan and cook the beans gently for 6–8 minutes until tender.

3 Season the stew with salt and pepper and garnish with chopped coriander. Serve with rice and extra chillies, if you like.

> **Cook's Tip**
> If you prefer, you can reduce the quantity of chillies used in the recipe to suit your taste buds, and omit the extra chillies served with the stew, if you like.

Curried Mushrooms Energy 154kcal/643kJ; Protein 10.4g; Carbohydrate 13g, of which sugars 4.9g; Fat 7.2g, of which saturates 1.7g; Cholesterol 6mg; Calcium 139mg; Fibre 2.6g; Sodium 133mg.
Yard-long Bean Stew Energy 200kcal/840kJ; Protein 5.5g; Carbohydrate 24.4g, of which sugars 22.9g; Fat 9.7g, of which saturates 1.5g; Cholesterol 19mg; Calcium 158mg; Fibre 3.4g; Sodium 384mg.

Tofu and Green Bean Red Chilli Curry

This is one of those versatile recipes that should be in every chilli-loving cook's repertoire. This version uses green beans, but other vegetables work equally well. The tofu takes on the flavour of the spice paste and also boosts the nutritional value.

Serves 4 to 6
600ml/1 pint/2½ cups canned
   coconut milk
15ml/1 tbsp Thai red curry paste
45ml/3 tbsp Thai fish sauce
10ml/2 tsp palm sugar (jaggery)
   or light muscovado
   (brown) sugar
225g/8oz/3¼ cups button
   (white) mushrooms
115g/4oz/scant 1 cup green
   beans, trimmed
175g/6oz firm tofu, rinsed,
   drained and cut into
   2cm/¾in cubes
4 kaffir lime leaves, torn
2 fresh red chillies, seeded
   and sliced
fresh coriander (cilantro) leaves,
   to garnish

1 Pour about one-third of the coconut milk into a wok or pan. Cook until it starts to separate and an oily sheen appears on the surface.

2 Add the red curry paste, fish sauce and sugar to the coconut milk. Mix thoroughly. Add the button mushrooms. Stir the mixture and cook for 1–2 minutes.

3 Stir in the remaining coconut milk. Bring the mixture slowly back to the boil. Add the green beans and tofu cubes. Reduce the heat and simmer gently for 4–5 minutes more.

4 Stir in the kaffir lime leaves and sliced red chillies. Heat the curry for a couple of minutes until bubbling. Spoon the curry into warmed individual bowls. Sprinkle the coriander leaves over the top of each serving as a garnish and serve at once.

Cook's Tip
Tofu or bean curd is quite bland in flavour but it readily picks up strong tastes, such as chillies and spices.

Courgette and Jalapeño Chilli Torte

This spicy dish looks like a Spanish omelette, which is traditionally served at room temperature. Serve warm or prepare it in advance and leave to cool, but do not refrigerate.

Serves 4 to 6
500g/1¼lb courgettes (zucchini)
60ml/4 tbsp vegetable oil
1 small onion
3 fresh jalapeño chillies, seeded
   and cut in strips
3 large eggs
50g/2oz/½ cup self-raising
   (self-rising) flour
115g/4oz/1 cup grated Monterey
   Jack or mild Cheddar cheese
2.5ml/½ tsp cayenne pepper
15g/½oz/1 tbsp butter
salt

1 Preheat the oven to 180°C/350°F/Gas 4. Top and tail the courgettes, then slice them thinly.

2 Heat the oil in a large frying pan. Add the courgettes and cook for a few minutes, turning them over at least once, until they are soft and beginning to brown. Using a slotted spoon, transfer them to a bowl.

3 Slice the onion and add it to the oil left in the pan, with most of the jalapeño strips, reserving some for the garnish. Fry until the onions have softened and are golden.

4 Using a slotted spoon, transfer the onions and jalapeños to the bowl with the courgettes.

5 Beat the eggs in a large bowl. Add the self-raising flour, cheese and cayenne. Mix well, then stir in the courgette mixture, with salt to taste.

6 Grease a 23cm/9in round shallow ovenproof dish with the butter. Pour in the courgette mixture and bake in the oven for 30 minutes until it has risen, is firm to the touch and golden brown all over. Allow to cool.

7 Serve the courgette torte in thick wedges and garnish with the remaining jalapeño strips. A tomato salad, sprinkled with chives, makes a colourful accompaniment.

Tofu and Bean Curry Energy 110kcal/460kJ; Protein 5.7g; Carbohydrate 10.2g, of which sugars 9.6g; Fat 5.5g, of which saturates 0.9g; Cholesterol 0mg; Calcium 282mg; Fibre 1.3g; Sodium 437mg.
Courgette Torte Energy 421kcal/1747kJ; Protein 18.8g; Carbohydrate 13.2g, of which sugars 3.2g; Fat 32g, of which saturates 12.9g; Cholesterol 216mg; Calcium 356mg; Fibre 1.7g; Sodium 359mg.

Stuffed Green Chillies

Stuffed chillies are popular all over Mexico. The type of chilli used differs from region to region. Poblanos and Anaheims are quite mild, but you can use hotter chillies if you prefer.

Makes 6

6 fresh poblano or Anaheim chillies
2 potatoes, total weight
   about 400g/14oz
200g/7oz/scant 1 cup
   cream cheese
200g/7oz/1³⁄₄ cups grated
   mature (sharp) Cheddar cheese
5ml/1 tsp salt
2.5ml/¹⁄₂ tsp ground black pepper
2 eggs, separated
115g/4oz/1 cup plain
   (all-purpose) flour
2.5ml/¹⁄₂ tsp white pepper
oil, for frying
chilli flakes to garnish, (optional)

1 Cut a slit down one side of each chilli. Dry-fry the chillies in a pan, turning frequently, until they blister. Place in a plastic bag and tie the top to keep the steam in. Set aside for 20 minutes, then peel off the skins and remove the seeds through the slits, keeping the chillies whole. Dry with kitchen paper and set aside.

2 Scrub or peel the potatoes and cut them into 1cm/¹⁄₂in dice. Bring a large pan of water to the boil, add the potatoes and return to the boil. Lower the heat and simmer for 5 minutes, or until the potatoes are just tender. Drain them thoroughly.

3 Put the cream cheese in a bowl with the mature cheese. Add 2.5ml/¹⁄₂ tsp of the salt and the black pepper. Mix in the potato. Spoon potato filling into each chilli. Put them on a plate, cover with clear film (plastic wrap) and chill for 1 hour to firm up.

4 Put the egg whites in a clean, grease-free bowl and whisk to firm peaks. In another bowl, beat the yolks until pale, then fold in the whites. Scrape the mixture into a large, shallow dish. Spread out the flour in another shallow dish and season it with the remaining salt and the white pepper.

5 Heat the oil for deep-frying to 190°C/375°F. Coat a few chillies first in flour and then in egg before frying the chillies in batches until golden and crisp. Drain on kitchen paper and serve hot, garnished with a sprinkle of chilli flakes for extra heat, if desired.

Chilli and Herb Grilled Polenta with Tangy Pebre

In this dish, polenta is flavoured with pasilla chillies. Serve with a tangy salsa from Chile called pebre.

Serves 6

10ml/2 tsp crushed dried pasilla
   chilli flakes
1.3 litres/2¹⁄₄ pints/5²⁄₃ cups water
250g/9oz quick-cook polenta
50g/2oz/¹⁄₄ cup butter
75g/3oz Parmesan cheese, grated
30ml/2 tbsp chopped fresh dill
30ml/2 tbsp chopped fresh
   coriander (cilantro)
30ml/2 tbsp olive oil
salt

For the pebre

¹⁄₂ pink onion, finely chopped
4 drained bottled sweet cherry
   peppers, finely chopped
1 fresh medium hot red chilli,
   seeded and finely chopped
1 small red (bell) pepper,
   quartered and seeded
10ml/2 tsp raspberry vinegar
30ml/2 tbsp olive oil
4 tomatoes, halved, cored, seeded
   and roughly chopped
45ml/3 tbsp chopped fresh
   coriander (cilantro)

1 Chop the dried chilli flakes. Put them in a pan with the water. Bring to the boil and add salt to taste. Add the polenta, whisking all the time. Reduce the heat and whisk for a few minutes. When the polenta is thick, whisk in the butter, Parmesan and herbs and season. Pour into a greased 33 × 23cm/13 × 9in baking tray. Leave uncovered to firm the surface and chill overnight.

2 About an hour before you plan to serve the meal, make the pebre. Place the onion, sweet cherry peppers and chilli in a mortar. Slice the skin from the red pepper. Dice the flesh and add it to the mortar with the vinegar and oil. Pound with a pestle for about 1 minute, then transfer to a serving dish. Stir in the tomatoes and coriander. Cover and leave in a cool place.

3 Remove the polenta from the refrigerator and leave for 30 minutes. Cut into 12 triangles and brush the top with oil. Heat a griddle and grill the polenta triangles in batches oiled side down for 2 minutes, then turn through 180 degrees and cook for a minute, to get a criss-cross effect. Serve with the chilled pebre.

Stuffed Chillies Energy 498kcal/2072kJ; Protein 14.9g; Carbohydrate 27.8g, of which sugars 3.2g; Fat 36.5g, of which saturates 18.6g; Cholesterol 127mg; Calcium 322mg; Fibre 1.8g; Sodium 374mg.
Chilli and Herb Polenta Energy 176kcal/732kJ; Protein 4.8g; Carbohydrate 16.4g, of which sugars 1.2g; Fat 10g, of which saturates 4g; Cholesterol 15mg; Calcium 87mg; Fibre 1g; Sodium 98mg.

Crispy Fried Tempeh with Chilli Spices

Often cooked at street stalls, this crispy fried tempeh can be served as a snack or as part of a selection of Indonesian dishes. For a substantial meal, try serving it with stir–fried noodles or rice and pickled vegetables.

Serves 3 to 4
45–60ml/3–4 tbsp coconut or
   groundnut (peanut) oil
500g/1 1/4lb tempeh, cut into
   bitesize strips

4 shallots, finely chopped
4 garlic cloves, finely chopped
25g/1oz fresh galangal or
   fresh root ginger, finely chopped
3–4 red chillies, seeded and
   finely chopped
150ml/1/4 pint/2/3 cup kecap manis
   (Indonesian sweet soy sauce)
30–45ml/2–3 tbsp unsalted
   peanuts, crushed
1 small bunch fresh
   coriander (cilantro) leaves,
   roughly chopped
noodles or rice, to serve

1 Heat 30–45ml/2–3 tbsp of the oil in a wok or large, heavy frying pan. Add the tempeh and stir-fry until golden brown all over. Using a slotted spoon, transfer the tempeh to kitchen paper to drain, then set aside.

2 Wipe the wok or frying pan clean with kitchen paper. Heat the remaining 15ml/1 tbsp oil in the wok or pan, stir in the shallots, garlic, galangal and chillies and fry until fragrant and beginning to colour. Stir in the kecap manis and add the fried tempeh. Stir-fry until the sauce has reduced and is clinging to the tempeh.

3 Transfer the tempeh to a serving dish and sprinkle with the peanuts and coriander leaves. Serve immediately with stir-fried noodles or cooked rice.

> **Variation**
> *Tempeh, which is fermented tofu, can be bought from Chinese and South-east Asian supermarkets. If you are unable to purchase it, then tofu can be used as an alternative.*

Tortillas with Salsa and Guacamole

This is just the right spicy dish to keep hungry guests from feeling the effects of too many preprandial drinks. The fieriness of the salsa will depend on the chilli sauce used, so choose one to suit your tastes.

Serves 6
30ml/2 tbsp chipotle or other
   chilli oil
15ml/1 tbsp sunflower oil
8 yellow corn tortillas

For the salsa
4 tomatoes
30ml/2 tbsp chopped fresh basil
juice of 1/2 lime
20ml/4 tsp good quality sweet
   chilli sauce
1 small red onion, finely chopped
salt and ground black pepper

For the guacamole
4 avocados
juice of 1/2 lime
1 fat mild chilli, seeded
   and chopped

1 Make the salsa one or two hours ahead to allow the flavours to blend. Cut the tomatoes in half, remove the cores and scoop out the seeds. Dice the flesh. Add the chopped basil, lime juice and sweet chilli sauce. Stir in the onion, then season to taste.

2 Make the guacamole. Cut the avocados in half, prize out the stones (pits), then scoop the flesh into a bowl. Add the lime juice, chilli and season. Mash with a fork to a fairly rough texture.

3 Prepare the barbecue. Mix together the chilli and sunflower oils. Stack the tortillas on a board. Lift the first tortilla off the stack and brush it lightly with the oil mixture. Turn it over and place it on the board, then brush the exposed side with oil. Repeat with the remaining tortillas, to make a new, second stack. Slice the whole stack diagonally into six pointed triangles.

4 Once the flames have died down, position a lightly oiled rack over the coals to heat. When the coals are hot, or with a light coating of ash, heat a griddle on the rack. Grill the tortilla wedges for 30 seconds on each side.

5 Transfer them to a bowl, so that they are supported by its sides. As they cool, they will shape themselves to the curve of the bowl. Serve with the salsa and guacamole.

Tortillas with Salsa Energy 340kcal/1421kJ; Protein 5.6g; Carbohydrate 34.8g, of which sugars 4.4g; Fat 20.7g, of which saturates 3.8g; Cholesterol 0mg; Calcium 69mg; Fibre 4.5g; Sodium 232mg.
Crispy Fried Tempeh Energy 258kcal/1071kJ; Protein 14.8g; Carbohydrate 7.7g, of which sugars 5.5g; Fat 18.9g, of which saturates 2.6g; Cholesterol 0mg; Calcium 682mg; Fibre 1.7g; Sodium 2680mg.

Aubergines in a Chilli Sauce

This dish is a great Indonesian favourite, both in the home and at the street stall. You can make it with large aubergines, cut in half and baked, or with small ones, butterflied. The dip is served in aubergine skins.

Serves 4

2 large aubergines (eggplants), cut in half lengthways, or 4 small auberines, butterflied
45–60ml/3–4 tbsp coconut oil
4 shallots, finely chopped
4 garlic cloves, finely chopped
25g/1oz fresh root ginger, finely chopped
3–4 red chillies, seeded and finely chopped
400g/14oz can tomatoes, drained
5–10ml/1–2 tsp palm sugar (jaggery)
juice of 2 limes
salt
1 small bunch fresh coriander (cilantro), finely chopped, to garnish

1 Preheat the oven to 180°C/350°F/Gas 4. Put the prepared aubergines on a baking tray and brush with 30ml/2 tbsp of the coconut oil. Bake in the oven for 40 minutes, until they are soft and tender.

2 Using a mortar and pestle, or a food processor, grind the shallots, garlic, ginger and chillies to a paste.

3 Heat the remaining 15ml/1 tbsp of oil in a wok or frying pan, stir in the spice paste and cook for 1–2 minutes, until it becomes fragrant and its colour begins to darken.

4 Add the tomatoes and sugar to the pan and cook for a further 3–4 minutes, until heated, then stir in the lime juice and a little salt to taste.

5 Put the baked aubergines in a serving dish and gently press down the flesh using the back of a wooden spoon to create a small hollow. Fill this with the sauce and spoon more of the sauce over the aubergines.

6 Garnish the aubergines with the chopped coriander and serve immediately if you want them warm, or leave to cool before serving at room temperature.

Crispy Rolls with Pumpkin, Tofu, Peanuts and Chillies

This is one of the best Vietnamese 'do-it-yourself' dishes. You place all the ingredients on the table with the rice wrappers for everyone to assemble their own rolls.

Serves 4 to 5

about 30ml/2 tbsp groundnut (peanut) or sesame oil
175g/6oz tofu, rinsed and patted dry
4 shallots, halved and sliced
2 garlic cloves, finely chopped
350g/12oz pumpkin flesh, cut into strips
1 carrot, cut into strips
15ml/1 tbsp soy sauce
3–4 green Thai chillies, seeded and finely sliced
1 crispy lettuce, torn into strips
1 bunch fresh basil, stalks removed
115g/4oz/2/3 cup roasted peanuts, chopped
100ml/3 1/2 fl oz/scant 1/2 cup hoisin sauce
20 dried rice wrappers
salt
chilli sauce (optional), to serve

1 Heat a heavy pan and smear with oil. Place the tofu in the pan and sear on both sides. Transfer to a plate and cut into thin strips.

2 Heat 30ml/2 tbsp oil in the pan and stir in the shallots and garlic. Add the pumpkin and carrot, then pour in the soy sauce and 120ml/4fl oz/1/2 cup water. Add a little salt and cook gently until the vegetables have softened but still have a bite to them.

3 Meanwhile, arrange the tofu, chillies, lettuce, basil, peanuts and hoisin sauce in separate dishes and put them on the table. Fill a bowl with hot water and place it on the table or fill a bowl for each person, and place the wrappers beside it. Transfer the vegetable mixture to a dish and place on the table.

4 To eat, dip a wrapper in the water for a few seconds to soften. Lay it flat on the table or on a plate and, just off-centre, spread a few strips of lettuce, then the pumpkin mixture, some tofu, a sprinkling of chillies, some hoisin sauce, some basil leaves and peanuts, to layer the ingredients. Pull the shorter edge (the side with filling on it) over the stack, tuck in the sides and roll into a cylinder. Dip the roll into chilli sauce, if you like.

Aubergines Energy 100kcal/419kJ; Protein 2.1g; Carbohydrate 9.4g, of which sugars 8.8g; Fat 6.4g, of which saturates 0.9g; Cholesterol 0mg; Calcium 42mg; Fibre 3.7g; Sodium 15mg.
Crispy Rolls Energy 402kcal/1669kJ; Protein 14g; Carbohydrate 29g, of which sugars 13g; Fat 26g, of which saturates 5g; Cholesterol 0mg; Calcium 321mg; Fibre 4.1g; Sodium 0.4g.

Aubergines and Peppers Stuffed with Lamb and Chillies

Aubergines and sweet peppers are stuffed with an aromatic lamb filling.

Serves 6
3 small aubergines (eggplants)
1 each red, green and yellow
    (bell) peppers
boiled rice, to serve

For the stuffing
45ml/3 tbsp corn oil
3 medium onions, sliced
5ml/1 tsp chilli powder
1.5ml/¼ tsp ground turmeric
5ml/1 tsp ground coriander
5ml/1 tsp ground cumin
5ml/1 tsp crushed ginger
5ml/1 tsp crushed garlic

5ml/1 tsp salt
450g/1lb minced (ground) lamb
3 fresh green chillies, chopped
30ml/2 tbsp chopped fresh
    coriander (cilantro)

For the fried onions
45ml/3 tbsp corn oil
5ml/1 tsp mixed onion, mustard,
    fenugreek and white cumin seeds
4 dried red chillies
3 medium onions, roughly chopped
5ml/1 tsp salt
5ml/1 tsp chilli powder
2 medium tomatoes, sliced
2 fresh green chillies, chopped
30ml/2 tbsp chopped fresh
    coriander (cilantro)

1 Prepare the vegetables. Slit the aubergines lengthways; keep the stalks intact. Cut the tops off the peppers and remove the seeds. Retain the pepper tops for lids once stuffed, if you like.

2 For the stuffing, heat the oil and fry the onions for a few minutes. Add the chilli powder, turmeric, coriander, cumin, ginger, garlic and salt, and stir-fry for 1 minute. Add the lamb and stir-fry for 10 minutes. Add the chillies and coriander towards the end.

3 Make the onions. Heat the oil in a large frying pan. Add the mixed seeds and the dried chillies, and fry for a minute. Stir in the onions and fry for 2 minutes. Add the salt, chilli powder, tomatoes, chillies and coriander. Cook for 1 minute, then set aside.

4 Fill the vegetables with the meat mixture. Place on top of the onions in the pan. Cover with foil and cook over a low heat for about 15 minutes until tender. Serve with plain boiled rice.

Shredded Cabbage with Chilli and Cumin

This cabbage dish is only lightly spiced and is a good accompaniment to many other dishes, or it will make a great main dish for a lunch or a mid-week dinner.

Serves 4
15ml/1 tbsp corn oil
50g/2oz/4 tbsp butter
2.5ml/½ tsp coriander
    seeds, crushed

2.5ml/½ tsp white cumin seeds
6 dried red chillies
1 small Savoy cabbage, shredded
12 mangetouts (snow peas)
3 fresh red chillies, seeded
    and sliced
12 baby corn cobs
salt, to taste
25g/1oz/¼ cup flaked (sliced)
    almonds, toasted
5ml/1 tbsp chopped fresh
    coriander (cilantro)

1 Heat the oil and butter in a wok or a large, heavy frying pan and add the crushed coriander seeds, white cumin seeds and dried red chillies. Stir-fry for 1–2 minutes until the spices release their fragrances.

2 Add the shredded cabbage and the mangetouts to the pan and fry, stirring constantly, for about 5 minutes, until the vegetables are just tender.

3 Finally add the fresh red chillies, baby corn cobs and salt, and fry for a further 3 minutes.

4 Garnish with the toasted almonds and fresh coriander, and serve immediately.

Variations
• Lots of other vegetables will work equally well in this dish. If mangetouts are out of season, you could replace them with any other green beans. Or try adding some bell peppers in place of the baby corn cobs.
• If you prefer a little more heat, you can keep the seeds in the chillies or increase the amount of chillies used.

Stuffed vegetables Energy 346kcal/1441kJ; Protein 19.6g; Carbohydrate 20.2g, of which sugars 15.1g; Fat 21.5g, of which saturates 5.6g; Cholesterol 57mg; Calcium 69mg; Fibre 5.4g; Sodium 81mg.
Shredded Cabbage Energy 230kcal/952kJ; Protein 6.2g; Carbohydrate 11.3g, of which sugars 7.1g; Fat 18.2g, of which saturates 7.3g; Cholesterol 27mg; Calcium 104mg; Fibre 3.8g; Sodium 416mg.

Fiery Prawn Noodles

In Malaysia and Singapore, there are endless stir-fried noodle dishes. Some of these are classic Chinese recipes; others have been influenced by the Chinese but adapted to suit the tastes of the different communities. The rice vermicelli in this popular snack is stir-fried with prawns and lots of chilli.

Serves 4
30ml/2 tbsp vegetable oil
1 carrot, cut into matchsticks
225g/8oz fresh prawns
    (shrimp), peeled
120ml/4fl oz/½ cup chicken
    stock or water
30ml/2 tbsp light soy sauce
15ml/1 tbsp dark soy sauce

175g/6oz beansprouts
115g/4oz mustard greens or pak
    choi (bok choy), shredded
225g/8oz dried rice vermicelli,
    soaked in lukewarm water until
    pliable, and drained
1–2 fresh red chillies, seeded and
    finely sliced, and fresh coriander
    (cilantro) leaves, roughly
    chopped, to garnish

For the spice paste
4 dried red chillies, soaked until
    soft and seeded
4 garlic cloves, chopped
4 shallots, chopped
25g/1oz fresh root ginger, peeled
    and chopped
5ml/1 tsp ground turmeric

1 Place all the ingredients for the spice paste in a mortar and pestle or food processor and grind to a smooth paste.

2 Heat the oil in a wok or heavy pan and stir in the spice paste until it begins to colour and become fragrant.

3 Add the carrots to the pan and cook, stirring constantly, for a minute. Then add the prawns to the pan and mix well.

4 Pour in the stock or water and soy sauces and mix well until combined. Cook for about 1–2 minutes. Add the beansprouts and mustard greens to the pan, followed by the noodles. Toss well to make sure the vegetables noodles are well coated and heated through.

5 Transfer the noodles to a warmed serving plate. Garnish with the sliced chillies and coriander.

Chinese Stir-fried Noodles with Red Chillies

This Chinese dish of stir-fried rice noodles and seafood is one of the most popular at the hawker stalls. Breakfast, lunch, supper, mid-morning, mid-afternoon or late evening, you will find this dish anywhere at any time of day. Variations include red snapper, clams and pork. Use the broad, fresh rice noodles available in Chinese markets.

Serves 3 to 4
45ml/3 tbsp vegetable oil
2 garlic cloves, finely chopped

2 red chillies, seeded and
    finely sliced
1 Chinese sausage, finely sliced
12 fresh prawns (shrimp), peeled
2 small squid, trimmed, cleaned,
    skinned and sliced
500g/1¼lb fresh rice noodles
30ml/2 tbsp light soy sauce
45ml/3 tbsp kecap manis
    (Indonesian sweet soy sauce)
2–3 mustard green
    leaves, chopped
a handful of beansprouts
2 eggs, lightly beaten
ground black pepper
fresh coriander (cilantro) leaves,
    finely chopped, to serve

1 Heat a wok or large frying pan and add the oil. Stir in the garlic and chillies and fry until fragrant.

2 Add the Chinese sausage, followed by the prawns and squid, tossing them to mix thoroughly.

3 Toss in the noodles and mix well. Add the soy sauce and kecap manis, and toss in the mustard leaves and beansprouts.

4 Stir in the eggs for a few seconds until set. Season with black pepper, garnish with coriander and serve immediately.

> **Cook's Tip**
> Kecap manis is an Indonesian soya bean condiment similar to soy sauce but sweeter and with a more complex flavour. If it is not available you can replace it with the same quantity of dark soy sauce mixed with a little sugar.

Fiery Prawn Noodles Energy 330kcal/1377kJ; Protein 17.5g; Carbohydrate 49.9g, of which sugars 4.5g; Fat 6.6g, of which saturates 0.8g; Cholesterol 110mg; Calcium 125mg; Fibre 1.9g; Sodium 960mg.
Chinese Noodles Energy 618kcal/2582kJ; Protein 24.8g; Carbohydrate 100g, of which sugars 1.1g; Fat 12.9g, of which saturates 2.1g; Cholesterol 217mg; Calcium 96mg; Fibre 0.5g; Sodium 717mg.

Red-hot Noodles with Chillies and Sesame

The Vietnamese have put their own particularly delicious stamp on spicy Singapore noodles, which are a popular dish throughout South-east Asia. At home, you can make this dish with any kind of noodles – egg or rice, fresh or dried.

Serves 4

30ml/2 tbsp sesame oil
1 onion, finely chopped
3 garlic cloves, finely chopped
3–4 green or red chillies, seeded and finely chopped
4cm/1½in fresh root ginger, peeled and finely chopped
6 spring onions (scallions), finely chopped
1 skinless chicken breast fillet, cut into bitesize strips
90g/3½oz pork, cut into bitesize strips
90g/3½oz prawns (shrimp), shelled
2 tomatoes, skinned, seeded and chopped
30ml/2 tbsp tamarind paste
15ml/1 tbsp Thai fish sauce
juice and rind of 1 lime
10ml/2 tsp sugar
150ml/¼ pint/⅔ cup water or fish stock
225g/8oz fresh rice sticks (vermicelli)
salt and ground black pepper
1 bunch each of fresh basil and mint, stalks removed, leaves shredded, and chilli dipping sauce, to serve

1 Heat a wok or heavy pan and add the oil. Stir in the onion, garlic, chillies and ginger, and cook until they begin to colour.

2 Add the spring onions and cook for 1 minute, add the chicken and pork, and cook for 2 minutes, then add the prawns.

3 Add the tomatoes, followed by the tamarind paste, fish sauce, lime juice and rind, and sugar. Pour in the water or fish stock, and cook gently for 2–3 minutes.

4 Toss the noodles in a pan of boiling water and cook for a few minutes until tender. Drain and add to the chicken mixture.

5 Season with salt and ground black pepper and serve immediately, with plenty of basil and mint sprinkled over the top, and drizzled with spoonfuls of chilli dipping sauce.

Spiced Stir-fried Noodles

Originally from China, spicy stir-fried noodles are very popular at street stalls throughout Indonesia, and are just as varied and equally delicious.

Serves 4

450g/1lb fresh egg noodles
15–30ml/1–2 tbsp palm, groundnut (peanut) or corn oil, plus extra for shallow frying
2 shallots, finely chopped
2–3 spring onions (scallions), finely chopped
2–3 garlic cloves, crushed
3–4 Thai chillies, seeded and finely chopped
15ml/1 tbsp shrimp paste
15ml/1 tbsp tomato purée (paste)
15–30ml/1–2 tbsp kecap manis (Indonesian sweet soy sauce)
4 eggs
salt

For the garnish

15ml/1 tbsp palm or corn oil
3–4 shallots, finely sliced

1 First prepare the garnish. Heat the oil in a heavy pan, stir in the shallots and fry until deep golden brown. Drain on kitchen paper and put aside.

2 Fill a deep pan with water and bring it to the boil. Drop in the egg noodles, untangling them with chopsticks, and cook for about 3 minutes until tender but still firm to the bite. Drain and refresh under running cold water.

3 Heat the oil in a wok or large, heavy frying pan and fry the shallots, spring onions, garlic and chillies until fragrant. Add the shrimp paste and cook until the mixture darkens.

4 Toss the noodles into the pan, making sure that they are thoroughly coated in the mixture. Add the tomato purée and kecap manis, toss thoroughly, and cook for 2–3 minutes. Season the noodles with salt to taste. Divide the noodles between four warmed bowls and keep warm.

5 Heat a thin layer of oil in a large, heavy frying pan, and crack the eggs into it. Fry for 1–2 minutes until the whites are cooked but the yolks remain runny. Place on the noodles and serve immediately with the fried shallots sprinkled over the top.

Red-hot Noodles Energy 420kcal/1756kJ; Protein 23g; Carbohydrate 59g, of which sugars 9g; Fat 10g, of which saturates 2g; Cholesterol 86mg; Calcium 119mg; Fibre 1.3g; Sodium 500mg.
Spiced Noodles Energy 549kcal/2317kJ; Protein 20.5g; Carbohydrate 82.9g, of which sugars 3.9g; Fat 17.6g, of which saturates 4.5g; Cholesterol 224mg; Calcium 68mg; Fibre 3.7g; Sodium 549mg.

Noodles and Vegetables in Coconut Sauce with Fresh Red Chillies

When everyday vegetables are given the Thai treatment, the result is a delectable dish which everyone is certain to enjoy.

Serves 4 to 6
30ml/2 tbsp sunflower oil
1 lemon grass stalk, finely chopped
15ml/1 tbsp Thai red curry paste
1 onion, thickly sliced
3 courgettes (zucchini), thickly sliced
115g/4oz Savoy cabbage, thickly sliced
2 carrots, thickly sliced

150g/5oz broccoli, stem sliced and head separated into florets
2 X 400ml/14fl oz cans coconut milk
475ml/16fl oz vegetable stock
150g/5oz dried egg noodles
15ml/1 tbsp Thai fish sauce
30ml/2 tbsp soy sauce
60ml/4 tbsp chopped fresh coriander (cilantro)

For the garnish
2 lemon grass stalks
1 bunch fresh coriander (cilantro)
8–10 small fresh red chillies

1 Heat the oil in a large pan or wok. Add the lemon grass and red curry paste and stir-fry for 2–3 seconds. Add the onion and cook over a medium heat, stirring occasionally, for about 5–10 minutes, until the onion has softened but not browned.

2 Add the courgettes, cabbage, carrots and slices of broccoli stem. Toss the vegetables with the onion mixture. Reduce the heat and cook gently, stirring occasionally, for 5 minutes.

3 Increase the heat to medium, stir in the coconut milk and vegetable stock and bring to the boil. Add the broccoli florets and the noodles, then simmer gently for 20 minutes.

4 Meanwhile, make the garnish. Split the lemon grass stalks lengthways. Gather the coriander into a small bouquet and lay it on a platter, following the curve of the rim. Tuck the lemon grass halves into the bouquet and add chillies to resemble flowers.

5 Stir the fish sauce, soy sauce and chopped coriander into the noodle mixture. Spoon on to the platter, taking care not to disturb the herb bouquet, and serve immediately.

Indonesian Spicy Fried Rice

This dish of fried rice is one of Indonesia's national dishes. Generally made with leftover cooked grains, the fried rice is served with crispy shallots and chillies or it is tossed with prawns or crabmeat, and chopped vegetables.

Serves 4
½ cucumber
30–45ml/2–3 tbsp vegetable or groundnut (peanut) oil, plus

extra for shallow frying
4 shallots, finely chopped
4 garlic cloves, finely chopped
3–4 fresh red chillies, seeded and chopped
45ml/3 tbsp kecap manis (Indonesian sweet soy sauce)
15ml/1 tbsp tomato purée (paste)
350g/12oz/1¾ cups cooked long grain rice
4 eggs

1 Peel the cucumber, cut it in half lengthways and scoop out the seeds. Cut the flesh into thin sticks. Put aside until it is required.

2 Heat the oil in a wok or large frying pan. Add the shallots, garlic and chillies to the pan and fry, stirring constantly, until they begin to colour.

3 Add the kecap manis and tomato purée and stir for about 2 minutes until thick, to form a sauce.

4 Add the cooked rice to the pan and continue to cook, stirring occasionally, for about 5 minutes until the rice is well coated with the sauce and heated through.

5 Meanwhile, in a large frying pan, heat a thin layer of oil for frying and crack the eggs into it. Fry for 1–2 minutes until the whites are cooked but the yolks remain runny.

6 Spoon the rice into four deep bowls. Alternatively, use one bowl as a mould to invert each portion of rice on to each individual plate, then lift off the bowl to reveal the mound of rice beneath. Place a fried egg on top of each serving and garnish with the cucumber sticks.

Noodles with Chillies Energy 293kcal/1235kJ; Protein 8.9g; Carbohydrate 44.7g, of which sugars 17.3g; Fat 10g, of which saturates 2.1g; Cholesterol 11mg; Calcium 131mg; Fibre 4.2g; Sodium 1007mg.
Indonesian Spicy Rice Energy 273kcal/1146kJ; Protein 9.9g; Carbohydrate 33g, of which sugars 4.7g; Fat 12.3g, of which saturates 2.5g; Cholesterol 190mg; Calcium 67mg; Fibre 1.1g; Sodium 884mg.

Spiced Vietnamese Chilli Rice

Although plain steamed rice is served at almost every meal in Vietnam, many families like to sneak in a little spice too. Chilli for fire, turmeric for colour, and coriander for its cooling flavour, are all that's needed.

Serves 4

15ml/1 tbsp vegetable oil
2–3 green or red Thai chillies, seeded and finely chopped
2 garlic cloves, finely chopped
2.5cm/1in piece fresh root ginger, chopped
5ml/1 tsp sugar
10–15ml/2–3 tsp ground turmeric
225g/8oz/generous 1 cup long grain rice
30ml/2 tbsp Thai fish sauce
600ml/1 pint/2½ cups water or stock
1 bunch of fresh coriander (cilantro), stalks removed, leaves finely chopped
salt and ground black pepper

1 Heat the oil in a large, heavy pan. Stir in the chillies, garlic and ginger with the sugar. As the spices begin to colour, stir in the ground turmeric.

2 Add the rice, coating it well, then pour in the fish sauce and the water or stock – the liquid should sit about 2.5cm/1in above the rice.

3 Season with salt and ground black pepper and bring the liquid to the boil. Reduce the heat, cover the pan and simmer for about 25 minutes, or until the water has been absorbed. Remove from the heat and leave the rice to steam for a further 10 minutes.

4 Transfer the rice on to a serving dish. Add some of the coriander and lightly toss together using a fork. Garnish with the remaining coriander.

Cook's Tip
This rice goes well with grilled (broiled) and stir-fried fish and shellfish dishes, but you can serve it as an alternative to plain rice. Add extra chillies, if you like.

Red-hot Mexican Rice

Versions of this dish, a relative of Spanish rice, are popular all over Latin America. It is a delicious medley of rice, tomatoes and aromatic flavourings.

Serves 6

200g/7oz/1 cup long grain rice
200g/7oz can chopped tomatoes in tomato juice
½ onion, roughly chopped
2 garlic cloves, roughly chopped
30ml/2 tbsp vegetable oil
450ml/¾ pint/scant 2 cups chicken stock
2.5ml/½ tsp salt
3 fresh fresno chillies or other fresh green chillies, trimmed
150g/5oz/1 cup frozen peas (optional)
ground black pepper

1 Put the rice in a large heatproof bowl and pour over boiling water to cover. Stir once, then leave to stand for 10 minutes. Transfer into a strainer over the sink, rinse under cold water, then drain again. Set aside to dry slightly.

2 Pour the tomatoes and juice into a food processor or blender, add the onion and garlic and process until smooth.

3 Heat the oil in a large, heavy pan, add the rice and cook over a moderate heat until it turns a delicate golden brown. Stir occasionally to ensure that the rice does not stick to the pan.

4 Add the tomato mixture and stir over a moderate heat until all the liquid has been absorbed. Stir in the stock, salt, whole chillies and peas, if using. Continue to cook, stirring occasionally, until all the liquid has been absorbed and the rice is just tender.

5 Remove the pan from the heat, cover it with a tight-fitting lid and leave it to stand in a warm place for 5–10 minutes. Remove the chillies, fluff up the rice lightly and serve, sprinkled with black pepper. The chillies may be used as a garnish, if liked.

Cook's Tip
Do not stir the rice too often after adding the stock or the grains will break down and the mixture will become starchy.

Spiced Vietnamese Chilli Rice Energy 252kcal/1066kJ; Protein 5g; Carbohydrate 51g, of which sugars 1g; Fat 5g, of which saturates 1g; Cholesterol 0mg; Calcium 24mg; Fibre 0.3g; Sodium 500mg.
Mexican Rice Energy 162kcal/676kJ; Protein 2.8g; Carbohydrate 28.4g; of which sugars 1.6g; Fat 4g; of which saturates 0.5g; Cholesterol 0mg; Calcium 11mg; Fibre 0.5g; Sodium 167mg.

Pak Choi in a Spicy Lime and Coconut Dressing

The coconut dressing for this Thai speciality is traditionally made using fish sauce, but vegetarians could use mushroom sauce instead. Beware, this is a fiery dish.

Serves 4
30ml/2 tbsp vegetable oil
3 fresh red chillies, cut into strips
4 garlic cloves, thinly sliced

6 spring onions (scallions), sliced diagonally
2 pak choi (bok choy), shredded
15ml/1 tbsp crushed peanuts
salt

For the dressing
30ml/2 tbsp fresh lime juice
15–30ml/1–2 tbsp Thai fish sauce
250ml/8fl oz/1 cup coconut milk

1 Make the dressing. Put the lime juice and fish sauce in a bowl and mix well together, then gradually whisk in the coconut milk.

2 Heat the oil in a wok and stir-fry the chillies for 2–3 minutes, until crisp. Transfer to a plate using a slotted spoon. Add the garlic to the wok and stir-fry for 30–60 seconds, until golden brown. Transfer to the plate.

3 Stir-fry the white parts of the spring onions for about 2–3 minutes, then add the green parts and stir-fry for 1 minute more. Transfer to the plate.

4 Bring a large pan of lightly salted water to the boil and add the pak choi. Stir twice, then drain immediately.

5 Place the pak choi in a bowl, add the dressing and toss to mix. Spoon into a large serving bowl and sprinkle with the peanuts and the stir-fried chilli mixture. Serve warm or cold.

Variation
This recipe can be adapted for diners who don't particularly like spicy food. Simply substitute red (bell) pepper strips for some or all of the chillies.

Chilli Cucumber Stuffed with Onions and Spices

A classic summer variety of kimchi, the refreshing natural succulence of cucumber is perfect on a hot, humid day. The spiciness of the chilli is cooled by the cucumber, with flavours that invigorate the palate.

Serves 4
15 small pickling cucumbers
30ml/2 tbsp sea salt
1 bunch Chinese chives

For the seasoning
1 onion, finely chopped
4 spring onions (scallions), thinly sliced
75ml/5 tbsp Korean chilli powder
15ml/1 tbsp Thai fish sauce
10ml/2 tsp salt
1 garlic clove, crushed
7.5ml/1½ tsp grated fresh root ginger
5ml/1 tsp sugar
5ml/1 tsp sesame seeds

1 If the cucumbers are long, cut them in half widthways. Make two slits in a cross down the length of each cucumber or cucumber half, making sure not to cut all the way to the end. Coat with the sea salt, and leave for 1 hour. Cut the Chinese chives into 2.5cm/1in lengths, cutting off and discarding the bulb.

2 Combine the onion and spring onions with the Chinese chives in a bowl. Add 45ml/3 tbsp of the chilli powder and add the Thai fish sauce, salt, garlic, ginger, sugar and sesame seeds. Mix the ingredients thoroughly by hand, using plastic gloves to prevent the chilli powder from staining your skin.

3 Lightly rinse the cucumbers to remove the salt crystals. Coat with the remaining chilli powder, and press the seasoning into the slits. Put the cucumber into an airtight container and leave at room temperature for 12 hours before serving.

Cook's Tip
Cucumber kimchi can be stored in the refrigerator, although it is best eaten within two days.

Pak Choi Energy 79kcal/329kJ; Protein 1.8g; Carbohydrate 4.5g, of which sugars 4.4g; Fat 6.1g, of which saturates 0.8g; Cholesterol 0mg; Calcium 99mg; Fibre 1.2g; Sodium 398mg.
Stuffed Chilli Cucumber Energy 32kcal/131kJ; Protein 2.5g; Carbohydrate 3.9g, of which sugars 3.4g; Fat 2.1g, of which saturates 0.2g; Cholesterol 0mg; Calcium 88mg; Fibre 1.4g; Sodium 2067mg.

Smoked Aubergine with a Spring Onion and Chilli Dressing

Aubergines can be placed in the flames of a fire, or over hot charcoal, or directly over the gas flame of a stove, and still taste great. This way of smoking or roasting them has its roots in North Africa, the Middle East, India and across South-east Asia, producing many delicious dips, purées and salads. This spicy Vietnamese version is served as a side salad to accompany meat and poultry dishes.

Serves 4
2 aubergines (eggplants)
30ml/2 tbsp groundnut (peanut) or vegetable oil
2 spring onions (scallions), finely sliced
1–2 red serrano chillies, seeded and finely sliced
15ml/1 tbsp fish sauce
25g/1oz/½ cup fresh basil leaves
salt
15ml/1 tbsp roasted peanuts, crushed, to garnish
chilli sauce, to serve

1 Place the aubergines over a barbecue or under a hot grill (broiler), or hold them on a fork or skewer directly over a gas flame on the stove and cook, turning them from time to time, until they are soft when pressed.

2 Carefully lift the aubergines by the stalk and put them into a plastic bag to sweat for 1 minute.

3 Holding the aubergines by the stalk once again, carefully peel off the skin under cold running water. Gently squeeze the excess water from the peeled flesh, remove the stalk and pull the flesh apart in long strips. Place these strips in a serving dish.

4 Heat the oil in a small pan and quickly stir in the spring onions. Remove the pan from the heat and stir in the chillies, fish sauce, basil leaves and a little salt to taste. Pour this dressing over the aubergines, toss gently and sprinkle the peanuts over the top.

5 Serve at room temperature and, for those who like a little extra fire, splash on some chilli sauce.

Mooli with Chilli and Ginger

Mooli kimchi from Korea is traditionally eaten as the autumn evenings start to draw in, with a spiciness that fortifies against the cold. The pungent aromas and tangy flavours make this one of the most popular and tasty kimchi varieties.

Serves 4
1.5kg/3½lb mooli (daikon), peeled
225g/8oz/2 cups coarse sea salt
5ml/1 tsp sugar

For the seasoning
75ml/5 tbsp Korean chilli powder
1 garlic clove, crushed
¼ onion, finely chopped
3 spring onions (scallions), finely sliced
15ml/1 tbsp sea salt
5ml/1 tsp Thai fish sauce
5ml/1 tsp fresh root ginger, peeled and finely chopped
22.5ml/4½ tsp light muscovado (brown) sugar

1 Cut the mooli into 2cm/¾in cubes. Place in a bowl and coat with the sea salt and sugar. Leave for 2 hours, draining off any water that collects at the bottom of the bowl.

2 Combine all the ingredients for the seasoning and mix well with the salted mooli. Place the mooli in an airtight container and seal. Leave at room temperature for 24 hours and chill before serving.

Cook's Tip
Kimchi is a pungent condiment served at almost every Korean meal. Various vegetables – such as cabbage or turnips – are pickled then traditionally stored in sealed pots to ferment.

Variations
• *Blend half an onion in a food processor and add it to the seasoning for a tangier taste and subtle sweetness.*
• *For extra kick you could add a finely chopped red chilli to the seasoning, but be warned, this will make the dish extremely hot.*

Mooli with Ginger Energy 73kcal/302kJ; Protein 3.1g; Carbohydrate 14g, of which sugars 13.6g; Fat 0.8g, of which saturates 0.4g; Cholesterol 0mg; Calcium 81mg; Fibre 3.7g; Sodium 1203mg.
Smoked Aubergine Energy 215kcal/890kJ; Protein 10g; Carbohydrate 6g, of which sugars 4g; Fat 17g, of which saturates 3g; Cholesterol 0mg; Calcium 425mg; Fibre 0.8g; Sodium 700mg.

Red-hot Chilli Cauliflower

Vegetables are seldom
served plain in Mexico.
The cauliflower here is
flavoured with a simple
tomato salsa and feta
cheese. The salsa could be
any table salsa; tomatillo is
particularly good. The
contrast of the hot spicy
salsa with the texture and
mild flavour of the
cauliflower makes for a
tasty dish.

Serves 6
1 small onion
1 lime
1 medium cauliflower
400g/14oz can chopped tomatoes
*4 fresh serrano chillies, seeded
  and finely chopped*
*1.5ml/¼ tsp caster
  (superfine) sugar*
75g/3oz feta cheese, crumbled
salt
*chopped fresh flat leaf parsley,
  to garnish*

1 Chop the onion very finely and place in a bowl. With a
cannelle knife (zester), peel away the rind of the lime in thin
strips. Add to the chopped onion.

2 Cut the lime in half and add the juice from both halves to
the bowl containing the onions and lime rind mixture. Set aside
so that the lime juice can soften the onion. Cut the cauliflower
into florets.

3 Place the tomatoes in a pan and add the chillies and sugar.
Heat the mixture gently. Meanwhile, place the cauliflower in a
pan of boiling water, reduce the heat and cook gently for about
5–8 minutes, until tender.

4 Add the onions to the tomato salsa in the pan, with salt to
taste, stir in and heat through, then spoon about a third of the
salsa into a serving dish.

5 Arrange the drained cauliflower florets on top of the salsa in
the serving dish and then spoon the remaining salsa on top of
the florets.

6 Sprinkle the feta cheese over the top – it should soften a
little on contact. Serve immediately, sprinkled with chopped
fresh flat leaf parsley.

Deep-fried Aubergine with Spicy Garlic Sauce

This dish is often served
at the many rice stalls
throughout Singapore as an
accompaniment to a main
rice dish. Many of the cooks
at the stalls, and in the
home, make up batches of
different sambals to be
stored and used for making
quick and simple dishes like
this one. Generally, the
aubergines will be cooked
by deep-frying at the
hawker stalls, but you could
bake them in the oven at
home. Serve this dish as a
spicy snack to go with a
chunk of fresh bread or as a
side dish to accompany a
more substantial rice dish
or grilled meats.

Serves 2 to 4
6 shallots, chopped
4 garlic cloves, chopped
2 red chillies, seeded and chopped
*1 lemon grass stalk, trimmed
  and chopped*
5ml/1 tsp shrimp paste
15ml/1 tbsp sesame oil
15–30ml/1–2 tbsp soy sauce
7.5ml/1½ tsp sugar
vegetable oil, for deep-frying
*2 slender, purple aubergines
  (eggplants), partially peeled in
  strips and halved lengthways*

To garnish
*1 green chilli, seeded and
  finely chopped*
*a small bunch each of fresh mint
  and coriander (cilantro), stalks
  removed, finely chopped*

1 Using a mortar and pestle or food processor, grind the
shallots, garlic, chillies and lemon grass to a paste. Beat in the
shrimp paste and mix well.

2 Heat the sesame oil in a small wok or heavy pan. Stir in the
spice paste and cook until fragrant and brown. Stir in the soy
sauce and sugar and cook until smooth. Remove from the heat.

3 Heat enough oil for deep-frying in a wok or heavy pan. Drop
in the aubergine halves and fry until tender. Drain on kitchen
paper, then press the centres to make a dip or shallow pouch.

4 Arrange the aubergine halves on a plate and smear with the
spicy sauce. Garnish with the chopped green chilli, mint and
coriander and serve at room temperature.

Red-hot Chilli Cauliflower Energy 63kcal/262kJ; Protein 4.2g; Carbohydrate 4.5g, of which sugars 4g; Fat 3.2g, of which saturates 1.9g; Cholesterol 9mg; Calcium 74mg; Fibre 1.9g; Sodium 192mg.
Deep-fried Aubergine Energy 158kcal/654kJ; Protein 1.6g; Carbohydrate 6.5g, of which sugars 5.1g; Fat 14.2g, of which saturates 1.8g; Cholesterol 0mg; Calcium 24mg; Fibre 2.7g; Sodium 271mg.

Black Gram in a Spiced Cream Sauce

Dhabas are highway cafés throughout India and are very lively eating places serving a variety of dishes. This bean recipe is commonly served, and is one of the most popular.

Serves 4 to 6

175g/6oz black gram, (lentils) soaked overnight
50g/2oz red gram (lentils)
120ml/4fl oz/½ cup double (heavy) cream
120ml/4fl oz/½ cup natural (plain) yogurt
5ml/1 tsp cornflour (cornstarch)
45ml/3 tbsp ghee
1 onion, finely chopped
5cm/2in piece fresh root ginger, crushed
4 green chillies, chopped
1 tomato, chopped
2.5ml/½ tsp chilli powder
2.5ml/½ tsp ground turmeric
2.5ml/½ tsp ground cumin
2 garlic cloves, sliced
salt

1 Drain the black gram and place in a heavy pan with the red gram. Cover with water and bring to the boil. Reduce the heat, cover the pan and simmer until the gram are tender. The black gram will remain whole but the red gram will be mushy. Gently mash with a spoon. Allow to cool.

2 In a bowl, mix together the cream, yogurt and cornflour. Mix into the gram without breaking the black gram grains.

3 Heat 15ml/1 tbsp of the ghee in a frying pan and fry the onion, ginger, two of the green chillies and the tomato until the onion is soft and translucent. Add the spices and salt and fry for a further 2 minutes. Add it all to the gram mixture and mix well. Reheat, transfer to a heatproof serving dish and keep warm.

4 Heat the remaining ghee in a frying pan and fry the garlic slices and the remaining chillies until the garlic is golden.

5 Pour over the gram and serve, folding the garlic and chilli into the gram just before serving. Place extra cream on the table for the diners to add more, if they wish.

Lentils with Chilli, Ginger and Coconut Milk

For the largely vegetarian South Indian population spicy dhal dishes such as this one are an important source of protein.

Serves 4

30ml/2 tbsp ghee, or 15ml/1 tbsp vegetable oil and 15g/½oz/ 1 tbsp butter
1 onion, chopped
4 garlic cloves, chopped
2 fresh red chillies, seeded and chopped
50g/2oz fresh root ginger, peeled and chopped
10ml/2 tsp sugar
7.5ml/1½ tsp cumin seeds
5ml/1 tsp ground turmeric
15ml/1 tbsp garam masala
225g/8oz/generous 1 cup brown lentils, washed thoroughly and drained
600ml/1 pint/2½ cups coconut milk
salt
natural (plain) yogurt or curry, rice and chutney, to serve

For the garnish

10ml/2 tsp mustard seeds
a small handful dried curry leaves
1–2 dried red chillies
15ml/1 tbsp ghee

1 Heat the ghee, or oil and butter, in a heavy pan. Stir in the onion, garlic, chillies and ginger and fry until fragrant and beginning to colour.

2 Add the sugar, cumin seeds, turmeric and garam masala, taking care not to burn the spices. Stir in the lentils and coat in the spices and ghee. Pour in 600ml/1 pint/2½ cups water, mix thoroughly, and bring to the boil. Reduce the heat and allow to simmer gently for 35–40 minutes until the mixture is thick.

3 Stir in the coconut milk and simmer for a further 30 minutes until thick and mushy – if at any time the dhal seems too dry, add more water or coconut milk. Season to taste with salt.

4 In a small pan, heat the mustard seeds. As soon as they begin to pop, add the curry leaves and chillies. When the chillies start to darken, stir in the ghee until it melts. Spoon the mixture over the dhal, or fold it in until well mixed. Serve the dhal with yogurt or with a curry, rice and chutney.

Spicy Gram Energy 283kcal/1181kJ; Protein 10.1g; Carbohydrate 23g, of which sugars 5.6g; Fat 17.4g, of which saturates 9.3g; Cholesterol 23mg; Calcium 86mg; Fibre 6.8g; Sodium 32mg.
Lentils with Chilli Energy 322kcal/1358kJ; Protein 14g; Carbohydrate 41.3g, of which sugars 10.6g; Fat 12.4g, of which saturates 5.7g; Cholesterol 0mg; Calcium 77mg; Fibre 3g; Sodium 186mg.

Dhal Seasoned with Fried Spices

Dhals, made with lentils, are cooked in every house in India in one form or another. This recipe is for a quick and easy version of this spicy classic.

Serves 4 to 6

115g/4oz red gram, washed and picked over
50g/2oz Bengal gram, washed and picked over
350ml/12fl oz/1½ cups water
4 whole green chillies
5ml/1 tsp ground turmeric
1 large onion, sliced
400g/14oz canned plum tomatoes, crushed
60ml/4 tbsp vegetable oil
2.5ml/½ tsp mustard seeds
2.5ml/½ tsp cumin seeds
1 clove garlic, crushed
6 curry leaves
2 whole dried red chillies
1.5ml/¼ tsp asafoetida
salt
fresh coriander (cilantro) leaves, to garnish

1 Put both kinds of lentils, the water, chillies, turmeric and onion in a heavy pan and bring to the boil. Cover the pan and simmer until the pulses are soft and the water has been absorbed.

2 Mash the lentils with the back of a spoon. When nearly smooth, add the salt and tomatoes and mix well. If necessary, thin the mixture with hot water.

3 Heat the vegetable oil in a large frying pan and cook the mustard and cumin seeds for 1–2 minutes until they start to splutter and release their fragrances.

4 Add the garlic, curry leaves, dried chillies and asafoetida to the pan. Fry until the garlic begins to turn brown. Ensure that it does not burn, otherwise it will taste bitter.

5 Pour the spice mixture over the lentils and cover the pan. Return to the heat. After 5 minutes, mix well, garnish and serve.

Cook's Tip
If you prefer a little more heat in your spicy dishes, then increase the number of dried chillies used in this dish.

Potatoes with Crushed Red Chillies and Spices

If you like chillies, you'll love these spicy potatoes. If you're not a fan of fiery flavours, leave out the chilli seeds and just use the flesh.

Serves 4

12–14 small new or salad potatoes, halved
30ml/2 tbsp vegetable oil
2.5ml/½ tsp crushed dried red chillies
2.5ml/½ tsp white cumin seeds
2.5ml/½ tsp fennel seeds
2.5ml/½ tsp crushed coriander seeds
5ml/1 tsp salt
1 onion, sliced
1–4 fresh red chillies, chopped
15ml/1 tbsp chopped fresh coriander (cilantro)
chopped fresh coriander (cilantro), to garnish

1 Cook the potatoes in boiling salted water until just tender. Remove from the heat and drain. Set aside until needed.

2 In a deep frying pan, heat the oil over a medium-high heat, then reduce the heat to medium. Add the crushed chillies, cumin, fennel and coriander seeds and salt and fry, stirring, for 30–40 seconds, until the spices start to release their fragrances.

3 Add the sliced onion to the pan and fry for 4–5 minutes until golden brown. Then add the potatoes, red chillies and coriander and stir well.

4 Reduce the heat to very low, then cover the pan and cook for about 5–7 minutes.

5 Serve the potatoes hot, garnished with fresh coriander.

Cook's Tip
To prepare fresh chillies, slit down one side and scrape out the seeds, unless you want a really hot dish. Finely slice or chop the flesh. Wear rubber gloves if you have very sensitive skin that is irritated by the oils in chillies.

Dhal with Fried Spices Energy 213kcal/893kJ; Protein 9.1g; Carbohydrate 25.7g, of which sugars 6.5g; Fat 9.1g, of which saturates 1.1g; Cholesterol 0mg; Calcium 50mg; Fibre 3g; Sodium 21mg.
Potatoes with Chillies Energy 101kcal/421kJ; Protein 1.4g; Carbohydrate 11.4g, of which sugars 1.8g; Fat 5.8g, of which saturates 0.7g; Cholesterol 0mg; Calcium 20mg; Fibre 1.2g; Sodium 501mg.

Potato Curry with Yogurt and Green Chillies

Variations of this simple Indian curry are popular in Singapore at market stalls, where it is served with flatbread. Generally, it is served with a meat curry and rice, but it is also delicious on its own, served with yogurt and a spicy pickle or chutney.

Serves 4

6 garlic cloves, chopped
25g/1oz fresh root ginger, peeled and chopped
30ml/2 tbsp ghee, or 15ml/1 tbsp oil and 15g/^{1}/$_2$oz/1 tbsp butter
6 shallots, halved lengthways and sliced along the grain
2 green chillies, seeded and finely sliced
10ml/2 tsp sugar
a handful of fresh or dried curry leaves
2 cinnamon sticks
5–10ml/1–2 tsp ground turmeric
15ml/1 tbsp garam masala
500g/1^1/$_4$lb waxy potatoes, cut into bitesize pieces
2 tomatoes, peeled, seeded and quartered
250ml/8fl oz/1 cup Greek (US strained plain) yogurt
salt and ground black pepper
5ml/1 tsp red chilli powder, and fresh coriander (cilantro) and mint leaves, chopped, to garnish
1 lemon, quartered, to serve

1 Using a mortar and pestle or a food processor, grind the garlic and ginger to a coarse paste. Heat the ghee in a heavy pan and stir in the shallots and chillies, until fragrant. Add the garlic and ginger paste with the sugar, and stir until the mixture begins to colour. Stir in the curry leaves, cinnamon sticks, turmeric and garam masala, and toss in the potatoes, making sure they are coated in the spice mixture.

2 Pour in just enough cold water to cover the potatoes. Bring to the boil, then reduce the heat and simmer until the potatoes are just cooked – they should still have a bite to them.

3 Season with salt and pepper to taste. Gently toss in the tomatoes to heat them through. Fold in the yogurt so that it is streaky rather than completely mixed in. Sprinkle with the chilli powder, coriander and mint. Serve immediately from the pan, with lemon to squeeze over it and flatbread for scooping it up.

Chilli Bombay Potatoes

A classic Indian vegetarian dish of potatoes slowly cooked in a richly flavoured curry sauce with fresh chillies for an added kick.

Serves 4 to 6

450g/1lb new or small salad potatoes
5ml/1 tsp ground turmeric
60ml/4 tbsp vegetable oil
2 dried red chillies
6–8 curry leaves
2 onions, finely chopped
2 fresh green chillies, finely chopped
50g/2oz coriander (cilantro) leaves, coarsely chopped
1.5ml/^{1}/$_4$ tsp asafoetida
2.5ml/^{1}/$_2$ tsp each cumin, mustard, onion, fennel and nigella seeds
lemon juice
salt
fresh fried curry leaves, to garnish (optional)

1 Chop the potatoes into small chunks and cook in boiling lightly salted water with 2.5ml/^{1}/$_2$ tsp of the turmeric until tender. Drain, then coarsely mash. Set aside.

2 Heat the oil in a large, heavy frying pan and fry the red chillies and curry leaves, stirring constantly, until the chillies are nearly burnt.

3 Add the onions, green chillies, coriander, the remaining turmeric, asafoetida and spice seeds to the pan. Cook for about 4–5 minutes, stirring occasionally, until the onions are soft and turning translucent, the seeds are spluttering and the spices are releasing their fragrances.

4 Fold in the potatoes and add a few drops of water. Cook on a low heat for about 10 minutes, mixing well to ensure the even distribution of the spices.

5 When the potatoes are heated through, remove the dried chillies and curry leaves from the pan.

6 Transfer the spicy potatoes to a warmed serving dish and serve immediately, with lemon juice squeezed or poured over, to taste. Garnish the potatoes with the fresh fried curry leaves, if you wish.

Potato Curry Energy 231kcal/967kJ; Protein 6.7g; Carbohydrate 26.2g, of which sugars 7.4g; Fat 12.4g, of which saturates 4.1g; Cholesterol 0mg; Calcium 110mg; Fibre 2g; Sodium 63mg.
Chilli Bombay Potatoes Energy 208kcal/869kJ; Protein 4g; Carbohydrate 24g, of which sugars 6g; Fat 12g, of which saturates 1g; Cholesterol 0mg; Calcium 59mg; Fibre 2.2g; Sodium 100mg.

Refreshing Fruit Salad in a Tangy Dressing

Entrenched in the Indonesian culinary culture, this salad appears in many guises – as a snack, as a salad to accompany fried and grilled dishes, or as a festive dish. Designed to be flexible, this refreshing salad, tossed in a pungent and tangy dressing, can include any choice of fruit and vegetables that you have available.

Serves 4 to 6
1 green mango, finely sliced
1 ripe, firm papaya, finely sliced
1–2 star fruit (carambola), finely sliced
½ pineapple, finely sliced and cut into bitesize pieces
½ pomelo, segmented
1 small cucumber, roughly peeled, seeded, and finely sliced
1 yam bean, finely sliced
a handful of beansprouts

For the sauce
10ml/2 tsp shrimp paste
225g/8oz roasted peanuts
4 garlic cloves, chopped
2–4 red chillies, seeded and chopped
15ml/1 tbsp tamarind paste
30ml/2 tbsp palm sugar (jaggery)
salt

1 To make the sauce, dry-roast the shrimp paste in a small, heavy frying pan, stirring, until browned and emitting a toasted, pungent aroma.

2 Using a mortar and pestle or an electric blender, grind the peanuts, garlic and chillies to form a coarse paste. Beat in the dry-fried shrimp paste, tamarind paste and the sugar. Add enough water to the mixture to make a thick, pouring sauce, then stir until the sugar has completely dissolved. Season the sauce with salt to taste.

3 Put all the fruit and vegetables, except the beansprouts, into a large bowl. Pour in some of the sauce and toss gently together. Leave the salad to stand for 30 minutes.

4 Transfer the salad into a serving dish. Sprinkle the beansprouts over the top and serve with the remaining sauce drizzled over the top.

Serrano Chilli and Spinach Salad

Young spinach leaves make a welcome change from lettuce and are excellent in salads. The roasted garlic is an inspired addition to the spicy dressing.

Serves 6
500g/1¼lb baby spinach leaves
50g/2oz/⅓ cup sesame seeds
50g/2oz/¼ cup butter
30ml/2 tbsp olive oil
6 shallots, sliced
8 fresh serrano chillies, seeded and cut into strips
4 tomatoes, sliced

For the dressing
6 roasted garlic cloves
120ml/4fl oz/½ cup white wine vinegar
2.5ml/½ tsp ground white pepper
1 bay leaf
2.5ml/½ tsp ground allspice
30ml/2 tbsp chopped fresh thyme, plus extra sprigs, to garnish

1 Make the dressing. Remove the skins from the garlic when cool, then chop and combine with the vinegar, pepper, bay leaf, allspice and chopped thyme in a jar with a screw-top lid. Close the lid tightly, shake well, then put the dressing in the refrigerator until needed.

2 Wash the spinach leaves and dry them in a salad spinner or clean dish towel. Put them in a plastic bag in the refrigerator.

3 Toast the sesame seeds in a dry frying pan, shaking frequently over a moderate heat until golden. Set aside.

4 Heat the butter and oil in a frying pan. Fry the shallots for 4–5 minutes, until softened, then stir in the chilli strips and fry for 2–3 minutes more.

5 In a large bowl, layer the spinach with the shallot and chilli mixture, and the tomato slices. Pour over the dressing. Sprinkle with sesame seeds and serve, garnished with thyme sprigs.

> **Cook's Tip**
> To roast garlic, place in a roasting pan in the oven at 180°C/350°F/Gas 4 for about 15 minutes until soft.

Refreshing Fruit Salad Energy 321kcal/1344kJ; Protein 12.3g; Carbohydrate 30g, of which sugars 27.2g; Fat 17.7g, of which saturates 3.3g; Cholesterol 8mg; Calcium 91mg; Fibre 6.2g; Sodium 81mg.
Serrano and Spinach Salad Energy 181kcal/748kJ; Protein 4.7g; Carbohydrate 4.2g, of which sugars 4.1g; Fat 16.3g, of which saturates 5.7g; Cholesterol 18mg; Calcium 209mg; Fibre 3.4g; Sodium 177mg.

Squid and Seaweed with Chilli Dressing

This chilled seafood salad makes a great appetizer, and really stimulates the appetite. The flavours of chilli and rice vinegar are balanced by sweet maple syrup, with the kelp providing a tantalizing aroma and taste.

Serves 2
400g/14oz squid, cleaned
    and gutted
180g/7oz dried kelp,
    roughly chopped

2 cucumbers, thinly sliced
10ml/2 tsp sesame seeds
6 spring onions (scallions),
    finely chopped
2 dried red chillies, finely chopped
salt

For the dressing
30ml/2 tbsp rice vinegar
2 garlic cloves, crushed
60ml/4 tbsp gochujang chilli paste
60ml/4 tbsp maple syrup
15ml/1 tbsp grated fresh
    root ginger

1 Use a sharp knife to score the squid with a criss-cross pattern, and slice into generous pieces about 4cm/1½in long.

2 Soak the kelp in cold water for 20 minutes and blanch in boiling water for 1 minute, draining it almost immediately to retain its texture and colour. Squeeze any excess water from the leaves by hand. Roughly chop the kelp into bitesize pieces.

3 Place the thinly sliced cucumber in a colander and sprinkle with salt. Leave for 10 minutes for the salt to draw out some of the cucumber's moisture, and then pour away any excess liquid.

4 Combine all the dressing ingredients in a large bowl, mixing well to ensure they are thoroughly combined.

5 Bring a pan of water to the boil over high heat. Blanch the squid for 3 minutes, stirring constantly, then drain under cold running water. Place the squid, cucumber and kelp on a serving platter and pour the dressing over the dish. Chill in the refrigerator, and sprinkle with the sesame seeds, spring onions and chillies before serving.

Spicy Seafood Salad with Fragrant Herbs

This is a spectacular salad. The luscious combination of prawns, scallops and squid makes it the ideal choice for a special celebration. Any chilli-lovers will appreciate the presence of plenty of red chillies, which give this fragrant salad a deliciously spicy kick. Should you want it to be any hotter, use the seeds from the chillies in the salad as well.

Serves 4 to 6
250ml/8fl oz/1 cup fish stock
    or water
350g/12oz squid, cleaned and
    cut into rings
12 raw king prawns (jumbo
    shrimp), peeled and deveined,
    with tails intact

12 scallops
50g/2oz cellophane noodles,
    soaked in warm water for
    30 minutes
½ cucumber, cut into thin batons
1 lemon grass stalk, finely
    chopped
2 kaffir lime leaves, finely
    shredded
2 shallots, thinly sliced
30ml/2 tbsp chopped spring
    onions (scallions)
30ml/2 tbsp fresh coriander
    (cilantro) leaves
12–15 fresh mint leaves,
    coarsely torn
4 fresh red chillies, seeded and
    cut into slivers
juice of 1–2 limes
30ml/2 tbsp Thai fish sauce
fresh coriander (cilantro) sprigs,
    to garnish

1 Pour the fish stock or water into a medium pan set over a high heat and bring to the boil. Cook each type of seafood separately in the stock for 3–4 minutes. Remove with a slotted spoon and set aside to cool.

2 Drain the noodles. Cut them into short lengths, about 5cm/2in long. Place them in a serving bowl and add the cucumber, lemon grass, lime leaves, shallots, spring onions, coriander, mint and chillies.

3 Pour over the lime juice and fish sauce. Mix well, then add the seafood. Toss lightly.

4 Garnish the salad with the fresh coriander sprigs and then serve immediately.

Squid and Seaweed Energy 321kcal/1354kJ; Protein 35.6g; Carbohydrate 30g, of which sugars 27.3g; Fat 7.3g, of which saturates 1.3g; Cholesterol 450mg; Calcium 247mg; Fibre 3.3g; Sodium 433mg.
Spicy Seafood Salad Energy 137kcal/578kJ; Protein 20g; Carbohydrate 10.2g, of which sugars 1.2g; Fat 1.8g, of which saturates 0.4g; Cholesterol 171mg; Calcium 61mg; Fibre 0.9g; Sodium 154mg.

Chilli Chicken and Prawn Salad

This delicious Indonesian salad is spicy and refreshing.

Serves 4
500g/1¼lb chicken breast fillets
 or thighs
225g/8oz prawns (shrimp),
 shelled and deveined
30ml/2 tbsp groundnut (peanut) oil
5ml/1 tsp blachan (shrimp paste)
10ml/2 tsp palm sugar (jaggery)
2 tomatoes, skinned, seeded
 and chopped
1 bunch fresh coriander (cilantro)
 leaves, chopped
1 bunch fresh mint leaves, chopped
juice of 1 lime
salt and ground black pepper

For the spice paste
2 shallots, chopped
2 garlic cloves, chopped
2–3 fresh red chillies, seeded
 and chopped
25g/1oz galangal, chopped
15g/½oz fresh turmeric, chopped,
 or 2.5ml/½ tsp ground turmeric
1 lemon grass stalk, chopped
2 candlenuts, chopped

To serve
1 lime, quartered
2 fresh green or red chillies,
 seeded and cut into quarters
 lengthways

1 Cook the chicken pieces according to your preference by steaming, roasting or boiling. When cooked, if using chicken breast fillets, cut the meat into thin strips and, if using thighs, shred the meat with your fingers. Set aside.

2 Boil or steam the prawns for 2–3 minutes, drain and refresh under cold running water, then drain again. Put aside.

3 To make the spice paste, using a mortar and pestle, grind the shallots, garlic, chillies, galangal, turmeric, lemon grass and candlenuts together to form a paste.

4 Heat the oil in a pan, stir in the spice paste and fry for a minute. Add the shrimp paste and sugar and stir for 3–4 minutes, until the paste browns. Add the tomatoes, coriander, mint and lime juice and cook for 5–10 minutes, until the sauce is reduced and thick. Season and put in a large bowl. Leave to cool.

5 Add the chicken and prawns to the bowl and toss well. Serve with the lime wedges, and the chillies to chew on.

Tangy Chicken Salad

This fresh and lively dish typifies the character of Thai cuisine. It is ideal for a spicy light lunch on a hot and lazy summer's day.

Serves 4 to 6
4 skinless chicken breast fillets
2 garlic cloves, crushed
30ml/2 tbsp soy sauce
30ml/2 tbsp vegetable oil
120ml/4fl oz/½ cup
 coconut cream
30ml/2 tbsp Thai fish sauce
juice of 1 lime
30ml/2 tbsp palm sugar (jaggery)
 or light muscovado
 (brown) sugar

115g/4oz/½ cup canned water
 chestnuts, sliced
50g/2oz/½ cup cashew nuts,
 roasted and coarsely chopped
4 shallots, thinly sliced
4 kaffir lime leaves, thinly sliced
1 lemon grass stalk, bruised and
 thinly sliced
5ml/1 tsp chopped fresh galangal
1 large fresh red chilli, seeded and
 finely chopped
10–12 fresh mint leaves, torn
2 spring onions (scallions),
 thinly sliced
2 fresh red chillies, seeded and
 sliced, to garnish
1 lettuce, separated into leaves,
 to serve

1 Place the chicken in a large dish. Rub with the garlic, soy sauce and 15ml/1 tbsp of the oil. Cover and leave to marinate for 1–2 hours.

2 Heat the remaining oil in a wok or frying pan and stir-fry the chicken for 3–4 minutes on each side, or until cooked. Remove and set aside to cool.

3 In a pan, heat the coconut cream, fish sauce, lime juice and sugar. Stir until the sugar has dissolved; set aside.

4 Tear the cooked chicken into strips and put it in a bowl. Add the water chestnuts, cashew nuts, shallots, kaffir lime leaves, lemon grass, galangal, red chilli, mint leaves and spring onions. Mix the ingredients together until well combined.

5 Pour the coconut dressing over the mixture and toss well again so that everything is evenly coated in the dressing. Serve the chicken on a bed of lettuce leaves and garnish with sliced red chillies.

Chilli Chicken Salad Energy 274kcal/1154kJ; Protein 41.6g; Carbohydrate 10.4g, of which sugars 8.7g; Fat 7.7g, of which saturates 1.1g; Cholesterol 197mg; Calcium 99mg; Fibre 2.2g; Sodium 193mg.
Chicken Salad Energy 404kcal/1691kJ; Protein 40.4g; Carbohydrate 11.3g, of which sugars 9g; Fat 22.3g, of which saturates 9.8g; Cholesterol 105mg; Calcium 25mg; Fibre 0.8g; Sodium 666mg.

Thai Chicken Salad

Chiang Mai is a city in the north-east of Thailand. The city is culturally very close to Laos. It is famous for its chicken salad, which was originally called 'laap' or 'larp'. Duck, beef or pork can be used instead of chicken.

Serves 4 to 6

450g/1lb minced (ground) chicken
lower 5cm/2in of 1 lemon grass
   stalk, root trimmed
3 kaffir lime leaves
4 fresh red chillies, seeded
   and chopped
60ml/4 tbsp fresh lime juice
30ml/2 tbsp Thai fish sauce
15ml/1 tbsp roasted ground rice
   (see Cook's Tip)
2 spring onions (scallions),
   finely chopped
30ml/2 tbsp fresh coriander
   (cilantro) leaves
thinly sliced kaffir lime leaves,
   mixed salad leaves and fresh
   mint sprigs, to garnish

1 Heat a wok or large, heavy frying pan. Add the minced chicken and moisten with a little water. Stir constantly over a medium heat for 7–10 minutes, until it is cooked through. Remove the pan from the heat and drain off any excess fat. Finely chop the trimmed lemon grass stalk and the kaffir lime leaves.

2 Transfer the cooked chicken to a large bowl and add the chopped lemon grass, lime leaves, chillies, lime juice, fish sauce, roasted ground rice, spring onions and coriander. Mix all the ingredients thoroughly.

3 Spoon the chicken mixture into a salad bowl. Sprinkle sliced lime leaves over the top and garnish with salad leaves and sprigs of mint.

> **Cook's Tip**
> Use glutinous rice for the roasted ground rice. Put the rice in a frying pan and dry-roast it until golden brown. Remove and grind to a powder, using a mortar and pestle or a food processor. When the rice is cold, store it in a glass jar in a cool and dry place.

Chilli Beef Salad

A hearty main meal salad from Thailand. It combines tender strips of sirloin steak with thinly shredded cucumber and a piquant chilli and lime dressing.

Serves 4

2 sirloin steaks, each weighing
   about 225g/8oz
1 lemon grass stalk, root trimmed
1 red onion or 4 Thai shallots,
   thinly sliced
½ cucumber, cut into strips
30ml/2 tbsp chopped spring
   onion (scallion)
juice of 2 limes
15–30ml/1–2 tbsp Thai
   fish sauce
2–4 fresh red chillies, seeded and
   finely chopped
Chinese mustard cress, salad cress
   or fresh coriander (cilantro),
   to garnish

1 Pan-fry the steaks in a large, heavy frying pan over a medium heat. Cook them for 4–6 minutes for rare, 6–8 minutes for medium and about 10 minutes for well done, depending on their thickness. (In Thailand the beef is traditionally served quite rare.) Alternatively, cook them under a preheated grill (broiler). Remove the steaks from the pan and leave to rest for 10–15 minutes. Meanwhile, cut off the lower 5cm/2in from the lemon grass stalk and chop it finely. Discard the remainder.

2 When the meat is cool, slice it thinly and put the slices in a large bowl. Add the sliced onion or shallots, cucumber, lemon grass and chopped spring onion to the meat slices.

3 Toss the salad and add lime juice and fish sauce to taste. Add the red chillies and toss again. Transfer to a serving bowl or plate. Serve the salad at room temperature or chilled, garnished with the Chinese mustard cress, salad cress or coriander leaves.

> **Cook's Tip**
> Look for gui chai leaves in Thai and Chinese groceries. These look like very thin spring onions (scallions) and are often used as a substitute for the more familiar vegetable.

Thai Chicken Salad Energy 135kcal/572kJ; Protein 27.4g; Carbohydrate 3.4g, of which sugars 0.4g; Fat 1.3g, of which saturates 0.4g; Cholesterol 79mg; Calcium 8mg; Fibre 0.1g; Sodium 424mg.
Chilli Beef Salad Energy 161kcal/674kJ; Protein 26.9g; Carbohydrate 1.8g, of which sugars 1.4g; Fat 5.1g, of which saturates 2.3g; Cholesterol 57mg; Calcium 14mg; Fibre 0.3g; Sodium 873mg.

Lemon, Chilli and Garlic Relish

This powerful relish is flavoured with North African spices and punchy preserved lemons, which are widely available in Middle Eastern stores. It is great served with Moroccan tagines.

Makes I small jar
45ml/3 tbsp olive oil
3 large red onions, sliced
2 heads of garlic, separated into
   cloves and peeled
10ml/2 tsp coriander
   seeds, crushed
10ml/2 tsp light muscovado
   (brown) sugar, plus a little extra
pinch of saffron threads
5cm/2in piece cinnamon stick
2–3 small whole dried red
   chillies (optional)
2 fresh bay leaves
30–45ml/2–3 tbsp sherry vinegar
juice of ½ small orange
30ml/2 tbsp chopped
   preserved lemon
salt and ground black pepper

I Gently heat the oil in a large heavy pan. Add the onions and stir, then cover and cook on the lowest setting for 10–15 minutes, stirring occasionally, until soft.

2 Add the garlic cloves and the coriander seeds. Cover and cook for 5–8 minutes, until soft.

3 Add a pinch of salt, lots of ground black pepper and the sugar to the onions and cook, uncovered, for a further 5 minutes.

4 Soak the saffron in about 45ml/3 tbsp warm water for 5 minutes, then add to the onions, together with the soaking water. Add the cinnamon, dried chillies, if using, and bay leaves. Stir in 30ml/2 tbsp of the sherry vinegar and the orange juice.

5 Cook very gently, uncovered, until the onions are very soft and most of the liquid has evaporated. Stir in the preserved lemon and cook gently for 5 minutes.

6 Taste the relish and adjust the seasoning, adding more salt, sugar and/or vinegar to taste.

7 Serve warm or cold (not hot or chilled). The relish tastes best if left to stand for 24 hours.

Chilli Strips with Lime

This fresh relish is ideal for serving with stews, rice dishes or bean dishes. The oregano adds a sweet note and the absence of sugar or oil makes this a very healthy choice.

Makes about 60ml/4 tbsp
10 fresh green chillies
½ white onion
4 limes
2.5ml/½ tsp dried oregano
salt

I Roast the chillies in a griddle pan over a moderate heat until the skins are charred and blistered. The flesh should not be allowed to blacken as this might make the salsa bitter. Place the roasted chillies in a strong plastic bag and tie the top to keep the steam in. Set aside for 20 minutes.

2 Meanwhile, slice the onion very thinly and put it in a large bowl. Squeeze the limes and strain the juice into the bowl, adding any pulp that gathers in the strainer. The lime juice will soften the onion. Stir in the oregano.

3 Remove the chillies from the bag and peel off the skins. Slit them, scrape out the seeds with a small sharp knife, then cut the chillies into long strips.

4 Add the chilli strips to the onion mixture, mixing well, and season with salt.

5 Cover the bowl and chill in the refrigerator for at least I day before serving. This will allow the flavours to blend together. The salsa will keep for up to 2 weeks in a well-covered bowl in the refrigerator.

Cook's Tip
This method of roasting chillies is ideal if you need more than one or two, or if you do not have a gas burner. To roast over a burner, spear the chillies, four or five at a time, on a long-handled metal skewer and hold them over the flame until the skins blister.

Lemon and Chilli Relish Energy 102kcal/422kJ; Protein 1.9g; Carbohydrate 11.4g, of which sugars 7.8g; Fat 5.7g, of which saturates 0.8g; Cholesterol 0mg; Calcium 28mg; Fibre 1.7g; Sodium 4mg.
Chilli Strips with Lime Energy 45kcal/189kJ; Protein 3.8g; Carbohydrate 6.2g, of which sugars 4.9g; Fat 0.7g, of which saturates 0g; Cholesterol 49mg; Calcium 49mg; Fibre 0.9g; Sodium 9mg.

Green Chilli Pickle

Southern India is the source of some of the hottest curries and pickles, which are said to help cool the body in the hot climate. This fiery pickle should be used sparingly as an accompaniment to spicy food.

Makes 450–550g/1–1¼lb/2–2½ cups

50g/2oz yellow mustard seeds, crushed

50g/2oz freshly ground cumin seeds

25g/1oz ground turmeric

50g/2oz garlic cloves, crushed

150ml/¼ pint/⅔ cup white vinegar

75g/3oz sugar

10ml/2 tsp salt

150ml/¼ pint/⅔ cup mustard oil

20 small garlic cloves, peeled and left whole

450g/1lb small green chillies, washed, dried and halved

1 Mix the mustard seeds, cumin, turmeric, crushed garlic, vinegar, sugar and salt together in a sterilized glass bowl. Cover with a cloth and allow to rest for 24 hours. This enables the flavours of the spices to mingle together and allows time for the sugar and salt to dissolve.

2 Heat the mustard oil in a wok or frying pan and gently fry the spice mixture for about 5 minutes until it releases its fragrances. (Keep a window open while cooking with mustard oil as it is pungent and the smoke may irritate the eyes.)

3 Add the whole garlic cloves to the pan and fry, stirring constantly, for a further 5 minutes until they turn a light brown colour. Ensure that the garlic does not burn, otherwise it will impart a bitter taste to the pickle.

4 Add the chillies to the pan and cook them gently until they are tender but still green in colour. This will take about 30 minutes over a low heat.

5 Cool the mixture thoroughly and then pour into sterilized bottles. Ensure that the oil is evenly distributed if you are using more than one bottle. Leave the pickle to rest for about a week before serving to allow the flavours to merge and mingle. Serve as an accompaniment to Indian curries and other spicy food.

Red-hot Lime Pickle

A good lime pickle is not only delicious served with any meal, but it increases the appetite and aids digestion. The tangy pickle is the perfect accompaniment to a curry, such as a biryani, and is delicious as a dip with poppadums and snacks such as pakora and samosas or spicy chicken wings.

Makes 450g/1lb/2 cups

25 limes

225g/8oz salt

50g/2oz ground fenugreek

50g/2oz mustard powder

150g/5oz chilli powder

15g/½oz ground turmeric

600ml/1 pint/2½ cups mustard oil

5ml/1 tsp asafoetida

25g/1oz yellow mustard seeds, crushed

1 Cut each lime into eight pieces and remove the pips (seeds), if you wish. Place the limes in a large sterilized jar or glass bowl.

2 Add the salt to the limes and toss together until well combined. Cover the jar or bowl and leave in a warm place until the limes become soft and dull brown in colour. This will take about 1 to 2 weeks.

3 Mix together the fenugreek, mustard powder, chilli powder and turmeric and add to the limes, mixing well to ensure the limes are evenly covered in the spices. Cover again and leave to rest in a warm place for a further 2 or 3 days.

4 Heat the mustard oil in a frying pan and fry the asafoetida and mustard seeds until the seeds begin to splutter. When the oil reaches smoking point, pour it over the limes.

5 Mix well, cover with a clean cloth and leave in a warm place for about 1 week before serving.

> **Cook's Tip**
> *Asafoetida is a pungent spice obtained from the resin of a fennel-like plant. It has a very strong odour of garlic and onion and should only be used sparingly.*

Lime Pickle Energy 4699kcal/19387kJ; Protein 57g; Carbohydrate 151.3g, of which sugars 64g; Fat 438.1g, of which saturates 53.4g; Cholesterol 0mg; Calcium 2173mg; Fibre 0g; Sodium 88610mg.
Chilli Pickle Energy 1953kcal/8134kJ; Protein 51.5g; Carbohydrate 176.9g, of which sugars 95.2g; Fat 123.3g, of which saturates 14.7g; Cholesterol 0mg; Calcium 488mg; Fibre 8.2g; Sodium 96mg.

Fiery Bengal Chutney

Not for timid tastebuds, this fiery chutney is the perfect choice for lovers of hot and spicy food. Although it can be eaten a month after making, it is better matured for longer.

Makes about 2kg/4½lb
115g/4oz fresh root ginger
1kg/2¼lb cooking apples
675g/1½lb onions
6 garlic cloves, finely chopped
225g/8oz/1½ cups raisins
450ml/¾ pint/scant 2 cups malt vinegar
400g/14oz/1¾ cups demerara (raw) sugar
2 fresh red chillies
2 fresh green chillies
15ml/1 tbsp salt
5ml/1 tsp ground turmeric

1 Peel and finely shred the fresh root ginger. Peel, core and roughly chop the apples. Peel and quarter the onions, then slice as thinly as possible. Place in a preserving pan with the garlic, raisins and vinegar.

2 Bring to the boil, then simmer steadily for 15–20 minutes, stirring occasionally, until the apples and onions are thoroughly softened. Add the sugar and stir over a low heat until the sugar has dissolved. Simmer the mixture for about 40 minutes, or until thick and pulpy, stirring frequently towards the end of the cooking time.

3 Halve the chillies and remove the seeds, then slice them finely. (Always wash your hands with soapy water immediately after handling chillies.)

4 Add the chillies to the pan and cook for a further 5–10 minutes, or until no excess liquid remains. Stir in the salt and turmeric.

5 Spoon the chutney into warmed sterilized jars, cover and seal them immediately, then label when cool.

6 Store the chutney in a cool, dark place and leave to mature for at least 2 months before eating. Use within 2 years of making the chutney. Once opened, store in the refrigerator and use within 1 month.

Hot Yellow Plum Chutney

It is well worth seeking out yellow plums to make this hot, fragrant chutney. They give it a slightly tart flavour and make it the perfect accompaniment to deep-fried Asian-style snacks such as spring rolls and wontons, or battered vegetables and shellfish.

Makes 1.3kg/3lb
900g/2lb yellow plums, halved and stoned (pitted)
1 onion, finely chopped
7.5cm/3in piece fresh root ginger, peeled and grated
3 whole star anise
350ml/12fl oz/1½ cups white wine vinegar
225g/8oz/1 cup soft light brown sugar
5 celery sticks, thinly sliced
3 green chillies, seeded and finely sliced
2 garlic cloves, crushed

1 Put the halved plums, onion, ginger and star anise in a large pan and pour over half the white wine vinegar. Bring to the boil and simmer gently over a low heat for about 30 minutes, or until the plums have softened.

2 Stir the remaining vinegar, sugar, sliced celery, chillies and crushed garlic into the plum mixture. Cook very gently over a low heat, stirring frequently, until the sugar has dissolved.

3 Bring the mixture to the boil, then simmer for 45–50 minutes, or until thick, with no excess liquid. Stir frequently during the final stages of cooking to prevent the chutney sticking to the pan.

4 Spoon the plum chutney into warmed sterilized jars, then cover and seal immediately. Store the chutney in a cool, dark place then allow to mature for at least 1 month before using. Use within 2 years.

> **Cook's Tips**
> • Once opened, store the chutney in the refrigerator and use within 3 months.
> • Be sure to use jars with non-metallic lids to store the chutney.

Fiery Chutney Energy 2789kcal/11889kJ; Protein 18.4g; Carbohydrate 717.3g, of which sugars 701.8g; Fat 3.5g, of which saturates 0g; Cholesterol 0mg; Calcium 573mg; Fibre 31.2g; Sodium 6163mg.
Hot Plum Chutney Energy 1243kcal/5312kJ; Protein 8g; Carbohydrate 320.4g, of which sugars 319g; Fat 1.3g, of which saturates 0g; Cholesterol 0mg; Calcium 313mg; Fibre 16.9g; Sodium 123mg.

Pickled Peach and Chilli Chutney

This is a spicy, rich chutney with a succulent texture. It is great served traditional-style, with cold roast meats such as ham, pork or turkey; it is also good with pan-fried chicken served in warm wraps. Try it with ricotta cheese as a filling for pitta bread.

Makes about 450g/1lb

475ml/16fl oz/2 cups
  cider vinegar
275g/10oz/1¼ cups light
  muscovado (brown) sugar
225g/8oz/1⅓ cups dried
  dates, stoned (pitted) and
  finely chopped
5ml/1 tsp ground allspice
5ml/1 tsp ground mace
450g/1lb ripe peaches, stoned
  (pitted) and cut into
  small chunks
3 onions, thinly sliced
4 fresh red chillies, seeded and
  finely chopped
4 garlic cloves, crushed
5cm/2in piece fresh root ginger,
  peeled and finely grated
5ml/1 tsp salt

1 Place the vinegar, sugar, dates, allspice and mace in a large pan and heat gently, stirring, until the sugar has dissolved. Bring to the boil, stirring occasionally.

2 Add the peaches, sliced onions, chopped chillies, crushed garlic, grated ginger and salt, and bring the mixture back to the boil, stirring occasionally.

3 Reduce the heat and simmer for 40–50 minutes, or until the chutney has thickened. Stir frequently to prevent the mixture sticking to the bottom of the pan.

4 Spoon the hot cooked chutney into warmed sterilized jars and seal immediately. When cold, store the jars in a cool, dark place and leave the chutney to mature for at least 2 weeks before eating. Use within 6 months.

Cook's Tip
To test the consistency of the chutney before bottling, spoon a little of the mixture on to a plate: if the chutney retains its shape then it is the right consistency.

Red Hot Relish

Make this relish during the summer months when tomatoes and peppers are plentiful. It enhances simple, plain dishes such as a cheese or mushroom omelette.

Makes about 1.3kg/3lb

800g/1¾lb ripe tomatoes,
  skinned and quartered
450g/1lb red onions, chopped
3 red (bell) peppers, seeded
  and chopped
3 fresh red chillies, seeded and
  finely sliced
200g/7oz/1 cup sugar
200ml/7fl oz/scant 1 cup red
  wine vinegar
30ml/2 tbsp mustard seeds
10ml/2 tsp celery seeds
15ml/1 tbsp paprika
5ml/1 tsp salt

1 Put the chopped tomatoes, onions, peppers and chillies in a preserving pan, cover with a lid and cook over a very low heat for about 10 minutes, stirring once or twice, until the tomato juices start to run.

2 Add the sugar and vinegar to the tomato mixture and slowly bring to the boil, stirring occasionally, until the sugar has dissolved completely.

3 Add the mustard seeds, celery seeds, paprika and salt to the pan and stir well to combine.

4 Increase the heat under the pan slightly and cook the relish, uncovered, for about 30 minutes, or until most of the liquid has evaporated and the mixture has a thick but moist consistency. Stir frequently towards the end of cooking time to prevent the mixture sticking to the pan.

5 Spoon the relish into warmed sterilized jars, cover and seal. Store in a cool, dark place and leave for at least 2 weeks before eating. Use the relish within 1 year of making.

Cook's Tip
Once opened, store the jar of relish in the refrigerator and use within 2 months.

Peach Chutney Energy 2039kcal/8684kJ; Protein 20.9g; Carbohydrate 517.3g, of which sugars 502.9g; Fat 2g, of which saturates 0.2g; Cholesterol 0mg; Calcium 407mg; Fibre 23.6g; Sodium 59mg.
Hot Relish Energy 1270kcal/5392kJ; Protein 17.8g; Carbohydrate 306.2g, of which sugars 294.1g; Fat 5.6g, of which saturates 1.4g; Cholesterol 0mg; Calcium 320mg; Fibre 23.5g; Sodium 121mg.

Thai Pickled Shallots with Chillies

Pickling Thai shallots in this way demands some patience while the vinegar and spices work their magic, but the results are definitely worth the wait. Thinly sliced, the shallots are often used as a condiment with South-east Asian meals.

Makes 2 to 3 jars

5–6 small red or green bird's
    eye chillies
500g/1¼lb Thai pink
    shallots, peeled
2 large garlic cloves,
    peeled, halved and green
    shoots removed

For the vinegar

40g/1½oz/3 tbsp sugar
10ml/2 tsp salt
5cm/2in piece fresh root ginger,
    peeled and sliced
15ml/1 tbsp coriander seeds
2 lemon grass stalks, cut in
    half lengthways
4 kaffir lime leaves or pared
    strips of lime rind
600ml/1 pint/2½ cups
    cider vinegar
15ml/1 tbsp chopped fresh
    coriander (cilantro)

1 The chillies can be left whole or halved and seeded, if you prefer. The pickle will be hotter if you leave the seeds in. If leaving the chillies whole, prick them several times with a cocktail stick (toothpick). Bring a large pan of water to the boil. Add the chillies, shallots and garlic. Blanch for 1–2 minutes, then drain. Rinse all the vegetables under cold water, then drain again.

2 Prepare the vinegar. Put the sugar, salt, ginger, coriander seeds, lemon grass and lime leaves or lime rind in a pan, pour in the vinegar and bring to the boil. Reduce the heat to low and simmer for 3–4 minutes. Leave to cool.

3 Remove and discard the ginger, then bring the vinegar back to the boil. Add the fresh coriander, garlic and chillies and cook for 1 minute.

4 Pack the shallots into sterilized jars, distributing the lemon grass, lime leaves, chillies and garlic among them. Pour over the hot vinegar. Cool, then seal and store in a cool, dark place for 2 months before eating.

Hot Pickled Mushrooms

This method of preserving mushrooms is popular throughout Europe. The pickle is good made with cultivated mushrooms, but it is worth including a couple of sliced ceps for their delicious flavour.

Makes about 900g/2lb

500g/1¼lb/8 cups mixed
    mushrooms, such as small ceps,
    chestnut mushrooms, shiitake
    and girolles
300ml/½ pint/1¼ cups white
    wine vinegar or cider vinegar

15ml/1 tbsp sea salt
5ml/1 tsp caster (superfine) sugar
300ml/½ pint/1¼ cups water
4–5 fresh bay leaves
8 large fresh thyme sprigs
15 garlic cloves, peeled, halved,
    with any green shoots removed
1 small red onion, halved
    and thinly sliced
2–3 small dried red chillies
5ml/1 tsp coriander seeds,
    lightly crushed
5ml/1 tsp black peppercorns
a few strips of lemon rind
250–350ml/8–12fl oz/1–1½
    cups extra virgin olive oil

1 Trim the mushrooms and wipe clean. Cut any large mushrooms in half.

2 Put the vinegar, salt, sugar and water in a pan and bring to the boil. Add the bay leaves, thyme, garlic, onion, chillies, coriander seeds, peppercorns and lemon rind and simmer for 2 minutes.

3 Add the mushrooms to the pan and simmer for 3–4 minutes. Drain the mushrooms through a sieve (strainer), retaining the herbs and spices, then set aside for a few minutes more until the mushrooms are thoroughly drained.

4 Fill one large or two small cool sterilized jars with the mushrooms. Distribute the garlic, onion, herbs and spices evenly among the layers of mushrooms, then add enough olive oil to cover by at least 1cm/½in. You may need to use extra oil if you are making two jars.

5 Leave the pickle to settle, then tap the jars on the work surface to dispel any air bubbles. Seal the tops, then store in the refrigerator. Use within 2 weeks.

Pickled Shallots Energy 129kcal/551kJ; Protein 3.9g; Carbohydrate 29.2g, of which sugars 29.2g; Fat 0.5g, of which saturates 0g; Cholesterol 0mg; Calcium 71mg; Fibre 305g; Sodium 1991mg.
Pickled Mushrooms Energy 579kcal/2392kJ; Protein 9g; Carbohydrate 7.2g, of which sugars 6.2g; Fat 57.4g, of which saturates 8.4g; Cholesterol 0mg; Calcium 33mg; Fibre 10.7g; Sodium 35mg.

Dill Pickles with Chillies

Redolent of garlic and piquant with fresh chilli, salty dill pickles can be supple and succulent or crisp and crunchy. Every pickle aficionado has a favourite type.

Makes about 900g/2lb
20 small, ridged or knobbly pickling (small) cucumbers

2 litres/3¹/₂ pints/8 cups water
175g/6oz/³/₄ cup coarse sea salt
15–20 garlic cloves, unpeeled
2 bunches fresh dill
15ml/1 tbsp dill seeds
30ml/2 tbsp mixed pickling spice
1 or 2 hot fresh chillies

1 Scrub the cucumbers and rinse well in cold running water. Leave to dry.

2 Put the measured water and salt in a large pan and bring to the boil. Turn off the heat and leave the salted water to cool to room temperature.

3 Using the flat side of a knife blade or a wooden mallet, lightly crush each garlic clove, breaking the papery skin.

4 Pack the cucumbers tightly into one or two wide-necked, sterilized jars, layering them with the garlic, fresh dill, dill seeds and pickling spice. Add one chilli to each jar.

5 Pour over the cooled brine, making sure that the cucumbers are completely covered. Tap the jars on the work surface to dispel any trapped air bubbles.

6 Cover the jars with lids and then leave to stand at room temperature for about 4–7 days before serving. Store the pickles in the refrigerator.

> **Cook's Tip**
> *If you cannot find ridged or knobbly pickling cucumbers, use any kind of small cucumbers instead.*

Spicy Pickled Limes

This hot, pungent pickle comes from Punjab in India. Salting softens the rind and intensifies the flavour of the limes, while they mature in the first month or two of storage. Pickled limes are extremely salty, so are best served with slightly under-seasoned dishes.

75g/3oz/¹/₃ cup salt
seeds from 6–8 green cardamom pods
6 whole cloves
5ml/1 tsp cumin seeds
4 fresh red chillies, seeded and sliced
5cm/2in piece fresh root ginger, peeled and finely shredded
450g/1lb/2¹/₄ cups preserving or granulated (white) sugar

Makes about 1kg/2¹/₄lb
1kg/2¹/₄lb unwaxed limes

1 Put the limes in a large bowl and pour over cold water to cover. Set aside and leave the limes to soak for 8 hours, or overnight, if preferred.

2 The next day, remove the limes from the soaking water. Using a sharp knife, cut each lime in half from end to end, then cut each of the halves into slices that are approximately 5mm/¹/₄in thick.

3 Place the lime slices in the bowl, sprinkling the salt between the layers, ensuring the slices are evenly covered. Cover the bowl and leave to stand for a further 8 hours.

4 Drain the limes, catching the juices from them in a large pan or a preserving pan.

5 Crush the cardamom seeds together with the cumin seeds. Add to the pan with the chillies, ginger and sugar. Bring to the boil, stirring constantly until the sugar completely dissolves. Simmer the mixture gently for about 2 minutes, stirring occasionally, and then set aside to cool.

6 Mix the limes in the syrup. Pack into sterilized jars, cover and seal. Store in a cool, dark place for at least 1 month before eating. Use within 1 year.

Dill Pickles Energy 76kcal/305kJ; Protein 5.3g; Carbohydrate 11.4g, of which sugars 10.7g; Fat 0.8g, of which saturates 0g; Cholesterol 0mg; Calcium 140mg; Fibre 4.6g; Sodium 10013mg.
Pickled Limes Energy 1963kcal/8354kJ; Protein 12.3g; Carbohydrate 502.3g, of which sugars 502.3g; Fat 3g; of which saturates 1g; Cholesterol 0mg; Calcium 1089mg; Fibre 0g; Sodium 2042mg.

Fiery Habañero Chilli Salsa

This is a very fiery salsa with an intense heat level. A dab on the plate alongside meat or fish dishes adds a fresh, clean taste, but this is not for the faint-hearted. Habañero chillies, also called Scotch bonnets, are very hot. Lantern-shaped, they range in colour from yellow to a deep orange red. Costeno amarillo chillies are yellow when fresh and have a milder level of heat and a sharp citrus flavour.

Serve sparingly

5 dried roasted habañero chillies
4 dried costeno amarillo chillies
3 spring onions (scallions),
    finely chopped
juice of ½ large grapefruit or
    1 Seville orange
grated rind and juice of 1 lime
bunch of fresh coriander (cilantro)
salt

I Soak the habañero and costeno amarillo chillies in hot water for about 10 minutes until softened. Drain, reserving the soaking water.

2 Wear rubber gloves to handle the habañeros to avoid them irritating your skin. Remove the stalks from all chillies, then slit them and scrape out the seeds with a small sharp knife. Chop the chillies roughly.

3 Put the chillies in a food processor or blender and add a little of the soaking liquid. Blend to a fine paste. Do not lean over the processor – the fumes from the chillies may irritate your eyes and face. Remove the lid and scrape the chilli mixture into a bowl.

4 Put the chopped spring onions in another bowl and add the fruit juice, with the lime rind and juice, and mix well together. Roughly chop the coriander.

5 Carefully add the coriander to the bowl and stir thoroughly. Then add the spring onion mixture to the chillies, mixing well. Taste a tiny amount of the salsa and add salt.

6 Cover the salsa and chill in the refrigerator for at least 1 day before use. Serve the salsa very sparingly.

Classic Spiced Tomato Salsa

This is the traditional tomato-based salsa that most people associate with Mexican food. There are innumerable recipes for it, but the basics of onion, tomato, chilli and coriander are common to all. Serve as a condiment with a wide variety of dishes.

Serves 6 as an accompaniment

3–6 fresh serrano chillies
1 large white onion
grated rind and juice of 2 limes,
    plus strips of rind, to garnish
8 ripe, firm tomatoes
bunch of fresh coriander (cilantro)
1.5ml/¼ tsp sugar
salt

I Use three chillies for a salsa of medium heat; up to six if you like it hot. Spear the chillies on a metal skewer and roast them over a gas flame until the skins blister. Do not let the flesh burn. Alternatively, dry-fry them in a griddle. Place them in a strong plastic bag and tie the top. Set aside for 20 minutes.

2 Meanwhile, chop the onion finely and put it in a bowl with the lime rind and juice. The lime juice will soften the onion.

3 Remove the chillies from the bag and peel off the skins. Cut off the stalks, then slit the chillies and scrape out the seeds with a sharp knife. Chop the flesh roughly and set aside.

4 Cut a small cross in the base of each tomato. Place them in a heatproof bowl and pour over boiling water to cover.

5 Leave the tomatoes in the water for 3 minutes, then lift out and plunge into a bowl of cold water. Drain. The skins will be peeling back from the crosses. Remove the skins completely.

6 Dice the peeled tomatoes and put them in a bowl. Add the chopped onion and lime mixture; the onion should have softened. Chop the fresh coriander finely.

7 Add the coriander, with the chillies and the sugar. Mix gently until the sugar has dissolved and all the ingredients are coated in lime juice. Cover and chill for 2–3 hours. The salsa will keep for 3–4 days in the refrigerator. Garnish with lime rind before serving.

Classic Spiced Tomato Salsa Energy 42kcal/176kJ; Protein 2g; Carbohydrate 8g, of which sugars 7g; Fat 1g, of which saturates 0g; Cholesterol 0mg; Calcium 31mg; Fibre 1.7g; Sodium 100mg.
Fiery Habañero Chilli Salsa Energy 62kcal/259kJ; Protein 5.3g; Carbohydrate 7.4g, of which sugars 7.1g; Fat 1.5g, of which saturates 0g; Cholesterol 0mg; Calcium 147mg; Fibre 3g; Sodium 31mg.

Red Chilli Salsa

Use this as a condiment with fish or meat dishes, or as a dipping sauce for baked potato wedges. It is often added to rice dishes.

Makes about 250ml/ 8fl oz/1 cup
3 large tomatoes
15ml/1 tbsp olive oil
3 ancho chillies
2 pasilla chillies
2 garlic cloves, peeled and left whole
2 spring onions (scallions)
10ml/2 tsp soft dark brown sugar
2.5ml/½ tsp paprika
juice of 1 lime
2.5ml/½ tsp dried oregano
salt

1 Preheat the oven to 200°C/400°F/Gas 6. Quarter the tomatoes and place in a roasting pan. Drizzle over the olive oil. Roast for about 40 minutes until slightly charred. Leave to cool slightly, then remove the skin.

2 Soak the chillies in hot water for about 10 minutes. Drain, remove the stalks, slit the flesh and then scrape out the seeds. Chop the flesh finely.

3 In a heavy frying pan, dry-roast the garlic until just golden. Ensure that it does not burn, otherwise it will impart a bitter taste to the salsa.

4 Finely chop most of the spring onions, retaining the top part of one for garnishing. Place the chopped onion in a bowl with the sugar, paprika, lime juice and oregano. Slice the remaining spring onion diagonally and set aside for the garnish.

5 Put the skinned tomatoes and chopped chillies in a food processor or blender and add the garlic. Process until smooth.

6 Add the sugar, paprika, lime juice, spring onions and oregano to the blender. Process for a few seconds, then taste and add salt.

7 Spoon into a pan and warm through before serving, or place in a bowl, cover and chill until required. Garnish with the sliced spring onion. The salsa will keep, covered, for up to 1 week in the refrigerator.

Chipotle Chilli Sauce

The delicious smoky flavour of this sauce makes it the ideal choice to go with barbecued food, either as a marinade or as an accompaniment. It is also wonderful stirred into cream cheese as a sandwich filling with chicken. Chipotle chillies are smoked dried jalapeño chillies.

Serves 6 as an accompaniment
500g/1¼ lb tomatoes
5 chipotle chillies
3 garlic cloves, roughly chopped
150ml/¼ pint/⅔ cup red wine
5ml/1 tsp dried oregano
60ml/4 tbsp clear honey
5ml/1 tsp American mustard
2.5ml/½ tsp ground black pepper
salt

1 Preheat the oven to 200°C/400°F/Gas 6. Cut the tomatoes into quarters and place them in a roasting pan. Roast for 45 minutes to 1 hour, until the skins of the tomatoes are charred and softened.

2 Meanwhile, soak the chillies in a bowl of cold water to cover for about 20 minutes, or until soft. Remove the stalks, slit the chillies and scrape out the seeds with a small sharp knife. Chop the flesh roughly.

3 Remove the tomatoes from the oven, let them cool slightly, then remove the skins. If you prefer a smooth sauce, remove the seeds. Chop the tomatoes and put them in a blender or food processor.

4 Add the chopped chillies and garlic with the red wine to the blender or food processor. Blend the mixture until smooth, then add the oregano, honey, mustard and black pepper. Process briefly to mix, then taste and season with salt.

5 Scrape the mixture into a small pan. Place over a moderate heat and stir until the mixture boils. Lower the heat and simmer the sauce for about 10 minutes, stirring occasionally, until it has reduced and thickened.

6 Spoon the salsa into a serving bowl and serve immediately if using hot, or set aside to cool before serving cold.

Red Chilli Salsa Energy 195kcal/818kJ; Protein 2.6g; Carbohydrate 20.6g, of which sugars 20.6g; Fat 12g, of which saturates 1.9g; Cholesterol 0mg; Calcium 35mg; Fibre 3.3g; Sodium 29mg.
Chipotle Chilli Sauce Energy 63kcal/265kJ; Protein 1g; Carbohydrate 10.4g, of which sugars 10.4g; Fat 0.3g, of which saturates 0.1g; Cholesterol 0mg; Calcium 12mg; Fibre 0.8g; Sodium 11mg.

Fiery Guacamole

One of the best loved Mexican salsas, this blend of creamy avocado, tomatoes, chillies, coriander and lime now appears on tables the world over. Store-bought guacamole usually contains mayonnaise, which helps to preserve the avocado, but this is not an ingredient in traditional recipes.

Serves 6 to 8

4 medium tomatoes
4 ripe avocados, preferably fuerte
juice of 1 lime
½ small onion
2 garlic cloves
small bunch of fresh coriander (cilantro), chopped
3 fresh red fresno chillies
salt
tortilla chips, to serve

1 Cut a cross in the base of each tomato. Place the tomatoes in a heatproof bowl and pour over boiling water to cover.

2 Leave the tomatoes in the water for 3 minutes, then lift them out using a slotted spoon and plunge them into a bowl of cold water. Drain. The skins will have begun to peel back from the crosses. Remove the skins completely. Cut the tomatoes in half, remove the seeds with a teaspoon, then chop the flesh roughly and set it aside.

3 Cut the avocados in half then remove the stones (pits). Scoop the flesh out of the shells and place it in a food processor or blender. Process until almost smooth, then scrape into a bowl and stir in the lime juice.

4 Chop the onion finely, then crush the garlic. Add both to the avocado and mix well. Stir in the coriander.

5 Remove the stalks from the chillies, slit them and scrape out the seeds with a small sharp knife. Chop the chillies finely and add them to the avocado mixture, with the chopped tomatoes. Mix well.

6 Check the seasoning and add salt to taste. Cover closely with clear film (plastic wrap) or a tight-fitting lid and chill for 1 hour before serving as a dip with tortilla chips. If it is well covered, guacamole will keep in the refrigerator for 2–3 days.

Black Bean and Chilli Salsa

This salsa has a very striking appearance. The pasado chillies add a subtle citrus flavour. Leave the salsa for a day or two after making to allow the flavours to develop fully.

Serves 4 as an accompaniment

130g/4½ oz/generous ½ cup black beans, soaked overnight in water to cover
1 pasado chilli
2 fresh red fresno chillies
1 red onion
grated rind and juice of 1 lime
30ml/2 tbsp Mexican beer (optional)
15ml/1 tbsp olive oil
small bunch of fresh coriander (cilantro), chopped
salt

1 Drain the beans and put them in a large pan. Pour in water to cover and place the lid on the pan. Bring to the boil, lower the heat slightly and simmer the beans for 40 minutes, or until tender. They should still have a little bite and should not have begun to disintegrate. Drain, rinse under cold water, then drain again and leave the beans until cold.

2 Soak the pasado chilli in hot water for about 10 minutes until softened. Drain, remove the stalk, then slit the chilli and scrape out the seeds with a small sharp knife. Chop the flesh finely.

3 Spear the fresno chillies on a long-handled metal skewer and roast them over the flame of a gas burner until the skins blister and darken. Do not let the flesh burn. Alternatively, dry fry them in a griddle pan until the skins are scorched. Then place the roasted chillies in a strong plastic bag and tie the top to keep the steam in. Set aside for 20 minutes.

4 Meanwhile, chop the red onion finely. Remove the chillies from the bag and peel off the skins. Slit them, remove the seeds and chop them finely.

5 Transfer the beans to a bowl and add the onion and both types of chilli. Stir in the lime rind and juice, beer, oil and coriander. Season with salt and mix well. Chill before serving.

Fiery Guacamole Energy 262kcal/1083kJ; Protein 3.2g; Carbohydrate 5g, of which sugars 3g; Fat 25.4g, of which saturates 5.4g; Cholesterol 0mg; Calcium 37mg; Fibre 5.5g; Sodium 15mg.
Bean and Chilli Salsa Energy 129kcal/544kJ; Protein 8g; Carbohydrate 17.6g, of which sugars 3.2g; Fat 3.5g, of which saturates 0.5g; Cholesterol 0mg; Calcium 67mg; Fibre 6.3g; Sodium 11mg.

Roasted Red Pepper and Chilli Jelly

The hint of chilli in this glowing red jelly makes it ideal for spicing up hot or cold roast meat, sausages or hamburgers. The jelly is also good stirred into sauces or used as a glaze for poultry.

Makes about 900g/2lb
8 red (bell) peppers, quartered
　and seeded
4 fresh red chillies, halved
　and seeded
1 onion, roughly chopped
2 garlic cloves, roughly chopped
250ml/8fl oz/1 cup water
250ml/8fl oz/1 cup white
　wine vinegar
7.5ml/1½ tsp salt
450g/1lb/2¼ cups preserving or
　granulated (white) sugar
25ml/1½ tbsp powdered pectin

1 Arrange the peppers, skin side up, on a rack in a grill (broiling) pan and grill (broil) until the skins blister and blacken.

2 Put the peppers in a polythene bag until they are cool enough to handle, then remove the skins.

3 Put the skinned peppers, chillies, onion, garlic and water in a food processor or blender and process to a purée.

4 Press the purée through a nylon sieve (strainer) set over a bowl, pressing it hard with a wooden spoon, to extract as much of the juice as possible. There should be roughly 750ml/1¼ pints/3 cups of purée.

5 Scrape the purée into a large stainless steel pan, then stir in the white wine vinegar and salt.

6 In a bowl, combine the sugar and pectin, then stir it into the pepper mixture. Heat gently, stirring constantly, until the sugar and pectin have dissolved completely, then bring the mixture to a rolling boil.

7 Cook the jelly, stirring frequently, for exactly 4 minutes, then remove the pan from the heat.

8 Pour the jelly into warmed, sterilized jars. Leave to cool and set, then cover, label and store.

Hot Chilli and Garlic Dipping Sauce

This dipping sauce is particularly strong and pungent, so warn any guests who are unaccustomed to spicy foods. This sauce is especially good for serving with satays and as a side dish to a simple bowl of rice.

Makes 120ml/4fl oz/½ cup
1 clove garlic, crushed
2 small red chillies, seeded and
　finely chopped
10ml/2 tsp sugar
5ml/1 tsp tamarind sauce
60ml/4 tbsp soy sauce
juice of ½ lime

1 Pound the garlic, chillies and sugar until smooth using a pestle and mortar, or grind in a food processor.

2 Mix in the tamarind sauce, soy sauce and lime juice.

Chilli Sambal

This ubiquitous Indonesian sauce, known as *sambal ulek*, will keep for several weeks in a well-sealed jar in the refrigerator, so it is worth making up a reasonable quantity at a time. Use a stainless-steel or plastic spoon to measure it out. This sauce is fiercely hot and so only small amounts are needed as an accompaniment. It is also useful as a source of ready-prepared chillies for adding some heat to other dishes.

Makes 450g/1lb
450g/1lb fresh red chillies, seeded
10ml/2 tsp salt

1 Plunge the chillies into a pan of boiling water and cook for 5–8 minutes. Drain them well and then grind in a food processor, without making the paste too smooth.

2 Turn into a screw-topped glass jar, stir in the salt and cover with a piece of baking parchment or clear film (plastic wrap). Then screw on the lid and store in the refrigerator.

3 Spoon into small dishes, to serve as an accompaniment, or use in recipes as suggested.

Pepper and Chilli Jelly Energy 2275kcal/9665kJ; Protein 18g; Carbohydrate 571g, of which sugars 565.1g; Fat 6.1g, of which saturates 1.5g; Cholesterol 0mg; Calcium 373mg; Fibre 24.8g; Sodium 89mg.
Chilli Dipping Sauce Energy 89kcal/378kJ; Protein 4.2g; Carbohydrate 18.4g, of which sugars 14.3g; Fat 0.3g, of which saturates 0g; Cholesterol 0mg; Calcium 27mg; Fibre 1g; Sodium 3208mg.
Chilli Sambal Energy 90kcal/374kJ; Protein 13.1g; Carbohydrate 3.1g, of which sugars 3.1g; Fat 2.7g, of which saturates 0g; Cholesterol 0mg; Calcium 136mg; Fibre 0g; Sodium 3962mg.

Index